BRAVE MEN AND TRUE

Pages from a Company Commander's Diary

*Joe Horden-n
our distinguished C.O.*

by
WALLACE CLARK *(tone)*

*with best wishes
from

Wallace Clark*

Maps and sketches by Ken Woods

ISBN 0-9509042-3-6

Printed by Coleraine Printing Company Ltd
117 Ballycastle Road, Coleraine, BT52 2DZ

Published by Wallace Clark Booksales
115 Kilrea Road, Upperlands, County Derry, BT46 5SB

November 2002

DEDICATION

TO THOSE MEMBERS OF

THE MAGHERA AND MAGHERAFELT COMPANIES

THE ULSTER DEFENCE REGIMENT

WHO GAVE THEIR LIVES TO PROTECT

THEIR HOMES FROM TERRORISM

BETWEEN 1970 AND 1992

CONTENTS

CHAPTERS

ACKNOWLEDGEMENTS

If mention were to be made of all the people who have helped with this book it would include almost everyone who has served in F and G Companies ,and many other members of 5 UDR.

This is impractical for several reasons.
Mentions by name are of necessity selective. A dozen or so members of 5 UDR have agreed to be named. On the advice of the Ministry of Defence other names have been deleted on security grounds. Some of those involved specifically did not want to be identified. Some names have been altered – others, including those who have helped most, are real. So the selection of names included is bound to appear illogical and therefore unfair. For this I ask the reader's understanding.

To name or not to name has been a major difficulty in writing this book. Even with these limitations the following pages will, I hope, help old comrades to remember bold deeds and ancient jokes; also that this will lead to every one of you looking back and enjoying a measure of satisfaction at a worthwhile job well done.

Among many civilians who have helped are author Davina Jones with invaluable sub-editing, Beverley Scott, as always, with typing and encouragement, Brian Scott and Gavin Hill with solving word processing problems, Ken Woods with maps and sketches, my brother Henry with his summary of the Sixties entitled *Optimism Before Storm*. Stanley Leacock with his remarkable memory for dates and places filled many gaps. My cousin Desmond Clark did an early useful proof read.

Above all Richard Scott has improved the story with criticism, valuable re-phrasing and many wise suggestions - also sniffing out grammatical clangers to which I am prone (Still a few left, I'm afraid, Richard!)
Tom Brown, himself a UDR company commander, made many shrewd criticisms. John Potter, author of the official regimental history *A Testimony to Courage* kindly took time to keep me right, from his vast knowledge, on military terminology, facts and dates. His angle on political events does not always coincide with mine but there is, I hope, mutual respect.

The staff of the Army Historical Branch in London and of the Royal Irish Regiment in Ballymena have been most courteous when checking the text.

To those who may feel let down at not being named, and for the errors which inevitably occur in a book relying so much on memory as this, I apologise.

Thanks to all those named and un-named for your reminiscences and your assistance. It's been a long job!

ILLUSTRATIONS

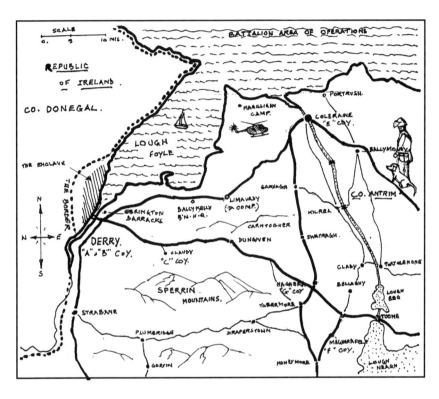

5 UDR Area

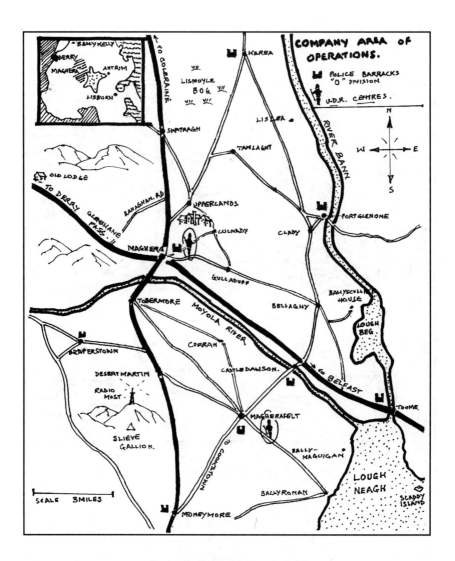

F and G Company Area

Technical Terms and Initials

Service communications today breed initials and abbreviations by the score. Most are familiar to soldiers and some are self evident.
For the general reader a hundred or so of the commonest of these can be found in a Glossary after the Appendices

FOREWORD

by
Brigadier Harry Baxter CBE GM KM
Colonel Commandant, The Ulster Defence Regiment

In January 1973 I was sitting at my desk in the British Embassy Athens studying a Spanish course prior to taking up my next appointment as Defence Attaché, Madrid. A second posting in this role was something to which I looked forward eagerly. The telephone rang. It was Brigadier Peter Leng of the Military Secretary's Department, an old friend from my time on the staff of Admiral Mountbatten. Now he was responsible for finding jobs for senior officers.
'I have a proposition,' he said, 'a change of posting, but only if you agree'.
It would be to command the Ulster Defence Regiment. I recall the words he used in description – 'Interesting – Challenging – No piece of cake.'

And then the sting in the tail. He, Leng, would be my boss. His enthusiasm and admiration for the Ulster Defence Regiment were infectious. These qualities he was to exhibit in great measure when, having agreed to take the job, I worked for him when he was Major-General Commanding Land Forces in the Province. I recall in particular his high regard for the volunteers, part-time men and, later, women Greenfinches, of the eleven battalions which then formed the Regiment. The part-timers came from all over the Province; many ex-B Specials, representing all social classes and professions; farmers (the backbone), factory workers, teachers, solicitors, butchers, bakers, shop managers, peers, postmen *et al.*

My introduction to the first battalion I visited made me quickly aware of what was in store for me. The Commanding Officer took me out to the Ballykinler ranges to see some training, which turned out to be a set-piece company attack.
"Surely not", I said, for training at this advanced standard and for such an unlikely contingency had been expressly ruled out by Brigadier Denis Ormerod, a friend and fellow Irish Fusilier from whom I had taken over as Commander. It was also outside our terms of service. Simple training, practising anti-ambush drills and vehicle checkpoints was the

limit of his training Directive. Leaving the CO, I moved with the attacking platoon observing the advanced age of many of the men. I noted one in particular, perhaps 50 years old, at the rear. Suddenly they came under fire from the 'enemy'. I waited to see what he would do – go to ground – roll over into a firing position – take cover. Not a bit. He sat down.

I prompted him. 'No, Sir', he said 'I'm dished.' (he used a much stronger adjective) 'All this capering is too much.' Months later he came to say goodbye to me in my office. A senior Bank Manager, he had completed two years of three night duties a week together with his full-time job, and he felt that at nearly sixty years he had done his bit. We downed a glass of sherry and before leaving he said to me, 'Remember we are NOT regular soldiers. Don't expect too much of us'. My education had begun. It continued and improved as I visited the other ten battalions, with their 60-plus company locations spread North and South of the Bann. Always my visits ended, usually at 0200hrs, in the combined Officers and Sergeant's Mess with a large Bushmills and great *crack*. And always, as I left, my understanding of the motivation of the part-timers became clearer.

'We are standing up to be counted.'

'We know the risks we are taking, but someone has to do it', was often said.

And the risks were frightful; farmers killed while on their tractors, postmen and bus drivers about their daily civilian tasks, managers shot at their office desks, rarely, if ever, when they were on duty in uniform. Among them, and forming a substantial part of the Regiment were the ex B Specials. Many were long in the tooth, not used to normal military ways of operation, but they provided much of the stiffening for the young part-timers, having a wealth of experience behind them, built up over 50 years of Province-wide fighting against the IRA. I, and subsequent Regular Battalion Commanders, learned much from them, as did the part-timers.

Among the companies I visited regularly were G and F Companies of 5 UDR, based in Maghera and Magherafelt. This book by Wallace Clark, G Coy commander, and incidentally employer in his mill of quite a lot of them, gives a detailed account of their service throughout the period 1970 to 1992 when the UDR and Royal Irish Rangers amalgamated to become the Royal Irish Regiment. It is an account which demands telling for it illustrates for the first time for public reading just what service in the UDR involved. Also of the bravery, dedication, unselfishness and many operational successes both companies scored.

As the then Commander and later Colonel Commandant, my visits to these two outstanding companies, who epitomised the spirit and dedication of the volunteers to whom the Province must always be indebted, was a humbling experience. As you follow the author's detailed accounts of incidents and actions you are drawn to the conclusion that he describes an extraordinary body of dedicated and gallant volunteers, risking so much and often paying the final price, for a cause in which they deeply believed, and providing invaluable support for the RUC and the Regular Army.

I commend this book to all past members of the Regiment, and to those now serving with the Royal Irish Regiment. They will find, as I have, that it is fascinating reading.

INTRODUCTION

The Sixties -- Optimism before Storm

The Irish Republican Army on 26th February 1962 made a formal admission of defeat. It came at the end of a seven year attempt, their third or fourth since Partition, to prise Northern Ireland out of the United Kingdom by force. Firm action by the Northern Ireland Government, the Royal Ulster Constabulary and Ulster Special Constabulary, familiarly known as *the B Men,* had prevented escalation of the attacks. There had been little sign of popular support for violence.

I described this campaign in a short book called Guns in Ulster. At the time as a B Special officer I felt, like thousands of others, that the use of guns was over and a good chance of peace and prosperity loomed for all in Ulster. In 1964 the liberal Terence O'Neill succeeded Lord Brookborough as Prime Minister of Northern Ireland. Terence had meetings with Sean Lemass, the Dublin Premier. His practical steps towards reconciliation coincided with a period of increasing prosperity. In the Sixties car ownership doubled to become the highest per head in all the UK. In the twenty years before 1970 a quarter of the Ulster population had moved into modern homes. Unemployment looked like falling to 6 % in Belfast and job opportunities spread into the countryside at a discernable rate. Inward investment brought better paid opportunities in firms like Chemstand, Du Pont and Enkalon. Ballymena and Larne, Protestant strongholds, elected popular Catholic Mayors. With the police achieving a detection rate of almost 75 %, crime was infrequent.

A decade of peace might have allowed a mature relationship to evolve between the two parts of Ireland, aided by common membership of the Common Market. Thus could a separatist war have been avoided. But the Sixties proved to be a period of challenge to authority worldwide. There were protest marches and mass demontrations in the Place de la Concorde in Paris, at Little Rock in USA and it took 4000 policemen to contain the one in Grosvenor Square in London. Irish activists would not wait. Investigative journalists were invited in. The Times Insight Team article of 1964 was one of the first things to de-stabilise Ulster. Journalists assumed that with a population of a million protestant Unionists and half a million nationalist Catholics armed conflict was inevitable and would make good copy.

What galled older people in Ulster in the late sixties was the way strife came so suddenly out of relative prosperity and increasing goodwill. A civil rights march on 5th Oct 1968 in Derry, which its organisers felt sure would oppose a Government ban and then be bound to draw full media coverage was the first step down the Gadarene slope. Television, still a popular novelty, caught the RUC wielding truncheons above their heads to stop the leaders. Police work in Ireland has always been on the robust side and the Civic Guards in the south no slouches at close quarters. But the media turned this incident into an international outcry against perceived repression.

By 1969 the stage was set for renewal of trouble. Each faction considered that its own end -- the destruction of Ulster as a community by the Nationalists, or its preservation within the UK by the Unionists, justified the means. The Nationalists favoured violence, the Unionistsm, more mildly, selective gerrymandering. Rioting and arson intensified. In August eight deaths resulted.

The Wilson Government in October 1969 summarily disbanded the Ulster Special Constabulary at the instance of Nationalist propagandists. They then reluctantly agreed to the creation of a new security force. This was to become the Ulster Defence Regiment. Of its life, and ultimate loss of identity by merger, you may read in the following pages.

The New Regiment

The best military authorities declare that the only way terrorists can be defeated is by the use of indigenous troops. Such local men and women can spot the arrival of evilly-disposed strangers, and the assembly of arms far more quickly than the most seasoned regular soldiers. Hence the Ulster Defence Regiment (hereinafter The UDR), from the moment it became operational in April 1970, comprised a major component of the Security Forces arrayed in Northern Ireland against the Irish Republican Army.

Few of the hundreds of books tackling the Irish troubles of the last thirty years have broached the subject of the UDR. It is high time for its story to be told from inside. So my tale is of life in two rifle companies in a rural area of high IRA activity. These were F (formed in 1970) and G (formed 1972) of the Fifth Londonderry Battalion; they were based in the small towns of Magherafelt and Maghera, ten miles apart, and each 35 miles from battalion headquarters Most of the operations described took place in an area ten by twenty miles, an hour and a half by car north of the Border. It was the base of the South Derry Battalion IRA and the home of several terrorists described at times as the most wanted men in Northern Ireland. F and G Companies often acted as Province Reserve for weekends on the Border. That gave a taste of what it felt like trying to prevent terrorist infiltration from the Irish Republic.

A linen weaver by trade, a naval officer and an offshore sailor by inclination, I suddenly found myself a khaki-clad soldier. As a part-timer for some seven years I was by turns platoon commander, operations officer, section leader and company commander, sometimes two or three of these at once--- because there was nobody else to do it. Initially we suffered an acute shortage of leaders. In time the UDR was to develop many fine ones at all levels, much better qualified than an ex-wartime naval lieutenant the likes of me. Much evilly-inspired nonsense has been written by pro-terrorist propagandists in efforts to demonise the UDR . Having seen their precursors the Ulster Special Constabulary destroyed by clever half- truths and enormous lies, the UDR had little reason to expect anything else. One way of combating the continuation of such distortions is by eye witness accounts.

The main thing I intend the following pages to illustrate is the courage, kindliness and humour of the men and women who were my contemporaries in F and G Companies --- their quiet acceptance of danger, and sadly the deaths of several at the hands of the IRA.

The names of most UDR personnel have been changed. This is because the risk of political assassination has been proved to continue long after departure from the Regiment. Real names are of those who were killed on service, or have since died, and of senior officers whose names were often mentioned in books, the press or regimental magazines. A few other members of G and F Companies are content, like myself, to have their real names recorded for posterity. **Only the names of those UDR members who have given written permission to be included are mentioned in the following pages.** As regards deeds it has been impossible for reasons of security and of space to record the bold actions of more than a fraction of those who volunteered to take the risks involved in joining the Ulster Defence Regiment.

My fellow soldiers were ordinary law abiding men and women who wanted to protect their homes and livelihood from destruction by terrorists . They came home from work to have an evening meal with their family, but two or three times a week hurried over their food . 'Many's a night all I got was a look the table and a kick at the cat', as one grey haired farmer told me, 'before I got on me oul' uniform and equipment'. Then out he and others sallied out, prepared if necessary to be in a gunfight a few minutes later. And many of them continued turning out like this for ten, even twenty two years. Such perseverance deserves to be recorded. History is best told anecdotally so in the following pages I have selected a few incidents out of the hundreds that occurred for description by participants.

Perhaps they will act as a cautionary tale.

PROLOGUE

An Ulster Defence Regiment Evening.............
28th July 1972

The pffft.... of a high velocity bullet cut through the dusk a few feet above our heads. 'Rotten shot!' said Platoon Sergeant Steve beside me. 'That sniper couldn't hit a stirk across the street.' The next shot was lower but Steve, tall, lean and stiff jawed, was unabashed.
'He'll not get no coconuts with that one'.
I reckoned it was high time to move. And we did. Our post was partly protected by a wall of sandbags built on the pavement of the Strand Road, Derry, beside the River Foyle. Whether they were thick enough to stop a Kalashnikov bullet time might tell.

It was about 9pm on July 28th 1972 and still daylight. Number 26 platoon of F Company, Fifth Battalion, the Ulster Defence Regiment (hereinafter 5 UDR) had been deployed to spend the night manning a checkpoint on the main route running north towards Donegal.

The Bogside, a low-lying area of housing and pubs half a mile from where we stood, had been for months a No Go area Two IRA units, entitled battalions but of unknown numerical strength, ruled it behind barricades and masked sentries. As dusk fell no more shots came in our direction. But one couldn't be sure that the risk had gone away. If the gunman was still around soldiers, standing in mid-road while questioning car drivers, were an easy target under sodium street lights. Chris, a recent recruit, tall and ginger-haired, was doing a stint as lookout man beside me. At my word he tried shooting out the light above us with his self-loading rifle. Two shots produced no effect.
'Jakers, man, are ye loadened with blank?', sniggered one of his mates. The high velocity shots had gone through the shade with no apparent effect. It was damned urgent to get that light out. Perhaps a low velocity bullet would make more of a shock. So I tried with my .38 revolver. The shade twanged; the light flickered; then gratifyingly went out. The wee bullets had done the trick. A once in a life time occasion followed as I walked down the main road and had the fun of shooting out street lights in the style of a Western Movie.

The resultant darkness was comforting. Derry was in such blitzed state that a few street lights would never be missed.

'Why don't you solder a few more, sir ?' said Corporal Willie, a small lean wiry man with sunken cheeks and bright eyes.

'Fired the rest of my ammo at that rat we couldn't catch at Fort William. Big as a wee cat he was.'

'Yep. But you needn't hae bothered: he'd been eating our Compo ration packs. That would have killed him anyway', was Willie's reply.

By midnight traffic had almost ceased. In the comparative calm I had time to think what the hell an aging juvenile like me was doing forty miles from home on the fringe of what might be quite a big party. Eight hours earlier sitting in a weaving factory the problem was where we could get some good warp yarn for a linen suiting. But I never located a yard. The phone rang at 3 p.m. with a code word meaning that 5 UDR was being mobilised. A few minutes later I was in uniform on the way to Fort William in Magherafelt.

If you want to find out what happened later that night and afterwards in Derry turn to Chapter Four. But better not be too impatient. I suggest that you read on now to learn how it all started. And if you think that's a bit disjointed, you're right. Disjointed is the only accurate way to relate UDR history. Life for UDR part-timers was always separate incidents — Patrol for an evening, then back with the family. Ambush the Border for a weekend and return to a civilian desk — Attend a high powered orders briefing — then home to porridge.

'There's but a twinkling of a star
between a man of peace and war'

CHAPTER ONE

Raising the Regiment

'The song of fighters great and small;
The song of pretty fighters all...'.
Ralph Hodgson -

In mid September 1969, almost three years before the incident described above, the idea of a new security force for Northern Ireland had been conceived.

As a result of alarm created in Westminster by a few day's rioting in the city of Derry the Ulster Special Constabulary or 'B Specials' who had kept the peace for 50 years were, in the words of a Government announcement, to be disbanded.

That spelled out to terrorists a huge acceleration in appeasement. Quick-fix politicians began to imagine the instant creation of a new regiment of Catholics and Protestants united in brotherly love, avidly restraining lawbreakers of every sort. In their innocence they left the IRA out of the planning. But pressure from on high was acute. Gestation of the new regiment was to take a mere matter of weeks. The birth announcement came in what is now known as the Hunt Report on 11 October 1969. Like most babies the force didn't at first have a name. But it was swaddled swiftly and christened in a year when democratic governments were learning that it was much more difficult to impose authority than flout it.

Two years earlier the Northern Ireland Civil Rights Association (NICRA) had been formed for peaceful protest. In the words of Conor Cruise O Brien in his book *Memoirs 'The Catholics of Northern Ireland suffered from a genuine sense of grievance, and also greatly exaggerated the extent of the same. Stormont had few delegated powers but abused those it had in relation to jobs, housing and local franchise. They justified this action as a means of preventing the destruction of the state, the first responsibility of any government.*

Many Catholics of good intent joined NICRA to take part in peaceful protest. This seemed initially to Unionists not unwelcome as the first Catholic concerted action in fifty years. But the leadership of NICRA was soon taken over for their own ends by members of the Irish

Republican Army. Moderates no longer held sway. Added to the NICRA demands already promulgated was the removal of the B Specials. This was the force that Sinn Fein historian Tim Pat Coogan described as *'the one rock on which any mass movement by the IRA in the North inevitably foundered.'*[1]

Next target of NICRA appeared to be the disintegration of the State they lived in followed by a creation of a United Socialist Ireland. In the first half of 1969 NICRA led a series of provocative demonstrations. Men with long memories rated the riots the worst since Northern Ireland was first set up in 1922. The troubles caused by these marches were mainly urban. They didn't bother us much in the County Derry[2] countryside where, following my father and grandfather, I was commanding a District of two hundred B Specials.

In most rural areas peace continued unbroken. But it was clear to any observer of Irish history that following the Nationalist political success a major IRA military campaign would follow. My story will concentrate on events in the county and city of Derry where I saw them unfold at first hand.

The month of August 1969 saw the RUC drawn into battle with Nationalist rioters who were determined to prevent the traditional Apprentice Boys Parade. Public and private buildings were burned as stoning and fire bombing raged for two long days. For the policemen, lacking reserves, it was 'watch on and stop on'. They had no relief and no respite By day four they were becoming exhausted and ineffective. The USC were mobilised but not for riot control in which they were considered to be untrained. My Number Three District USC , 40 miles east of Derry City, guarded Maghera Police Station and patrolled locally under RUC control. This released regular policemen for riot duty. But Derry City continued to worsen and the NI Government called for help from the army. The Prince of Wales' Regiment moved into the Nationalist Bogside. They were welcomed as saviours with smiles and cups of tea. But the honeymoon proved as short as the political strings were long. A few days later, on orders from Westminster, the elected Londonderry Council was suspended as being biased and unfit to rule. A Commission was appointed to run the City on the lines demanded by NICRA. The Harbour Board was sacked and replaced by another quango with a wider representation and membership. Compared to what lay ahead the 1969 riots were sporadic and up until July un-lethal. But after

50 years of peace in Ulster London ministers had no experience of local violence, knew little about counter-measures and could think of nothing but appeasement.

Premier Harold Wilson was naïve enough to believe that a few more quick concessions would buy off the terrorists and produce peace - at least until the General Election he planned in 1970. He announced on television on 22 August, without having checked its record, that the 8,000 strong Ulster Special Constabulary[3] would be phased out — a mealy mouthed euphemism for a terminal pay off.

The Derry Citizens Defence Association at once stepped up its demands. Their daily News letter Number Eleven includes :

Item 7

A military supervisory watch to be maintained over Ulster Special Constabulary arms storage. The military to control the issue of these arms.

Item 9

No USC to be used within the City or anywhere west of the Foyle. This is what the military promised to do if we took down the barricades The Defence Association refused the terms for a number of reasons...the fact that the barricades are protection against attack from any quarter. The fact that our holding this area is the symbol of our continous struggle against the Unionist Government. We hold 888 acres and two roods ...Within this are are 25,000 people.

The single sheet was available from eight centres in shops, schools and pubs. It indicates the extent to which citizens were arming while the IRA remained at a low ebb in men and equipment. Having found little popular support in their 1956 campaign and been thoroughly defeated by the Royal Ulster Constabulary and USC, they were now said to have been staggered at such an unexpected bonanza as Wilson's announcement. If so. they soon recovered their composure. Foreseeing the long gap in security which would follow the disappearance of the B Specials, the IRA godfathers swiftly planned to make use of it to add to their weapons and manpower. They would soon enjoy a golden opportunity to move around arms and explosives un-hampered, to train recruits, establish caches and identify safe houses.

Vociferous protests by Unionists at Wilson's statement reached Ian Freeland, General Officer Commanding Nortern Ireland and recently appointed Head of Security. He did not appear to have been consulted and denied any plans to disband the USC. Few people knew Wilson's real intentions. He gave the impression of hardly knowing himself.

Lest the reader should assume that opinions above are the distorted view of an ex- B Specials officer I will here quote with kind permission Charles Moore. He is now Editor of the Daily Telegraph and wrote on 21 September in 1981 ...

'The UDR was born out of the chaos resulting from British indecision over the disorders in the Province at the end of the sixties. Believing the largely phoney accusations made by Republicans and repeated in the Press the Government of Harold Wilson disbanded the B Specials, the men most vital in the defeat of previous IRA campaigns. Thanks to the insistence of the military that some equivalent of the B men were essential the Government reluctantly formed the UDR.'

Charles Moore commented further in 1994: *'The people of Northern Ireland killed very few of their number between 1922 and 1969. They did not suddenly turn into psychopaths and fanatics 25 years ago, although, like any people, they have a few such among them. The killing in Northern Ireland started because order broke down and order is the responsibility of the civil power. The civil power got it wrong. In that sense it is, for all its altruism, to blame for the bloodshed. The first business of politics is to keep the peace in the country for which you are responsible. In this Britain has failed for a generation. It is the worst failure of our leaders in our time'*

Lord Hunt, of Everest fame, was beguiled into becoming a tool of the disbandment process. He was given a month to make a Northern Ireland Security Review. This was to include a recommendation to get rid of the USC. As a District Commandant (equivalent rank of major) in the USC I was interviewed by a weary Lord Hunt and his courteous henchmen, senior London and Glasgow police officers, Robert Mark and Sir James Robertson. Asked a direct question Hunt assured me that he was not going to leave Ulster without an effective internal security force, even temporarily. His intentions were honourable but to leave Ulster relatively undefended was exactly what his report was to do. When a few days later we read the Hunt Report it contained very little criticism of the USC but confirmed its disbandment. Paragraph 27 showed the limitations of Hunt's understanding, and the low quality of his briefing.

'.... a realistic assessment of the capacity of the IRA to mount serious terrorists attacks would not rate it very high, particularly as the

Weapon training at Shackleton Barracks, Ballykelly

Two G Company Marksmen

Government of the Irish Republic has stated publicly that it is opposed to the use of force on the Border'.

As well as disbanding the B Specials this report included the disarming of the Royal Ulster Constabulary. They were no longer to carry firearms, something they had found it essential to do since their formation in 1922. The steel doors and shutters were to be removed from all RUC Stations. Then the birth of a new defence force was announced. Two thousand strong it should be recruited locally as part of the regular army under the control of the GOC Northern Ireland ie not the police or Stormont Government. IRA leaders exulted afresh at this double stroke of luck — the RUC toothless and B men on the way out. If a week of Rent-a-Crowd riots could produce dividends like this, they thought, surely it won't take much more to topple the Northern Ireland Parliament.

'Yon man should a' stuck to climbing mountains', was among the mildest of the opinions of Hunt voiced by those B men and policemen who had to face the terrorists on the ground. Rushed discussions started as to the name, structure, size and equipment of the new force. A committee of mixed political views chose from many suggestions the name Ulster Defence Regiment. They also ruled that the new Regiment be kept distinct from any regular unit.

Half the committee wanted the B men to join because they knew they couldn't form a regiment in three months without a core of trained officers and men. The other half wanted nothing to do with them. Conflicting decisions were inevitable. The UDR, as the Chief of the General Staff remarked to me in 2001. was 'a political football from birth'. By December 1969 application forms to join the UDR were handed out as freely as religious tracts.

In January 1970 teams consisting of a training major and a posse of instructors started work at Army Barracks in each County. Locally, we learned that there would be a 600 strong battalion based in HMS Sea Eagle, the joint RAF and Royal Naval Anti-Submarine School in Derry. This establishment was now to come the full circle. It had been an army barracks since 1850. On the outbreak of World War 11 it was converted to naval use. Now in 1969 as a naval economy it was about to close. The base was saved from extinction when 8 Brigade under Brigadier Peter Leng was airlifted there from Plymouth in late 1969. The pre-war name of Ebrington Barracks was re-introduced and as one good result of the impending troubles hundreds of civilian staff were able to continue in employment there.

Headquarters staff in Thiepval Barracks, Lisburn started to open UDR applications on January 1, 1970. Vetting was then commenced by a curious assortment of commissioned and warrant officers from all three armed services brought in from England; some were retired, others in gaps between jobs. Most were tasked for reasons difficult to understand. The common denominator seemed to be that all of them, like Lord Hunt, knew nothing about Ireland.

As a sponsor I met many of these well meaning but ill-informed men. They rejected lots of excellent lads on flimsy allegations. This was often a suspected but unsubstantiated connection with a Protestant vigilante group. For a good man to be rejected was a slur on his character—a slur which soon became known locally. It inhibited neighbours from applying lest they suffer the same rebuff. Meanwhile the vetters approved others with extreme political views and in some cases criminal records. Mistakes were bound to happen since very limited means of cross checking statements on application forms were made available. The RUC appeared to be excluded from the process, being considered, quite unreasonably, to be too biased to give fair opinions. Not all admissions of extremists were accidental. In a neighbouring battalion the Commanding Officer Lt. Colonel Michael Torrens-Spence was asked by Regimental HQ why a certain Roman Catholic had been rejected. He replied that the man concerned had a criminal record and IRA associations. HQ told him to reverse the decision and take him on. The arbitrary impositions were political. Personally I found UDR HQ most helpful in such matters.

In South Derry after a positive vetting Sammy Hudson, USC Sub-District Commandant and I were granted UDR commissions. We had applied early to give a lead to others. This was rewarded by a letter from Her Majesty The Queen a few months later, sending greetings to each of those similarly honoured, addressing us as *Trusty and Well beloved. 'We, reposing especial trust in your loyalty, courage and good conduct do here by appoint you to be an officer in Our Land Forces.. .* So the handsome certificate went on.

A pleasant anachronism. Perhaps her staff had forgotten that her father had already commissioned me as a wartime Royal Naval officer

25 years earlier. It was good to feel doubly well loved. Many other USC men decided to take the coming disbandment in good part and do their best for the new regiment. Promises of better uniform and equipment, up to date radios, transport and training facilities, the availability of helicopters and Land Rovers for patrols had certain attractions for carrying on the fight which we knew would continue against the IRA.

The vetting process took so many weeks that young applicants often lost interest and decided not to turn up for interview. Those volunteers from our part of the country who survived the process were sworn in at a Territorial Army Centre in Magherafelt starting about 20th January In spite of many delays F Company of 5 UDR had a handful of signed up members to start training by February 1970. We taught the recruits how to wind puttees on the right way round and adjust the ribbon on a beret to make it fit comfortably; then to assemble web equipment to hold ammunition pouches. Sergeant Alfy instilled basic foot drill and rifle drill. We knew what an irksome business it can be to reduce oneself to an automaton, to become Number One, Two or Three of a squad. Worse still to concentrate for hours upon instantly adjusting the anguished frame to strange angles in obedience to hoarse commands. Square bashing was kept to a minimum. The B men meanwhile continued to do duty but were confined to static guards so unable to prevent enemy movements.

Roy Moore, a USC Sergeant and production manager in a local brick and tile company, was one of the earliest to be accepted. Today he remains as he was then round faced, broad-shouldered and impervious to cold, brimming over with cheerfulness and good nature.

'We were in the both outfits at the one time', he recalls with his ready smile .

Other families hung back to see which way the cat was going to jump. Wives hearing of IRA threats to applicants were not enthusiastic. Archie who was to become a famous battalion piper found that his wife had burned the Application Form and had to start all over again. Mothers of younger would-be joiners did the same thing. So recruiting was sluggish. Many fathers with dependant families reasonably decided not to add so greatly to the normal hazards of life. Humiliation at the abrupt disbandment of the USC and the possibility of the same fate awaiting the UDR was another inhibitor -- probably a major one. The IRA too were recruiting and taking new chums south to be trained at camps in the Republic where there were more than 30 to choose from. Worry about inflexibility of military working hours put plenty of good men off the UDR .

'This force will be under strictest Army Discipline and fully trained', had been bellowed loud by generals and politicians alike. Many potential joiners feared that under a severe regime a farmer would not be allowed to miss a duty if his cow was calving, or to refuse Annual Camp if it came at harvest time. Others didn't like the idea of unnecessary battle school type training. Neither of these worries were well founded. For the first eight years in F and G Companies all consideration was given to a man with important private business. But the early doubts were understandable. In terms of time the price of joining looked stiff. All that training was going to take a lot time. Would an already busy man be able to manage it? But in spite of these and other objections lots of determined men accepted the uncertainties and signed up. A couple of lines by Robert Browning summed up their attitude

'So battled we like men*
Nor boy- like sulked or whined'.

The main motivation was to defend one's homeland from a terrorist and left wing takeover. The words of an American politician just before USA entered the Hitler War vented my own feelings.

'Let us not rely for our shameful security upon the British Forces.*
Let us do our own fighting'.

A liking for adventure and a desire to test one's nerves under fire was a necessary ingredient in the decision to volunteer. Incidental attractions like a chance to learn to fire the latest weapons, to play the bagpipes, to make new friends, were influential. Family tradition was a strong incentive. I had seen my father and grandfather give large chunks of their lives to protecting local families and warding off terrorist attacks. Many F Coy recruits were proud to be able to say, 'My father did it before me'.

We had observed as we grew up many IRA assaults on Ulster. Terrorist campaigns starting with *Give 'em the Lead* O'Duffy in 1923, had arisen about every seven years since the Treaty in 1922 and were unlikely to stop now.

Pay was not initially important—the monthly cheque was looked on as pocket money at first but after some time it did come be counted as income. Good income too.

Doubtless there were other more subtle reasons for joining. Perhaps the best answer to the slightly embarrassing question, 'Why did you join?' was an honest, 'Augh, I don't really know'. But of one thing I remain sure — The Regiment comprised with few exceptions the boldest and best of Ulster's manhood.The volunteers knew that there would be no golden moments when one man would turn the battle or win victory in a set piece encounter—it was going to be just steady slogging.

Let me introduce a few early joiners — Willy Currie an electrician by trade, short, bright-eyed and inventive. A good hand with a car engine too, he was soon to make himself useful with our radio sets and Land Rovers. Another was Willis Hessin, a Housing Executive staffer, keen-eyed, lithe and active, who was in his element as a Section Leader, specially on isolated reconnaissance missions.[4]

Hughie Patterson, farmer from Culnady was like Roy a sturdy figure with rugged good looks and an experienced USC Sergeant He soon took a lead in F Company. Farmers, as others have remarked, formed the finest army material. Linen workers too as proved by both Hughie's tall brothers who followed him into the Regiment, to form an upright and un-flappable trio.

Billy Hatrick, short and sturdy with the weathered face of a man who has lived his life in good clean country air. He comes from one of the four oldest Plantation families in County Derry, a hardworking farmer but always ready to come in for duty when extra help was needed.

Malachi Conway, a GPO worker with long service as a regular infantryman seemed to smell the battle like an old warhorse. His rubbery smile and kindly manner made him an ideal trainer of recruits.

Bobby Lennox a postman, strong-jawed and weather-beaten, had served throughout World War Two in the local Anti Aircraft Battery, so was already a trained soldier. All were 'rarin' to go' and impatient to get on with action.

But first we had to get kitted up. The way the green baggy combat uniform was first doled out with sparse choice of sizes brought alive all the Old Bill jokes.

'If it fits, bring it back, we'll change it.', was said to be the sign over the quartermaster's counter. A curious decision was to issue black USC style web equipment. It must have upset those anxious to discard any links with the past but in fact there just wasn't enough khaki stuff to go round. One sportsman having been asked to dye his web equipment black dyed his trousers and blouse too! We kept him for searching coal holes. In spite of three months of mail-shots, press advertising, tub-thumping by politicians of various colours and exhortations on the media, F Company had by March achieved less than a quarter of the planned strength of 200.

The Regiment as a whole was slightly better with 2000 or a third of establishment. The wife of a colonel of a famous Scottish regiment faced with similar slow intake had promised a kiss for every volunteer. She got a thousand men in a day and sore lips for weeks. Perhaps we should have asked Brigadier Logan Scott-Bowden, our first Commander, to fix something similar. As a man who had won a DSO while reconnoitering the beaches before D Day, and leading Landing Craft Obstacle Clearance Units on the day itself he commanded respect in any society. Red of face and white of hair, enthusiastic in manner, he soon became widely known and liked. We learned later that he had objected to the word Defence in the chosen title on the grounds the no war has ever been won by defensive tactics alone. His prophetic opinion which would have much support in South Derry was not accepted by the establishment.

On 31 March 1970 the USC punctiliously handed in all its weapons, uniform and equipment.

Next day **APRIL FIRST 1970** The Ulster Defence Regiment was declared   operational. F Company from its tarred and rust-streaked Nissen Hut base in Magherafelt, County Derry was of course ready for action   at the same moment. That meant being ready to guard vital points, patrol on foot, in vehicles or by helicopter, check traffic, search for arms, and do stints on the Border as well as in is own home areas. 'You're on active service now', we were told. In real life it seemed remarkably in-active. The start date may not have been inappropriate — with the Government starring as The April Fool — they dithered so much in subsequent handling of the Regiment they had so hurriedly created. See what you think when you've read further!

At this time Bill Craig's Vanguard Force and talk of an Independent Ulster made the politicians jumpy. A competent Unionist Minister in his day Bill had left the Unionist Party and failed to support my brother Henry against Ian Paisley in a recent General Election. Bill, the UDR tended to think , 'was a right man when he was at himself.' Now he had gone over the top in advocating a military take-over and was considered by realists to be 'just wind and piss.'

At first F Company had only twenty rifles to be shared among fifty men. This shortage appeared deliberate, a precaution lest hotheads should join the Vanguards. Locally as I recall none did. Many Loyalist organisations preceded and succeeded Vanguard in common response to IRA atrocities — Ulster-Protestant Volunteers, Ulster Volunteer Force, Red Hand Commandos, Ulster Safety Organisation (a local one), the numerically strong Ulster Defence Association and half a dozen more. They were in my time not well supported in South Derry and fortunately we had no local Shankill Butchers. F and G Company clashed with some occasionally when they staged masked road checkpoints. But no doubt these irregular outfits played a major part, being at times when army activity was politically restricted, virtually the only active players in thwarting IRA tactics and strategy. F Company rifles were kept in those early days at the home of the last user. There was a penny notebook with each weapon, to be signed on hand over for duty--primitive accountancy but it worked. Joiners of my generation, born between the Wars, were mostly frontiersmen, used to the danger of sudden attack, to handling weapons safely and to keeping a well-oiled pistol under the pillow, or at least handy, at night. A rifle hidden in the house was nothing new. One F Company man kept his in the grandfather clock in the hall with the bolt stored elsewhere. Recruits in Magherafelt after April 1970 continued at a trickle rather than a rush. They were now being sworn in by Major Joe Cantley, a long service regular officer who had been Adjutant of the USC, appointed to the same position in our 5 UDR.

In spite of all the haste and the muddle, the UDR started with many good men in it and the admirable ideal of being a force containing a fair mix of the two religious communities. The RUC had tried hard to do the same 40 years earlier. The IRA had then threatened to shoot anyone who joined, especially Catholics. Now, being conservative folk, they made the same promise of death to the UDR. Many brave Catholics none the less welcomed in 1970 what seemed a good opportunity to do their bit for peace. They volunteered with the intention of taking part in even-handed security work. Applications from Catholics living in the Bogside and Creggan areas in Derry seemed to Recruiting Officers particularly welcome. Having drawn their kit — weather proof uniform and excellent boots — they returned home much better clad than their neighbours. In a majority of cases neither they or the kit were ever seen again. HQ at Lisburn did their best to avoid such blatant abuse. But let us not forget that some determined 'Bogsiders' continued to serve faithfully and not a few died for their temerity at the hands of the terrorists. Entry to the UDR was clogged from early days by a largely avoidable delays and marred by errors of admission and omission. After early mistakes were discovered, the RUC began to be consulted in doubtful cases before a man or woman was signed on.

Training by May was more advanced. Recruits had to learn how in danger spots to be ready for instant action by keeping the rifle muzzle on high and the butt on hip, a position soon known as the Derry Port, also to walk backwards an art needed by the rear man in a foot patrol as he kept a lookout for snipers astern --- how to shoot fast and straight by day and night. Later came action drills such as taking stations for a road check point, with cover and torch men, searchers and note takers. How to search vehicles, houses and bridges for possible bombs, and not least how to avoid ambush and react to it when it happened. Never bunch. Always have lookout men in each direction and, to borrow a naval command, 'have guns at standby bearings'. Section Leaders learned to give orders in theoretical situations such as --

'A civilian car comes up to your checkpoint and suddenly turns away.'
or
'The front truck in your patrol has just been blown up. The Lance-Corporal in charge of it is wounded. Radio is out of action. How do you deploy the six men in the rear truck?
or
'A man comes up and tells you of suspicious lights in an isolated house.'
     Oh, I nearly forgot to mention saluting!
The Ballymena Nod, like its near relations, the Tyrone Twitch or Fermanagh Flick, is a sideways jerk of the chin, the Ulster countryman's way of greeting a friend. Fine, but from the nod derives The Ballymena Salute which has driven generations of drill sergeants near to despair. In this variant the head comes over almost 45 degrees to the right. Then curled fingers rise up to touch the temple. It's nearer to a pulling of the forelock than the regimental chop of the Training Manual. We did our best to follow the drill book but traces of the Twitch remained. I didn't mind too much. The Ballymena Salute is pleasantly familiar to anyone

who has served with soldiers from Northern Ireland - that is to say the best fighting men in the world — men whom you can lead to hell and back, but not drive an inch.

To ease the strain of all that training. some sport and relaxation was organized as soon as possible.

Ulster Defence Regiment Company Organization

A UDR Company was commanded by a major, if one was available. Under him were three platoons, each under a lieutenant or senior sergeant. The platoon had three ten-man sections, each commanded by a corporal, with a lance corporal as his second in command (2 I/C). These were all part timers. Conrate or full time service men, later known as Permanent Cadre, comprised initially a few armoury guards. This category was not widely introduced until about 1976. It was on the sections of part-timers, most frequently acting on their own, that the effectiveness of the Company depended.

Full time Company staff in early days was minimal. It comprised a Permanent Sergeant Instructor and at times a civilian clerk, a quartermaster-sergeant and storeman. Company strength, if recruiting was good, could rise to two hundred, allowing additional platoons to be formed. Companies in the country were so remote as to have a considerable degree of independence. F and G Companies were ten miles apart, and 30 miles from Battalion Headquarters.

Our transport consisted of Land Rovers. At times later we had Shorlands, light armoured cars built on a Land Rover Chassis.The members of F and later G Company were all volunteers and all neighbours. Each lived within a ten mile circle round our base, most much closer. Ours was the discipline of mutual respect of which there was at times little outside evidence. We kept heel clicking and saluting to a minimum. I found it difficult, in spite of reminders by the PSI, to address as Corporal Jones the man I knew daily at work as Billy.

In each company we aimed to create a close knit group of friends, Catholic and Protestant, who knew and would trust their lives to each other. It was a mix which had succeeded so admirably in local factories. In early days recruits were trained within the company or battalion and there was time for a company commander to talk to each volunteer and make him feel welcome and part of a friendly team. Later on recruits were trained at Regimental HQ and I didn't see them until they arrived as trained soldiers. The training was better but the process could lose the vital personal touch.   It is important in the Army, even as a part-timer, to decide at an early stage if you want to be a major or major-general. Promotion within the UDR could mean more time spent in dreary meetings and on administration. And to leading from the rear — an art Very Senior Officers who have 'got their bravery over young' need to master. It never appealed to me. Having no ambition outside a company, one could relax and let the career boys steam ahead.

There was talk after a year or two of UDR part timers commanding battalions. They never actually did command but later some did admin. jobs at colonel level. That carrot was enough to keep ambitious young chaps on their toes, keen to get on courses and read up that extremely dull publication Queens Regulations. As a recruiter I was no more than re-active. That meant going to all possible lengths to make volunteers welcome. But not begging families to send in their sons. The risks ahead were too great for the decision to join to be anything other than the freely made choice of the individual.

Our great advantage, specially in early days, was that the burden of administration was carried by the full time staff, while the part-timers like me got on with planning and carrying out Operations. That just made it possible to do concurrently a full time civilian job and run a family. The mantra of a 19th Century general might have suited F Company part timers.

'*Damn your writing. Mind your fighting*'.

The common denominator of a UDR Company in early days was that we were all neighbours and shared the object of keeping the peace.

Battalion Organisation

In charge of the companies was battalion Headquarters. (Bn.HQ) with a Lieutenant-Colonel as Commanding Officer (C.O.) The intention in the White Paper was that initially Battalion Commanders should be local retired regular officers - County Commandants in the USC or men from the other services of equivalent rank. A Captain and a Commander, Royal Navy were among the first and best. We were lucky to have as CO the affable Ken Davidson (died 1996). He had served through World War 11 in the Argyll and Sutherland Highlanders and seen much fighting in Palestine, the desert and Italy. More recently he had served for six years as a Special Constable USC until promoted in turn Adjutant and County Commandant.

Answering to the CO was a part- timer as second-in-command, a full time adjutant, quartermaster, regimental sergeant major and a group of warrant and non-commissioned officers. Sometimes we had a regimental Medical Officer too; Trevor was a memorable one who to kept us all in stitches.

Commanders UDR

Fifty miles away in Lisburn was Regimental HQ, on whom F and G Company never looked. It was situated in Thiepval Barracks, a sprawling 200 acre fenced enclosure which housed the Army NI Headquarters. We became aware of them only from an occasional visit by the Brigadier Commanding. He was a busy man, controlling initially seven battalions. The visits were, as I recollect , always constructive. We were blessed throughout with excellent Commanders UDR — soldiers of fair minds, proven courage and administrative skills. For Operations 5UDR came under the control of 8 Brigade at Ebrington Barracks in Derry.

The IRA

Also neighbours were IRA members and supporters, with whom one traded and passed the time of day. These lads were victims of their own propaganda. Taught by parents and mentors, by the slant of school text books and teachers, by priests and political leaders, they blamed everything from the weather to the measles on the British, especially on the Ulster Protestants. They learned above all to hate. Sean O' Callaghan who joined the IRA aged 15 in 1970 has described his IRA experiences and the events that persuaded him to join.

He wrote in the Spectator of April 20th 1996

'The Catholic Church has long been a law unto itself. In many respects it is a rather unique form of criminality. Why unique? Because it consistently conspires with the worst elements of extreme nationalism to produce a dogma based on racial purity of a mythological 'Irish race'. We were taught that Irish Catholics were special to God and that the Virgin Mary was an Irish Colleen. Padraic Pearse and Easter Week were inextricably woven into a seamless mix of blood and sacrifice for country and Church. The Catholic Church's crimes against decency and

humanity on this island threatened to submerge us in a sea of superstition, ignorance and hatred of all that was not totally obedient to its will. The Nationalist cause was preached from the Pulpit and in the Dail and, fool that I was, I fell for it.

The Irish Press, ably led by Tim Pat Coogan, played its part with distinction. Hatred of Britain and the Unionists was vomited daily from its pages

Above is reproduced by kind permission of The Spectator Magazine Ltd

Sean goes on to tell how after helping to murder a soldier he was wined, dined, feted and lionized by the local priesthood.

Weapons for the IRA were mixed. The trusty old Tommy gun was popular in the early seventies. Shot guns, initially good news, went out of fashion as high velocity automatic rifles became available. Later twelve bores were popular again because forensic traces from small shot as opposed to bullets were minimal. Weapon technology and armament steadily increased as the IRA employed experts to design firing mechanism for bombs, booby traps and home-made mortars. They purchased with money from overseas rocket propelled grenades, heavy calibre machine guns and sniper rifles like the Barrett Light Fifty which could penetrate body armour and kill at over a thousand yards. The UDR had continually to keep learning to remain abreast.

As regards motivation and objects a version of the Sinn Fein oath[5] gives an idea of the IRA's objects. In aiming to unite Ireland by terrorizing the Protestants out of their homes the IRA had good material from which to recruit. Britain's Special Forces during WWII always contained a high proportion of Irishmen.

John Lodwick remarks in The Filibusters (Methuen 1946): *'Scotsmen and Irishmen will always predominate in any raiding force drawn from natives of the United Kingdom. I do not know why this is but it is a universal truth. Jocks are deadly in drink and can smash cafe tables more quickly than any other troops, but they can also carry greater loads and carry them farther. The Micks are incurably sentimental and obstinate as be-damned but well officered will go anywhere.'*

The Irish have a talent for guerilla warfare. That made the IRA tough enemies. Their ranks in 1970 contained a number of brave and clever men. The IRA also recruited skilled public relations men and propagandists. The latter, free of any of the obligations felt by democracies to broadcast the truth, were more deadly than the gunmen. Some IRA men fought clean; to them I bear no malice. In the words of a Scotsman of old, 'My enemy is my friend; he sharpens my wits, tests my skill and courage.' The UDR coming mainly from Ulster-Scots stock, which combined the fighting virtues of both nations, were even tougher. But they fought under enormous handicaps. Strict observance of the law under which democracies must operate makes the suppression of terrorism a most inefficient process.

The IRA were in their view free to torture or shoot any of us at any time without warning or wearing uniform and yet when arrested to claim prisoner of war status under the Geneva Convention. Government policy was to accept this and often appeared to stand not, as one might expect, behind the security forces and against the terrorists but evenly between the terrorists and their victims. PIRA activity varied from season to season. Assaults on RUC Stations at one time, car bombs and booby traps at another, ambushes of vehicles, attacks on army locations or off duty soldiers, blowing up of power and railway lines at others. It depended, one heard, on the bounty offered — so much for shooting a soldier, so much for killing a policeman, so much for a successful road mine or booby trap. Sniping attacks on individuals off duty was the most disagreeable tactic for the UDR and was soon to become top of the IRA pops.

The UDR was the target of several varieties of terrorists. To the soldier being shot at it didn't matter much, if at all, which group took the discredit — Irish National Liberation Army (INLA), Provisionals (PIRA) or Officials (OIRA). Our local impression was that PIRA and OIRA swapped guns and explosives and shared information much of the time. PIRA's objects varied from time to time. One could take it as getting the whole of Ireland under their own control; and shooting as many policemen and soldiers as possible along the way. The end justified any means.

James Connolly had in 1916 expressed as his desire *the expulsion of Imperialism in all its forms, political, economic, military and cultural.* As in any long struggle the motivation tended to get blurred. At times the object seemed to be just to keep going. One might interpret some of their actions in the words of Dalrymple in the New Statesman 2002 —

'few things are more enjoyable than unutterable cruelty committed in the name of justice and virtue'

The Officials obligingly issued   an update in early   1972 which showed how far that particular segment had moved from its traditional stance As quoted in a Friends of the Union Leaflet called The Extreme Left   this read *'We are not a Catholic organisation. We never said we were. If there is anyone in the community who is giving us support in the belief that we are some sort of militant Catholic nationalist organisation then let them withdraw their support now We are nothing of the sort We are out to build a revolutionary socialist party of the Irish working class'.* That must have limited their support quite a bit .

The UDR's biggest handicap was top Government policy.   The Foreign Office, it came through gradually to us at grass roots, did not want to defeat Ulster's enemies.   A major factor in this attitude was the fear of upsetting England's relationship with USA where the White House depended heavily on the Irish pro-IRA vote.

Tension between Unionists and Nationalists does not exist principally as a result of differences in religious beliefs. It arises as a result of differences in allegiance -- with almost all Protestants, and a significant minority of Roman Catholics, wishing to remain in the United Kingdom and the majority of Roman Catholics wishing to be part of a United Ireland. It was a separatist war we were fighting, not a religious one.

The Africans say that *'When two Rhinoceroses fight only the ground underneath is damaged.'* That in essence is what happened in Ulster.

Footnotes

1:   THE IRA . *Harper Collins Paperback Edition 1970 P. 37)*

2:   *DERRY ; The choice of Londonderry or Derry as a place name has sadly been turned during last few years into a bone of contention. My family and most of our neighbours   have always used Derry for the simple reason that it is shorter ands easier to pronounce: so Derry it will be in this book. Londonderry was adopted only some 300 years ago when the City of London Guilds furnished the money to improve the fortifications and provide settlers with tools and equipment. Derry, the oak wood in Irish, goes back 1500 years to the days of St Columba .*

3 : *THE ULSTER SPECIAL CONSTABULARY*
     In 1920 with Ulster under heavy attack from terrorists the British Government created to assist the Royal Irish Constabulary three categories

of Special Constables--As full time, Bs part time and C part time for static guards only .

When the IRA had been beaten in 1923 only the B Specials were retained in support of the RUC. They came to be referred to as the' B Men', wore police uniforms and were armed with Lee Enfield . 303 rifles.

There ware eight USC battalions, one in each of the six counties, in Derry and Belfast. They were commanded by a County or City Commandant . Within the battalion were districts of company strength and sub-districts of platoon strength. ie about 30 men. Their wide coverage, sharp eyes and ears to the ground made it very difficult for the IRA to assemble for operations, or even plan them, without the USC being aware of what was going on. One measure of their efficiency is their excellent skill at arms. In the Northern Ireland Command Rifle Meeting in April 1968 nineteen teams took part representing the Regular Army, Territorial Army, RAF, RUC and USC. The USC took first, second, and third prizes.

The 10.000 B Specials were administered with remarkable economy by less than one hundred full time staff, mostly retired regular soldiers. In 50 years between 1920 and their disbandment in 1970 the USC lost only 20 weapons. The Army in Northern Ireland in the same period lost from armouries several hundred.

During the fifty years civilians killed by the USC in accidental shooting numbered less than a dozen. The security forces in the seventies killed more than that in single years. Deaths of USC members at the hands of terrorists were seven only between 1922 and 1970. These figures show how peaceful the Province was from the end of the 1922 troubles and 1969 and the excellent discipline of the USC.

Better armed and equipped and with a lower age limit for retirement they could have been doing the same for the community today. Anti-Propagandists fastened on the fact that the USC contained very few and at times no Roman Catholics. This was in spite of substantial efforts early on to recruit them. The effort failed because the IRA showed their determination to murder any Catholic who joined -- the old Republican game of refusing cooperation and then crying discrimination.

In 50 years the IRA managed to penetrate to some degree all branches of the security forces. The B men were never penetrated.

Some B Men were members of the Orange Order but the Order had no control whatsoever in the manning or management of the Force.

The details of how the Special's reputation was destroyed by carefully fabricated lies and innuendo is told in with great clarity and detail in The 'B' Specials by Admiral Sir Arthur Hezlet KVO DSO DSC, a historian of international standing.

(Reprint and update by Mourne River Press, 1997)

SOME SPECIFIC ATTEMPTS TO DISCREDIT

Here are examples of the sort of fabrication attempted. Dan Breen, a well known IRA leader, was getting away after an operation in County Louth with two fellow Volunteers Frank Aiken and Oscar Traynor at high speed in side car. The road was bumpy. Dan fell out so heavily that his colleagues took him for dead.

'Let's put a few bullets into him' ,said one 'dump him north of the Border and say there's been a B Special atrocity'. At this juncture Dan came to and while applauding the idea suggested they find another victim. Another example is the attempt to prove that the USC took part in the stoning of the NICRA marchers en route from Belfast at Burntollet Bridge near Derry on 4th January 1969

Mr Paddy Devlin, Northern Ireland Labour MP for Falls, between 6th May and 8th July 1969 asked no less than 442 questions of the Minister of Home Affairs. He produced 180 names, presumably from photographs taken at the incident, and asked the Minister if they were members of the USC. Of these 117 had never been in the USC ; 47 had been members in the past but were not serving at the time. Some had been out for years. Twenty five of the names were serving members but there was only evidence that two were at Burntollet .One who lived nearby was watching 250 yards away from the bridge. The other was not known to have acted unlawfully in any way.In spite of these answers a disappointed Mr Devlin repeated his allegations on 25 June saying that a hundred members of the USC were present at the affray.

This statement re-appeared in print under the title Burntollet. The suggestion that the USC was used officially or deliberately to support attacks on civil rights demonstrations is utterly false and was refuted in the lengthy Cameron report on the incidents Two Special Constables who allowed themselves to be embroiled in a riot in Maghera on Jan 4th were fined in the Magistrates Court. Both the men were required to resign.

A different sort of incident illustrates the use of local knowledge and swift riposte which B men were well equipped to carry out. In the winter of 1957 two brothers were sitting by their fireside near the Tyrone Border when they heard an explosion. They judged it to be an attempt on a police station two miles away. Instantly they donned their high necked USC jackets which cover any sort of under garment. Grabbing their rifles they made for a bridge over the Border and lay in wait Five minutes later along at the trot came a pair of IRA bombers. Challenged they promptly dropped their arms and surrendered. That is the sort of 'cop' that the time involved in reporting for orders and drawing weapons from an armoury would have made virtually impossible for the UDR.

In 25 years service with the USC as a constable, sergeant and commandant I never witnessed any illegal behaviour, physical abuse or saw anything done that would not appear well on television. We were ordinary law-abiding citizens who were prepared to turn out when needed to prevent terrorist attacks on our homes.

4: *Captain Willis Hessin, having fought gallantly to the end, died in his bed of cancer in 1999*

5: *THE SINN FEIN OATH*
   (Version found by my father in a raid on an arms dump about 1922)

   'I . . . swear by Almighty God...by the blessed Virgin Mary , Mother of God and by Saint Patrick .....

   To fight until I die, wading in the Red Gore of the Saxon Tyrants and Murderers of the glorious cause of Nationalism, until there is not a vestige or footprint left to tell that the holy soil of Ireland was trodden by the Saxon Tyrants and Murderers
   And when the English Protestants and brutes shall be murdered and driven into the sea, like the swine Jesus caused to be drowned, we shall take Ireland ,root out the accursed heretics, adulterers and murderers of Henry VIII.
   And possess the treasures of the beasts that kept our Beloved Isle of Saints in bondage and us in foreign lands and shall wade in the blood of Orangemen and heretics who do not join us and become one of us.'
   Whether was this oath was required of recruit in 1970 is open to question. The words may have changed; the objects have apparently not.

CHAPTER TWO
PHONEY WAR
1970

Phoney War was a phrase used to describe the inert period at the start of World War Two.

'It is a law of life that is yet to be broken that a nation can only earn the right to live soft by being prepared to die hard in defence of its living'.

Field Marshall Wavell. 1945

For a few months after its activation 5 UDR trained in what seemed a no-risk situation. At battalion level there was little sense of urgency. But some of us felt very uneasy. It is hard to realize looking back how quiet things appeared on the surface but certain incidents give the feel of the period. About February 1970 a promotional CTP was held at Ebrington Barracks to sell the regiment to the great and good. Present were civic dignitaries and clergy of all denominations. Having driven 40 miles to attend I slid down a couple of quick drinks, then got myself into trouble with the Colonel Commandant. (not for the last time).

'How are things going, Wallace?', he asked as I joined a group.

'Terrible, sir,' I replied. 'We haven't done a day's work yet, and here we are drinking while the enemy is arming'.

'Well, I've done a day's work,' he snapped back and turned away. Next day I was ordered to apologize. Lucky it wasn't demand for 'Reasons in Writing', a form of naval torture which I had endured in WW 11.

General John Anderson, a great man and the founder of the regiment, bore no malice but the lesson was simple. I should have known always to tell senior officers what they want to hear. That should be added to the essential maxims for young soldiers—Never volunteer, Never be separated from your kit, and Never march on Moscow.

The very first checkpoint by F Coy was on April 3rd on a main road near Toome Bridge. Sergeant Roy Moore recalls his men being un-armed and ordered from HQ what to tell each driver,

'I wish to inform you that this is an Ulster Defence Regiment security check.'

At another slightly later stage we were ordered that cover men only should be armed and must keep well out of sight. As if the motorists cared .... The intended public relations exercise was as ineffective as it was harmless. For grown men who had been carrying out real life anti-IRA patrols for years, it just seemed silly.

'It's a wonder we didn't all resign in disgust from this barmy army ', is the recollection of one man who later became a battalion field officer.

Perhaps the strongest indication in this guerre de petit pois was the way that Malachi Conway, a Catholic ex- Regular soldier who lived nine miles from our base, travelled in uniform to attend training. He often thumbed a lift, at other times took a bus wearing UDR uniform. A few months later such a practice would have led to abduction and death. We soon got together to fix him a lift. In mid-April my cousin James Chichester-Clark, on the way home from his Prime Ministerial desk at Stormont, stopped at one of our VCP's to ask how things were.

'Very short of weapons, Sir. Only 15 among 45 men,' said newly fledged Lieutenant Sammy Hudson. He'd been wearing a Sub District Commandant USC 's two black pips a few days earlier.

'I'll see about that', said Major James, as the PM was affectionately known by his neighbours.

Within three days we got a rifle for every man.

Our military Land Rovers drew their petrol from civilian filling stations. Without a secure base to store MOD supplies there was no other way. The owner of one pump we patronized was not known for army sympathies. We later found that he had been noting car numbers and names of soldiers.

In May we were ordered, while attending a day's training, to form an Officer's Mess. Captain Jim Hood in a loud aside remarked, 'I think we're in a big enough mess already'.

Jim, a big quiet man, was always worth listening to. He had a son in the regiment and another in the Police. The USC, in which he was a senior officer, had managed, like the RUC, without any form of Mess. We had our social life in each other's houses and as a result cut down on bases which absorb so much manpower by needing guards. Experienced men like Jim knew that when the balloon went up — which it could at any minute — there was no way that 500 half-trained UDR men could

keep the peace or hold terrorists in check as well as had been done in the
County for 50 years by 1500 experienced B Specials, famed for
marksmanship and intelligence. A bit of planning unsuitable to the
threatening conditions was locating a new company headquarters half a
mile from the Border in what came to be known as the Enclave. That is
a half moon slice of Northern Ireland lying west of the Foyle.
Duncreggan Camp was opened with great éclat by the Lord Lieutenant.
But later when the sniping started in earnest the site proved to be
militarily untenable. B Coy moved back to Ebrington beside Battalion
HQ.

Some Special Forces at this time allowed themselves to be
photographed driving round NI wearing their cap badges. 'Doing a
recce,' they said. I suspect they were doing more than that but would
have been much better getting stuck in when the enemy was weak. This
Fool's Paradise was to continue for many months.

Area of Operations
(Known later as a Tactical Area of Responsibility or TAOR)

The countryside which became F Company's care is the west side of
the Bann Valley, a rectangle about 15 miles east/west by 20 north/south.
Its south-east boundary is the broad expanse of Lough Neagh, it's east
the placid River Bann and west the thousand foot rampart of the Sperrin
hills. The graceful peak of Slieve Gallion, with spruce plantations
hanging on its shoulders like a cloak, marks the south west limit. The
town of Kilrea lies just inside the northern edge and Moneymore is
similarly placed in the south.

Low ridges and round hillocks punctuate every view. Between them
are small plains and valleys, divided into irregular fields by thorn hedges
and stone walls. The glowing green of well-kept meadows is at its most
striking in May when the patches of rushy bog beside them are still in
the camel-colour of winter and the thickets of whins shine in cadmium
yellow. This is when visitors exclaim, 'Here I see why Ireland's called
the Emerald Isle!'

There are a few places where hills have been cut through to make
sunken roads and lots of dips and sharp bends, ideal for ambushers.
Surfaces are good and blind bends being eliminated Councillor Charlie
O'Hara of Maghera used to say in the fifties, 'The Romans were great
road builders but if they'd come to Ireland they'd have learned a lot from

the Derry County Council.' We are proud of our roads.

There is not much in the way of forestry but many tall trees – ash, oak, beech and sycamore — decorate the pleasantly shaggy hedgerows. Population is light and in 1970 there wasn't the need of a traffic light in the whole area. Economic importance comes from in its position at the centre of Ulster where the main road A29 north from Armagh to the North Channel crosses the A5 linking Belfast to Derry. This means easy access, about an hour by car, to the coast on the one hand and the Border on the other. South Derry where I have spent all my life is a good country to live in and it is not surprising that both factions consider it worth fighting for.

'When the gunmen are active on the Border South Derry is quiet and vice versa' was a 1920 saying which still has some truth. Like so many battlegrounds this patch lay maddeningly at the junction of three sheets of One Inch OS maps -- a curse for navigators. In practice our local knowledge was usually sufficient without referral. Perhaps that was one of our blessings, because soldiers say that the biggest danger in war is an officer with a map.

The Denominational Split

Recruiting continued to be slow. Regimental strength in September 1970 was 3,000, in F Company still about 50.

HQ were set on recruiting from the minority. Quite rightly but at times the aspiration seemed to reach the point of paranoia. 'Our very first application opened was from a Catholic', a senior officer had chortled in January 1970. Further reports about the even balance were issued at short intervals. F Coy sympathised with the motives and made Catholic recruits welcome but history told us that the chances of any proportion being allowed by the IRA to remain in the regiment were negligible. It was not long before HQ stopped issuing bulletins because the figures didn't encourage disclosure.

In the case of our 5th Battalion by late summer 1971 some 70 Catholics had signed on in response to the recruiting of Lt. Colonel Davidson. Of these by 1972 only three remained to serve under our new Catholic CO, Lt. Colonel John Lys. Two had been shot, the rest resigned, mostly because of death threats by the IRA. So the appointment of a Catholic CO did nothing to stop the rot. One who stuck to his post was the brave Malachi Conway, later our Company Sergeant-

Major.   The overall percentage of Catholics peaked at 19% then after a rapid decline due to intimidation settled down at 3%.

The End of The Beginning

The records say that Province–wide there were 170 bombs in 1970. Most as I recall were in the latter half of year.

The IRA suffered a fatal own goal in June when a bomb factory in Derry exploded, and another in September when a bomb meant for an electricity transformer in Belfast went off too soon. They needed time to give their bombers training. Content to rule the Bogside where the RUC found it almost impossible to serve a summons, the IRA godfathers kept offensive activity at a low level. On August 3 the army in Belfast made its first use of water cannon and rubber bullets. These so called baton rounds 6" long by 1" diameter and weighing five ounces, were propelled by loose discs of cordite. F Coy were trained in their use on certain guard duties but never fired any in anger in my time. The missiles became prized as souvenirs. At the same time rioters began to fire vicious steel tipped arrows.

Four nights of rioting in Belfast at the end of September 1970 might be said to mark the beginning of the end of the Phoney War. The RUC were being re-armed as Hunt Report predictions of enemy weakness proved inaccurate. The army was becoming more and more involved. But not the UDR . We were specifically banned from riot control.

By November 1970 F Company was busy patrolling but the chance of effective use of the UDR as a whole seemed to me remote. We received little in the way of intelligence and enemy contacts so far had been nil.

I was summoned from bed about midnight in October by a phone call from Corporal Jim Smyth. He was a competent quietly spoken section leader who later became a captain and sadly died in 1995. An ex-service civilian had reported a bomb at the door of a wooden hut near the police station on the Tobermore Road. This had been used for training by the USC and was now a base for occasional use by a platoon of the Royal Greenjackets.

There was still novelty value in a bomb. On arrival I saw policemen keeping a crowd back and narrowed my eyes to make out a tin alarm clock beside a milk churn at the hut door. When the crowd stopped chattering, it could be heard ticking. RUC Sergeant Dan gently carried a 94 year old woman wrapped in a blanket out of her house. She appeared unconcerned, perhaps unaware of what was going on. After a few minutes the bomb went off, but feebly. It barely shattered the milk churn.

'Good old Stickies; another bloody dud', said a voice behind me. It sounded as if the primer only had fired. A pity for us it hadn't worked better; the hut was shortly due for demolition. Attention switched to a nearby car, hijacked presumably by the bomber. The crowd waited, eager to see some action. The Bomb Disposal Officer (ATO) arrived from Derry, looking sunken-eyed and tired from dealing with many hoaxes. He drank a pint of coffee and approached the car reluctantly. A helper handed him a gun and torch; he fired an incendiary round into the car without visible effect, then another. On the third the car slowly became ringed in red, like a display at Portrush fireworks. A couple of fireballs shot out of it, Roman Candle style. The crowd went. 'Ooh' and 'Aah', and when nothing else happened for fifteen minutes slowly dispersed towards Regan's Bar .

That was a bomb night in Maghera. Soon to become all too familiar. From our view point this one was near home, and the risks of sniping minimal. It could have been a lot worse — a bomb night in the Brandywell.

We observed these things and did some searches. One of these followed a soldier's report of an unusual cross marked on a gatepost on the busy A5. In a sheugh on the opposite side of the road was a .300 rifle in a temporary hide. Good work but no way were we allowed to get up and go after the bombers or snipers by means of area sweeps or house searches.

Business pressure at home was acute and the need to make overseas sales trips increasing. Regretfully I applied to resign my commission. Looking back I wonder why I didn't simply ask to be dormant; i.e excused duty for a spell. But perhaps that option was not then on offer. The company, now numbering 70, was still under strength but training hard. We had been given an ex-Ministry of Agriculture Nissen hut for training in Magherafelt and an ex-USC Hut in Tobermore. Each man now a Lee Enfield .303 Rifle which he kept hidden at home when off duty. By February 1971 the four months it took for my release to come through was up. I handed over with mixed feelings to my stout second-in-command Captain Sammy Hudson.

The bliss of evenings and weekends at home was enjoyed as never before. But my timing was wrong, for I was departing just as the balloon was about to go up. In March 1971 Major James Chichester–Clark resigned as Prime Minister after the Westminister Government refused his requests to increase security force levels and re-occupy the No-Go areas. The experienced Brian Faulkner succeeded him in the hot seat. In June 1971 Ken Davidson our Commanding Officer who had been appointed for *'an initial period of one year'* and led to expect an extension was replaced by John Lys, a serving gunner. Most of the other ex-USC commanding officers were treated the same. One exception was Jack Riley, a young retired Royal Naval officer and ex-County Commandant of Tyrone. He had been so outstandingly successful in recruiting that he was retained for years. And one or two others stayed on for a while. I know that Ken Davidson who had put his all into the creation of the 5th Battalion and succeeded in recruiting 550 men was deeply hurt. He and his peers had been led to expect longer appointments.

Most of the new commanding officers were very good but nearly all lacked local knowledge. This meant a six month initiation period before each became effective. Meanwhile the opposition had been allowed to become much more sophisticated and soon the burden of command was too demanding for part-timers to be considered.

Internment and the First UDR Casualty.

Army and police deaths began to mount by March 1971 but it was to be another four months before the UDR took its first fatal casualty. This was to come in August 1971 at the time of internment when Brian Faulkner ordered the arrest of what was supposed to be a long list of known terrorists. The Army had reservations about internment, predicting correctly that the resentment caused would outdo any benefits. But Ted Heath listened to Faulkner. The UDR was not, I hasten to say, involved in the arrests but suffered sorely from the aftermath.

Internment without trial had been widely employed by European governments with security problems during the early twentieth century. In Ireland, promptly and briefly applied in The North and the Republic, it had proved highly effective as an anti-terrorist measure. Quite recently when the IRA launched what they intended to be a major offensive in 1956 swift internment played a major part in their defeat. This time there had been so much brinkmanship and warning that most leading terrorists had gone into hiding, locally and across the Border. On the first night some 250 men were rounded up.

Many of the arrests were carried out at night by soldiers who were inclined to break down the door if a man did not emerge at once. Policemen carrying out the same job would, unless the man was exceptionally dangerous, knock on the door, give him a minute or two to pull on some clothes, then take him off with minimum force. One army snatch squad in our area travelled in a Pig-troop carrier with a Special Branch policeman as guide. Their first call was on a 75 year old. He'd had nil terrorist connections for twenty years, and was allowed to go back to bed, flattered to be still considered active. At the next house there were four brothers; the soldiers got them to walk them past the Pig so that the Special Branch man who had to remain anonymous could identify the dangerous ones through a spy hole in the armour. They and other arrestees were handcuffed and laid on the floor of the troop-carrier. From there they were driven to an aircraft hangar at Ballykelly, then still handcuffed by helicopter to HMS Maidstone, a prison ship in Belfast Lough. A lot of unnecessary pain and humiliation was caused. Arrests continued until over 800 suspects were in the bag. Many were released after initial questioning. Past experience proved that after arrest of this sort internees give a great deal of information, mainly in trying to establish innocence. This time however the intelligence so available was not strongly followed up.

The legal complications of the arrests were expensive, long drawn out and equally unnecessary. Major Michael Armstrong UDR, ex B Special

District Commandant in Armagh and a member of the UDR Planning Committee, was a barrister by profession. He had pointed out to the General Officer Commanding in my presence that under current legislation soldiers did not have Powers of Arrest and advised that this should be amended by Parliament. His words were ignored. The failure to pass a corrective Act cost the Exchequer large sums in compensation.

A day or two later after the arrests started Winston Donnell, a private in our neighbouring UDR battalion, was on duty near the Border on a routine checkpoint. This had been set up at the bottom of a steep hill west of Strabane where the Clabby salient projects towards Donegal. Donell was one of two cover men concealed in the hedge on the Border side of the checkpoint. The IRA devised a clever plan of attack.

A car with its rear window removed was allowed to free wheel backwards down the hill enabling a gunman in the back to get in a burst of fire at the soldiers on the road. As soon as he had done so the driver was to engage a forward gear and speed away. Seeing the car coming towards the VCP and perhaps also the gunman, the brave Donnell stepped into the middle of the road to intercept it. He was shot down before he could open fire, but his action saved the lives of one or more men at the check point. If only he had remained concealed he could have been ideally placed to take the retreating enemy on the flank. Hindsight is a wonderful thing, and Winston did not die in vain, as subsequent checkpoints changed procedures after learning from his gallant death. There was still a year to go before F Coy suffered its first fatality. From internment there followed a huge increase in IRA attacks, resulting in an equally huge increase in UDR applications. Mine to rejoin was among them.

Then came personal experience of the frustration caused by delays in vetting recruits. The process was seriously flawed and defeated all efforts by the Advisory Council to speed it up. The RUC, now being consulted late in the day, were very slow to reply. There was still an acute shortage of officers but in October I was told it could take up to six months to be accepted. My request at first was to return as private soldier as that way demands on time and responsibility would be much less. My close friend Captain Marcus McCausland of D Company, Limavady, agreed that this idea might suit him too. He had been in process of attempting to resign since September because he felt that internment was morally and politically wrong. But as we learned later with sorrow, he was talked out of leaving because he was a Catholic and hence doubly valuable to the regiment. So he agreed to stay on, dormant without appointment. The OIRA then formed the impression that he was acting as a spy because they easily found out that he was on the UDR books and observed that he was not doing uniformed duties. As regards being a private, I meant it. Another friend Harry Stevenson from a neighbouring battalion wanted to do the same but both of us were persuaded to take commissions. After I'd telephoned the Commander UDR direct and asked him to speed things up, my posting came through in four months. That happened in January 1972 and was accompanied by a drop in rank. After a nine months absence I was allocated command of 26 Platoon in my old company. What a big plus that turned out. Lots of familiar faces to work with and it was far more to my taste to work at platoon than company level. Less administration hassle, and you could be out on the ground most of the time. I found that F Company strength had increased to 200 and an enormous improvement had taken place in weapon training, checkpoint and anti-ambush drills. Personal kit, accommodation and weapons were all better. Except perhaps in one respect. The good old Lee Enfield .303 had served Britain so well in two World Wars, and me for 25 years, was replaced by a semi-automatic weapon. Since a UDR soldier carried only twenty rounds and seldom fired at hard targets the advantages of high velocity and rapid fire were unclear. Public attitudes had hardened against the terrorists and our permitted reaction been toughened to meet it. All passengers of suspect cars could be got out, spread-eagled and searched. I felt out of touch for the first few patrols but the lads, bless 'em, looked after me and covered my areas of ignorance. Now what we needed was more intelligence. The organization to get it was being created and we all hoped that should lead to plenty of enemy contacts.

CHAPTER THREE
Patrols, Pickets and Checkpoints 1972

'We shall not weaken or tire. Neither the sudden shock of battle or the long drawn out trials of vigilance and exertion will wear us down'.

Winston Churchill

26 Platoon, F Company

If you'd looked along the road running south out of Magherafelt at 7.45 of an evening in January 1972 you'd have seen arriving a dozen or more cars. Under the street lights you might make out that the drivers were wearing civilian raincoats pulled over khaki combat jackets. Their green UDR berets would be concealed in a side pocket or on their knees. Armed only with puny private pistols, or nothing at all, they were at that moment relatively easy terrorist targets. The cars would be checked by a sentry wearing a flak jacket and armed with a rifle before disappearing through a high gate painted a sickly yellowish green. Other men who lived locally would be arriving on foot.

At 8 pm every third or fourth night 26 Platoon assembled on rough gravel that passed for a parade ground in front of a group of corrugated iron Nissen huts within a barbed wire enclosure. It had a name now — Fort William. As Duty Platoon they had been doing so at about the same time for the previous eighteen months. They'd form up in three ranks under the eye of the Platoon Sergeant on high summer days to patrol until the afterglow blended into dawn. They'd fallen in as the sun cast long shadows on balmy Indian summer evenings, fallen in on wet misty November nights, fallen in shivering on icy black nights in January, and stamping snow off their boots on white nights in February.

These were hard times. In Derry 26 platoon had seen the IRA taunt the army in weeks of verbal provocation, by sniping, by stoning and by bombing. Especially hard to endure for the regulars were mixed showers of missiles, mostly stones for which a shield was adequate protection but including an occasional 'knacker bomb', a small charge surrounded by nails which could maim, and sometimes high explosive grenade which could kill. To deal with these a keen-eyed rifleman had to be appointed on special lookout, calling 'Stone!', or. 'Bomb!', so that correct action could be taken. Days of taunting were interrupted only about 6 pm when the teenage would-be terrorists went inside to see themselves on television. The stoners had become skilful in planned withdrawals or feigned flight which led pursuing soldiers past carefully posted snipers. And scarcely an arrest had been made Inevitably this provocation and frustration lead to the necessity of a snatch squad and a gunfight during a Civil Rights march on Jan 30th. The terrorists got the worst of it. But they managed to label it Bloody Sunday. F Company were there that day manning check points on approach roads from Strabane and Dungiven. They were ordered to stop all traffic early on and that was when they heard the unmistakable fire of a Thompson sub-machine gun which the army never used. Later they let through some well searched vehicles.

A PART-TIME PRIVATE'S VIEW

(This was contributed in Spring 1972 to a local paper by a member of the Ulster Defence Regiment who wished to remain anonymous)

The whins in the hedgerows are starting to become a mass of gold and early daffodils show yellow heads. The lovely Ulster countryside is quickening with spring.

Glimpses of these annual pleasures are doubly delightful to members of a small fast growing body of Ulstermen who have become closely knit as The Ulster Defence Regiment. They are often too sleepy by day to enjoy the feel of spring, and sometimes wonder if they'll ever see these things again. Their regiment is now two years old. It has already suffered 10 deaths and many wounded at the hands of the IRA, the majority of these murdered off-duty .

Every three days I finish work at 5.30 and hurry home to join my wife in listening to the news. Not long ago the Northern Ireland news was a dull recital of domestic minutiae, now it is a war bulletin. Today's crop – ten more bombs and another policeman shot in cold blood. You can get used to anything, I suppose, but the closer parallel to older people in the United Kingdom is that this is like being back in World War II. There is just time to see the children to bed, gobble a meal and get dressed. It looks like a frosty night. Long underpants and a long-sleeved vest, thick stockings over a pair of socks, the huge army rubber-soled boots, clumsy, but warm with their nylon insulating liner (That's one part of me that won't be cold), combat trousers of double proofed cotton, a khaki shirt, army pullover, a civilian waistcoat, a combat jacket, a stocking cap comforter. A check on doors and windows in the house, a reiterated warning to my wife not to open to anyone, and then off on an eight mile drive to join the platoon. Most of us try to go in pairs or groups, but as no one in the platoon lives near by I travel alone. I vary the route as much as possible, but the options are limited. A wave from the sentry at the gate lets me into our base. I grab a flak jacket; lucky there's one left. They cost the taxpayer £150 each, so there are only enough for about half of us; the one I find is small. With it on my arms are restricted and I feel as clumsy as a knight of old must have felt in his armour. In silhouette we all could be taken for American footballers

We fall in. The Platoon Sergeant details us, most are dispatched to guard the police stations, power installations and pumping units for which my company is responsible. On these duties a man gets three or four hours sleep out of the eight hour 'stag'.

The regular army are given television sets to pass the time, cakes from local women's associations, and in most cases blankets and bunks to sleep in. We have to make do with a pack of cards and what we can provide ourselves; often one is glad of a piece of floor to sit on. I'm for the mobile patrol tonight; we climb into the back of a Land Rover, listen to the familiar routine of the radio check and pass a joke or two about what has happened since we last met. Sunray, our commander reports to the Operations Room. Tonight four regular soldiers have joined us, two in each Land Rover. Army vehicles always operate on pairs We are glad to have them with us, for the extra fire power and someone new to talk to. They appreciate the way we know every hole in the hedge. Four of our section go off in their Land Rover. The front Land Rover is armoured, ours is not. I sit at the rear with my rifle pointing out into the darkness. At any minute machine gun fire or a sniper shot may come out of the darkness. We pull up for a few minutes here, half an hour there, stop cars, look in the boots, under the bonnets, frisk the inmates with formal politeness, laugh off the insults or jybes. The search is superficial but it is all we can do. The night passes slowly, the sense of comradeship, the good humour make up for the fact that we'd much rather be at home in bed.

One thing I admire is the almost incredible bravery of the Roman Catholics, in our ranks, stubborn to the point of foolhardiness; many of them already warned to get out by the IRA, but refusing to do so. One was special chum of mine at school three years ago. These are the sort of men you'd like to have beside you in scrap. The nearest UDR patrol is 20 miles away. There are not nearly enough of us, but we are growing in strength. To beat the terrorists we need patrol no more than every five miles apart as we were able to in the B Specials. At a lonely crossroads four of us are sent off with the Army to investigate a deserted house from which lights have been reported. The Army move at a smart jog tro; we keep up as best we can. The heavy clothing, right for sitting in the Land Rover, is desperately clumsy across country. The house proves a blank, we walk back a little more slowly; but I have sweated so much that for the next hour I am chilled by clammy undergarments. At half time we stop and share the tea and sandwiches we brought with us. These are enjoyable friendly brew-ups in the warmth of thicket or the shelter of a hedge. At 4am we get back to the fort, I hand in my rifle and flak jacket and wonder which is the safest route home. Half an hour later it's flop wearily into bed, three hours later the alarm clock goes off and it is time to go to work. It takes a couple of days to sleep it off and feel fully alert again; just ready for the next sortie. Strong men can stand it, Ulstermen can stand it, but we need all the support we can get, both moral and physical. Our Company Commander tells us that nightly some 2000 UDR soldiers leave their firesides as I left mine to take on a James Bond role – because they are not prepared to give in to terrorism. By our combined efforts we relieve the weight for the regular army of some ten battalions.

Organisation and Equipment

Mobile phones which might have enabled an isolated man to call support were not yet available at this period. We never made use of them in my UDR Days. The time and place of the Duty Platoon's assembly in Magherafelt should for security reasons have been frequently altered .But in real life that was usually impossible.With a Weapons-Out policy (ie: rifles held at men's homes) some variation could be made. Assembly could be for example be at one of the men's houses. That had worked well for B Specials but under army rules for signing arms in and out there were difficulties. Our weapons were to be Out for another year or so (except for a few men living very exposed areas) but once Weapons-In became the rule the only place we could assemble was beside the armoury where they were stored. Weapons in armouries appeared more secure but statistically were less. Several spectacular bulk arms thefts had made that point very clear. Policy about arms In or Out varied from city to country and even within battalions. In areas along the Border, where arms thefts became frequent and violent at times and in the cities of Belfast and Derry arms had to be in. I know that F and G Companies operated better in the early seventies when arms were out. A man with his weapon at home could be on the scene of an incident some twenty minutes faster than when he had to drive to a central point and queue to sign for an issue.

But the price came when our Garvagh Company lost a weapon in an frightening incident. A house was raided and a wife beaten at pistol point until her husband's rifle was handed over. To add insult to injury the man concerned was fined £50 for the loss by Lt . Colonel John Lys. His mates clubbed together to pay the fine. Only afterwards did John admit that he had been wrong.

The time of fall-in at Magherafelt was controlled by civilian working hours. Few men could get home, feed and change and travel to be on parade before 8 oclock. To start later was to waste time on the ground, so 8 o'clock it had in general to be.

In addition on weekends 26 platoon reported for such activities as company operations, planned searches, shooting practice and recognition training. Also at any time there could be 24 hours mobilisations following a major incident or to cover an election when Polling Stations had to be guarded. Courses of instruction prior to promotion, or in specialized subjects like signals or sniping, took up more time. Some of 26 platoon had volunteered for ski patrols in powder snow around Christmas. That had been fun and it kept communications open to isolated units when roads were blocked. With the assistance of RAF helicopters we helped hill farmers to fodder their sheep and kept an eye out for tracks in the snow that might lead to arms caches. Some men went off for periods on the Royal Navy patrol boats which boarded coastwise shipping to prevent arms smuggling. Corporal Angus, popular with regular units on account of his skill as a piper, was 'volunteered' for a fortnight of marine training in Portsmouth, piped at several major functions and later went to sea for a month. He enjoyed himself!

The risk of enemy attack was always there, and so were 26 platoon.

Little wonder that when one weary squaddy got home from patrol at 3 am, his wife asked ,'

'Who's this strange man climbing into to bed beside me?'

These stout lads had not the whetted knife alertness of regulars doing a four week stake-out. But alert they were at a level that could be maintained year after year after year. That meant enduring the everyday risk of a bullet in the back by day, abduction from the home at night, a booby-trapped car on the way to work or a road mine ambush on patrol. The alertness varied a little with the tempo of the time. It could reach very high peaks after local incidents. At other times commanders had to meet the problem which occurs in any anti-terrorist campaign --- the lower the level of enemy activity, the harder it is to keep everyone on their toes. And by and large the commanders succeeded because they had such good material to work on. I think it was Lord Rosebery who said:

'You may talk of the dourness of the Scots, the hardihood of Lancastrian and the toughness of the Cockney but when I come to the bravery of the men of Ulster, I am lost for adequate words of description.'

After the fall-in Steve the Platoon Sgt told off sections for the various duties; Headquarter Guard, Red 18, Foot Patrol, Mobile Patrol and sometimes a special duty requested by the regular army or Police. The policy behind the patrolling was to inhibit enemy movement. At a certain level which the UDR never was numerically strong enough to reach it could have interdicted arms and explosive re-supply.

Steve carefully rotated duties so that sections took each task in turn. If I was away from home on business he became Platoon Commander. Red 18 was the least popular task--- static defence of a vital electricity switchover point. It occupied a three acre enclosure surrounded by high netting and multiple coils of barbed wire. Overhead a spaghetti-like tangle of wires strung on a forest of poles sparked and crackled eerily all night fortissimo if it was wet and windy. There was a minimum chance of the action most of us hoped for, but at least the men on this duty got a chance to lie down and try to sleep in the guard hut by turns for part of the eight hour stag. And thereby hung a tale. Terrorists short of a target would occasionally fire a few rounds at Red 18; sometimes the guard would fire in reply but I don't recall any casualties arising. A long battle with Battalion HQ was fought to get the hut protected at least against small arms fire. Months had elapsed with no response to this simple request. As part time soldiers we could challenge authority in a way that no regular could without risking court martial. At last we refused to do the Red 18 guard until protection was provided. Feathers were ruffled but no one was charged with mutiny. Sandbags and steel plating arrived with remarkable speed.

Once jobs had been detailed there was usually a few minutes for the lads have a to smoke, exchange jokes and gossip. This was while in the Ops Room section leaders were brought up to on date on intelligence, enemy activity and location of other security forces in the area and briefed for the night's task. As well as its own three sections, 26 Platoon had 'visitors' most nights; that is men from other platoons volunteering to do an extra duty. As 'visitors' some energetic individuals, often those unemployed or with not- too-demanding civilian jobs, did over 20 duties a month. Some managed as many as thirty. One man still has his leg pulled because in April he claimed to have done thirty two.We were always glad to see additional hands and provided the records were properly kept the Paymaster never questioned the expenditure. At that time money to pay the UDR was almost unlimited. Perhaps this was the Government's way a way of making up for its frenzy of indecision about how to defeat the terrorists.

Yellow Cards and ID Cards

Mike Eveleigh's well thought out book *Peace Keeping in a Democratic Society — The Lessons of Northern Ireland* — made many suggestions for making the law more effective. His ideas would have made the soldier's role easier in keeping terrorists on the jump and winning over hearts and minds. He had seen the problems at first hand commanding a Battalion in Derry. But few of his suggestions were taken up.

A simple one would have been the compulsory carrying of Identity Cards by all Northern Ireland citizens and visitors - that alone would have been worth two extra battalions on the ground. Then there was Enoch Powell's point that the IRA in demanding Prisoner of War status after arrest were admitting that a state of warfare existed. That implied that their volunteers as combatants could be shot on sight. No change of the Rules of Engagement resulted.

It was as well that, busy with the real world of marching and shooting in those early days, we did not realize the feebleness of our elected politicians and the deviousness of the Foreign Office .

The Yellow Card which all soldiers carried stressed the use of Minimum Force and in effect forbade us to fire until accurately fired at. Explaining it to soldiers we tended to emphasise the moral side -- one's own conscience in fact was a stronger imperative than any bit of cheap pasteboard. None of us wanted to wound or kill an innocent third party and to live with that for the rest of one's life. That applied especially operating near home. But the rules about reacting to armed gunmen could have been more realistic.

As a squaddie put it, ' You had to wait until wounded yourself or the man beside you killed before returning fire.'

At this time we passed round the story of an aggressive driver who when being questioned by one of our patrols snarled ;

'I know ya. I'll get ya! You're wee Tommy, the rent man', to which Platoon Sergeant Tommy McGuckin said quietly[2]

'Aye and I'll be round for the money next week as usual'.

For training there was limited time or appetite; volunteers joined to go on Ops, not square-bash or listen to lectures. An officer's job was to see that his potential heroes had bullets in their pouches that would fire out of well maintained rifles and wore web equipment properly fitted so as not rattle during stealthy approaches, could shoot straight by day or night and identify local men from the Wanted List supplied by the RUC. In country districts like ours every patrol could with imaginative planning be made different and usually some point of interest arose.

Help from Employers

By now you will be getting an idea of the time consuming dedication demanded of those who joined the UDR. Most employers at this early stage were accommodating towards men taking time off work or being heavy-eyed in the mornings. They got little credit or thanks for doing so at the time, nor have since. It would still be dangerous to name them, much as I'd like to. If any directors of those helpful companies read these lines please understand that your support was vital and greatly appreciated. Almost every business house in our area suffered a loss of efficiency from the necessarily weary workers

The UDR will always remember such understanding bosses with gratitude. Their names can not yet be listed The IRA never forgives or forgets.

In the same way our regular officers at Battalion HQ were sympathetic when duties had to be missed because of family or business commitments. We could cover for each other knowing that we were part of a team that could beat the IRA and believing that the Government were behind our efforts. In later years both business and military authorities took a less sympathetic view.

In 1972 as regards that most precious of all commodities-- personal time --- we took the line of 'In for a penny, In for a pound 'We gave lavishly of our leisure in the hope of bringing terrorism to a halt.

Memories Great and Small

As platoon commander I usually went with the foot patrol or mobile. One remembers individual patrols for a variety of minor reasons. Smells were among them, because they are so nostalgic and also are more noticeable at night — and the bulk of my memories are of cross-country soldiering in the dark — the linseedy smell of new putty when taking cover under a window, the goodly smell of fresh hay, the milky smell of cows, night scenting stock and flowering currant, the earthy smell of manure, the musky odour of whins. Other things one doesn't meet in every day life like hairy caterpillars dropping off a bush into your mouth, spiders in autumn when webs and strands continually brush your face, a woodcock almost trodden on when flushed out of an open drain which was also a sewer, lovely country sounds things like the drumming of a snipe close over head on a still May night, the click of a owl's beak as it went by in downy flight. And of course for the banter and laughter of the members of the section and the different senses of humour of the English, Jocks or Taffies who often joined us.

'Dear Mum, It's a bastard', a scouse from Liverpool would say when the rations didn't turn up. 'Dear Son, so are you, but don't tell Dad', his mate would chorus.

'Do ye think a'm daft, man?' would come from a Scotsman.

'Nark it, mate,' from a Cockney Greenjacket.

'Yakky dah,' from a Welshman and of course from the Booties, alias Royal Marines naval chestnuts like, 'Did he marry poor blind Nell? and 'Up yours, Jack, I'm inboard.'

F and later G Company soldiered alongside many regiments. This meant joint patrols, shared billets, messes and Operation Rooms. Of almost all we formed the highest opinion. In many cases cordial friendships developed. We observed that very few armies could have kept their temper as well as did The Brits in face of the cleverly orchestrated and continuous provocation aimed at them by Sinn Fein. Among our 'chummy' units were the Royal Hampshire Regiment, under the aimiable and valiant Colonel Bob Long They were proud of being ' men who fought at Minden'. Their Two Hundred and Seventy Fifth Anniversary was celebrated while they were on active service in our part of Ulster. That made our span seem like a dogwatch. The Hamps had all the Marlborough Battle Honours but that didn't save them from amalgamation about 1980.

Other regular units based in our compound were the Royal Marines, Royal Anglians (inevitably referred to as Anglicans), Black Watch, Paras, Glosters, Kings Own Border Regiment, 4/7 Royal Dragoon Guards, The Lancers ('9th/12th,old boy. Don't forget it'), Coldstream Guards and especially the Royal Greenjackets with whom we had family connections. And that's not forgetting Peter Mitchell and his splendid Battalion of Welly Boots, alias Duke of Wellington's. The only time they irritated us was when they or their wives talked about being 'out here' or made remarks like, 'The natives are restless,' indicating that the speaker shared the Foreign Office view of Ulster as a third world Crown Colony. Plenty of reports. real or fabricated have been circulated about suspicion, distrust and abuse of information as between Regulars, RUC and UDR. In my day with a common enemy we acted as one in ninety eight per cent unanimity.

More memories …. a procession of cars we stopped about two am in Draperstown homeward bound from what must have been the Wake of the Century. Drivers were so gloriously drunk as to have no shred of thought for breathalisers or law courts; they got out of their cars and pranced in the street, brandishing bottles and offering drinks all round.

'I declare to God, Sergeant, we sent oul' Paddy to heaven flying', said the lead dancer. UDR patrols rarely bothered to book drunks – it meant a lot of paper work and time consuming appearances in court thereafter. So we saw this merry crowd home with good wishes, and a tinge of envy.

Another drunk ended differently in the main street of Portglenone. A lady of a certain age cursed us as Orange Bastards with ferocity in a vocabulary I had to admire. Thought I'd learned all the best insult in the Navy but she excelled the lot. When she started to take off her ragged clothing and throw malodorous garments at our heads in quick succession it was time to drive off. The extraordinary thing was that she telephoned me at home next morning with profuse apologies. How she got my name and number was a mystery – we were outside our usual area. I assured her I'd often done worse myself and that there'd be nothing more about it! A stranger out with the patrol could be good news. An officer from the 6th Ghurkas joined us for a week or two to observe anti-terrorist tactics — he taught us more than he learned but was disappointed that he didn't to get a chance to use his kukri! So were we. Bruce was the last man I'd accuse of medal hunting — he had good reason to be there. But others of the base rat variety had only to wangle a four week attachment in order to qualified for the Northern Ireland gong.

Good company was Brigadier Miles Smeeton of Green Howards and Probyn's Horse fame who spent hours with us at night. He was able to give some tips about patrolling in thick scrub and point out that our wet bogs had some resemblance to the paddy fields he'd fought across in Burma. Roy Mason as Secretary of State visited F Coy and went out on patrol with the soldiers. Later GOC Tim Creasey did the same, insisting on entering a Swatragh Pub. In spite of absence of any badges of rank his tall figure and air of authority was quickly bubbled and announced loudly by mine host.

Mobile patrol impressions were the khaki inside of the Land Rover, the smell of half burned exhaust, the light reflecting on the criss-cross pattern of the Macrolon armour on the bonnet, two dim dials on the facia, the driver's rifle in clips just under the windscreen, the steel floor under your feet, your own nobbly rifle between you knees, the white grey ribbon of the road, black hedges sliding by, an odd tree or signboard picked out by the headlights. At intervals the rapid de–buss for a ten minute checkpoint, cover men on guard at each end hidden in hedgerows, torch men with 'Bardic' lamps (to show red, green and yellow thro' filters), millboard men to record numbers, search men to examine vehicles. Then a whistle from the section leader; mount and off again to set up shop somewhere else.

I was lucky usually to ride in front and be kept busy navigating; for the boys in the back it was sitting face to face, jammed flak jacket to flak jacket on low hard benches, trying to brace against the swaying jerky motion. Just once I remember at the end of a grilling night hallucinating to the extent of imagining that a rabbit crossing the road was a six foot kangaroo! But my faithful drivers Lexy at times, Willie Currie at others, kept us safe between the hedges and never let the patrol down. Not once.

It is worth repeating that on all these patrols the rules of the Yellow Card which every soldier was trained to observe, meant that he had to wait to be shot at before opening fire. For breaches of the rules many regular soldiers were given long jail sentences.

Let us look at nights when something bigger than drunks were encountered.

The Abandoned Car

One January evening Private Jim Byndman telephoned to report that while returning from his civilian employment he had seen a large car stopped across the road in Ballymacpeak about 5 miles east of Maghera. The windows were open, key in ignition; and children's clothes on the back seat. Our mobile patrol got there within minutes and an examination by torchlight found the boot locked. But there were no depressed rear springs to indicate a big bomb. On the floor were three Tommy Gun empty bullet cases. Had it been a get-away car? Corporal Hughie radio-ed the Magherafelt Ops. Room. The flat English voice of the regular watch keeper told him to stake it out.

'Don't touch anything. Wait for ATO.'

This was the standard instructions, of a sort loathed by us part-timers. If ATO was busy forty miles away it could involve the six hour discomfort of hanging about in icy conditions. Plus the risk that it might be a Come–On and we had been lured into a position where a sniper could pick one of us off. The local RUC, also thinking it might be a Come-On, refused to investigate. I arrived a bit later, drove to the to Portglenone Police Station and after a lengthy identification process outside the high steel gate got admitted. There was the man we needed — a most resourceful sergeant who'd helped on many an occasion. We pieced together the story — The IRA had set up a check point on a nearby main road and stayed there for about half an hour. Before moving they'd fired 20 rounds from a Tommy Gun, probably from bravado, perhaps just to clear the rust from the barrel. They'd left two hijacked cars blocking the road, and probably used a third one for a getaway. That was about an hour ago. Had the gunmen, perhaps hearing the noise of a Land Rover engine as they fled, left the getaway car and made off overland to the nearest safe house? Was this the car they'd abandoned?

There was every sign of a hasty disembarkation. But these signs might be faked and part of a booby trap. Unlikely — on second thoughts — The time scale had scarcely allowed of precise preparations. Sgt Fenton and I sallied forth once more.

I'd trained as a Bomb and Mine Disposal Officer in WW 11 but usually kept very quiet about it. It had been one of the Royal Navy's worst decisions to put a ham-fisted matelot like me into a job needing delicate touch. Now was the time to make a little use of that experience. Particularly as I was still feeling raw after a mysterious box had been reported as a bomb at a petrol station a hundred yards from the gate of my house. Twelve men had spent almost twelve hours staking that out until ATO investigated. It turned out to be four bricks wrapped up in paper and cardboard. I had been taken for mug, just as some low ranking PIRA courier had intended .

We checked the car over for nylon line attached to the air valve on a wheel. If there was one it would lead to a clothes peg which if withdrawn as the wheel rotated would allow the terminals of an electric detonator to close. That device had killed half a dozen men in recent months. We belly-crawled to scan the underbody.

Was there a pressure plate under a tyre...? or a wooden box containing a charge hung under the body? A neighbouring company commander had used one of his nine lives when such a box fell off the exhaust pipe of his car as he backed it out of his garage.

After an hour still no signs of ATO, but we were reasonably sure of an all clear.

The owner of the car turned up. A soldier on the cordon reported him as, 'Badly shook; but he's ris' an oration about getting yon car back'.

'Tell him we're doing our best' .

We questioned the owner. Then the intrepid police sergeant insisted on getting into the driving seat. We all stood well back as he turned the ignition key. All was well and he took the big red Jaguar back to the Station.

Well done, Sergeant Alan Fenton! He was later awarded a well earned MBE .

At midnight we resumed our patrol.

The Burnt Out Minor

What might have happened if we'd waited for ATO? Let me relate the outcome of an earlier incident in Moneymore. A Morris Minor of that popular beetle contour had been hijacked from outside its owner's house. Hours later it was found parked in a street where a bomb within it could have destroyed the police station. We posted sentries and waited for ATO. His distinctive pair of windowless strongly armoured vans arrived. A long-haired fellow in corduroys, scruffy tee-shirt and anorak got out and surveyed the car carefully. This was ATO himself, a member of the most decorated group of all the combatants.[1] You could pick them out, when seen in uniform, by the bomb flash on a cuff. Next thing ATO, lithe and alert, with the hands of a pianist did an electronic check to see if any device inside the car was to be triggered by radio signal. Fired a couple of snub-nosed Carl Gustav rockets from a distance to see if the charge could be shattered. No effect. Tried a Torpex incendiary candle on the ground under the engine compartment — too much rain — she wouldn't burn. From the rear of one van a ramp was lowered and out crawled Goliath, a remote-control tracked vehicle about the size of a large wheelbarrow. It had a flood light and a searchlight, two closed circuit TV scanners, a projecting arm that could act as a probe or fire a variety of projectiles and a selection of other devices undisclosed. Probably had a fist too. I felt like shaking hands with it. But ATO didn't wheel it up to the suspect car just yet.

'Last bloke in my billet had two of these blown up. Can't afford it. Cost £ 50.000 apiece,' he remarked as his assistant, a sapper Sergeant helped him to accouter. Seven League boots and a rigid carapace for body protection, topped by a thick visor on a huge casque – Star Wars style but not so glittery – All tastefully coloured in shades of crushed olive, as a fashion magazine might have put it. In the rain we continued to wait. Mac our signaler was called into the RUC Orderly room for a message.

'What time at HQ in the morning?' I heard him ask.

'Crikey; 9.30 ? We don't leave here until at 8,30.'

'Going home first, are you ? Can't do without it, eh?'

'Well 'er, yes. I mean no.'

'Corporal Dick will tell you what its about'.

'Ok. At the speed he drives we'll be at Ballykelly in 15 minutes from start.'

Meanwhile the Dalek-in-Khaki had delicately fingered the control box He was not called Felix for nothing. Goliath fired two more solid rounds. They smashed the rear window, and went through the driver seat into the engine. No results, so Goliath, its projector recharged, tossed in another Torpex candle.

It was at this stage that the elderly owner of the Morris arrived, to be stopped by a sentry one street back .

'You've got ma wee car', he said in tones of gratitude with a happy laugh..

'I've driv' her for twenty years'.

The Torpex was now fully alight. When he was allowed to look round the corner I've never seen a man's face fall so quickly.

'Lord save us', he said and wept as she became six pieces of twisted tin. It may have been the smoke but there were tears in my eyes too as I offered the poor man my flask.

It was four am when we got back to base, checked in arms and separately set out for our homes. That was when one felt most exposed. We tried to leave some members of the section direct at home or help them approach by an unusual route. To have a member of family stay awake, gun in hand, until one returned, as done in 8 UDR on the Border, would add to the already heavy strain on family life. I don't think many of us went that far. But once the patrol was over it had to be each man for himself.

Often one was too weary to do more than stagger inside the house to comparative safety as quick as possible. This night,(or was it another one?), a Black Watch Patrol was about to go out. So I asked them to escort a couple of us three miles home. For the last bit we approached the cottage across fields instead of up the normal lane.

At a hedge junction there were sounds of footsteps where none should be.

The Scottish corporal scouted stealthily forward. After a delay came the winged words,

'It's a'right. The're coos.' A pair of Aberdeen Angus must have heard the whisper, they lumbered off and we all relaxed.

An Easter Tale

And another car hijack story. A yachtsman who kept his immaculate ocean-going yawl at Coleraine Marina had spent many shekels and much time on having made in County Down a new wooden hollow mast. The time had come to bring the 60 foot stick on a low loader trailer to the sea. But as well as being the time of year when dormant yachties stir Easter is the occasion for atavistic gunmen to celebrate the 1916 Easter Rising. The boat owner requested a clear route from Rucsac (the Police). He was advised to proceed via County Antrim and the coast road. En route he was stopped by an army patrol.

'This way's unsafe. Go via Swatragh.'

'Swatragh?' he asked, 'What? An Official IRA village?

'All right We know it's clear.'

Swatragh when he got there us was blocked by masked gunmen. Their supporters were accumulating material for an Easter bonfire, all set to win an accolade for the best one in the county. They ordered him out of his car.

'Take my car.' said the yachtie. 'Burn it if you wish and the trailer too. Burn me if you must. But please, please, don't burn my mast.'

The OIRA Commandant was sympathetic. Sport in Ireland, let it be foxhunting, game shooting, football or even sailing, almost always transcended politics.

'Ok. Leave it here. We'll look after your mast. Come and collect it later' .

Yachtie, relieved, withdraws a mile or so up road. Up comes a One Pip Wonder in charge of an army patrol, tasked to clear the village.

'Don't worry, sir', said the keen young officer.

'We're the professionals. Go home and relax, sir. We'll get that mast safe to the Marina for you, I promise.'

While his men cleared the village the Second Lieutenant saw the slender mast laid safely to one side, its straight grain gleaming under manifold coats of varnish. Then the great army brain began to work and

One Pip's orders were issued.

The mast was indeed delivered as promised but only after it had on his instructions been chain-sawed into four pieces. Why? Because it might have been used for another road block. A task for which a hollow mast is hopeless. Built to act as a strut in compression, the lateral pressure of a couple of push bikes trying to force their way past would have bent and destroyed it.

That's why the good ship Daydream missed most of the summer's sailing and eventually had to settle for a nasty alloy mast. And H.M. Forces had to meet another stiff claim for damages .

A Bellaghy Arms Find.

One spring evening Lt. Walter Hotfun took the mobile to Bellaghy, accompanying it in his own car. He and a private called Dave decided to check on a house suspected of being used for IRA meetings. Walter and Dave went forward together and saw three cars at the house. The owner was a bachelor so something was on. They hid their car in a nearby field and scouted back. Two men with a plastic bag were observed in the back garden making their way through a hedge. The bag did not look bulky enough to have anything in it; however Walter decided to challenge. The only weapons he and Dave had were their pistols. The bag carriers when asked what they were doing said they were stopping up the gap in the hedge. One of them suddenly made off. Walter had been in trouble over shooting too fast on previous occasions and so chary of opening fire. So they lost the bolter but held his companion and the bag which held three pistols.

There seemed to be two men still in the house. One on hearing the challenge made off out of the front. Walter called on him to halt and when he didn't fired over his head but he went on. The other remained in the house and was arrested , so two men and one bag of arms were now in custody and only the two pistols to guard them. The bolter might be returning with armed accomplices at any minute. Walter managed to get in touch with the Ops Room to get support but the Duty Officer seemed disbelieving and was finding it difficult to contact the Mobile. There were radio black spots in the area. At last after telling the Mobile to join Walter the signaler suggested they click the pressel switch if receiving him. That seemed to work; The Mobile on approaching the house saw a car with two men at what appeared to be an army checkpoint 200 yards short of it but the Lance Corporal uncertain of what was happening decided to bypass this and approach from another direction. The RUC had refused to move, giving every excuse they could think of in case it might be a come-on.

Walter was unwilling to use the captured weapons and felt very exposed. but kept shouting orders to imaginary men in the field to keep him covered. The prisoner swore he had only one bag and begged to be let back into the house to get his coat but of course was not allowed to do so. When at last the Mobile arrived Walter found a second bag and two more pistols. The Mobile then handed over the prisoner to Rucsac and staked out the house until a full search could be made in daylight.

Back at the Fort two hours later Walter opened the bar and he and Dave sank a bottle of champagne. In a full war situation Walter with nerve, quick reactions and loads of guts would have been a hero in Special Forces.

I'm glad they drank that champagne. He didn't have so long to go; brain cancer got him a few years later. If only all patrols had been half as successful as that one!

But the biggest Op. ever was now close ahead.

Weapons find for 3 RRF in Derry

I'm Wondering Why
By a Soldiers Wife

I wonder why I'm here.
I wonder why the tears.
My husband is a soldier
And I know he's bolder .
I wonder why I'm here .
I'm here to love and cherish
To give him my support
To make him cups of coffee
And even watch the sport.
He doesn't cry. I don't know why.
He must see some awful sights
In Derry and on the Border.
God bring him home tonight.
The children are in bed
And that's the time I get so sad
It's eleven pm and I'm wondering when
My love will be home tonight.

Anon - From Visor Magazine

Footnotes

1: *Twenty two ATO officers were killed between 1970 and 1990. Sixteen were in same period decorated.*

2: *Sergeant Tommy McGuckin, wise, quiet and fearless, died as I was working on this book in July 2000.*

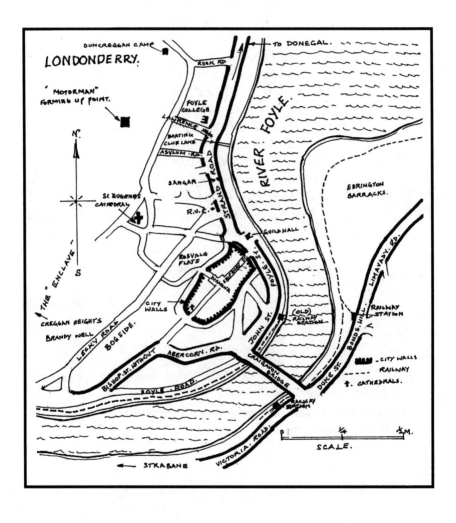

CHAPTER FOUR

OPERATION MOTORMAN
July and August 1972

Breaking into the Bogside

*'Those things which are hard to endure are pleasant
to look back upon'*

Marcus Aurelius

On July 28th 1972, a sunny Friday evening, 26 Platoon was busy on the Strand Road, Derry. If you scanned the Prologue to Chapter One you may recall that by ten oclock we'd come under fire and decided to shoot out the street lights. *'Aids to Better Street Lighting,'* had been an intended headline in the local paper a few weeks back. When some weary compositor had run it as *Aids to Better Street Fighting* – it seemed so apt that we glued it to the wall in the company office. Beside it was an advertisement for Clark's Commandos — walking shoes in case you don't remember—but more importantly our company's occasional nickname. Now we were making the improvements to street lighting ourselves. Our job, alternating with other platoons in eight hour stags, was to maintain three standing check points, one on the Craigavon Bridge and two known as Sierra Six and Seven at road junctions on the Strand Road and quay.

The whole UDR had been called out although we at grass roots didn't realise the full extent at the time. Or that the callout was to last for three weeks. Later we learned that 5000 men had turned out Province-wide. The effort, we hoped, was to cover a major operation to re-assert the rule of law and order in No-Go areas. Surely the regular battalions we'd seen massing at Ebrington Barracks were there for something big.

'Sssh! The're going to invade Donegal and clean out the IRA bases just over the Border', one civvy told us with an air of authority.

There was no need to go so far. In the Bogside the Queen's Writ had not run for months. Two 'battalions' of IRA there held sway. They recruited and trained in security, held their own courts and punished offenders with beatings, knee capping or execution.[1]

After we'd dowsed the lights, no more shots came in our direction. Maybe the sniper was the one who (according to rumour next day) had been shot between the eyes by a Scots Guards marksman. More likely the rifleman had handed his gun over to the local quartermaster, got a discreet lift over the Border and was now being regaled with big black pints in a Buncrana pub amid clouds of cigarette smoke and hero worship.

How it looked from the Grass Roots.

Let me try to explain how UDR soldiers felt at that time. The Northern Ireland Parliament had been forced to resign on the issue of security in March by Ted Heath after he had tired of the hubbub over Bloody Sunday and requests by Brian Faulkner for stronger anti - terrorist measures. Direct Rule from Westminister was instigated via the Northern Ireland Office based at Stormont. At this deed which looked like a major piece of appeasement a few UDR soldiers resigned in disgust. None as I recall in F Company but our faith in the Government's resolve was once again dented. Now we wanted as a minimum to see IRA rule abolished as smartly as had been the Stormont Members of Parliament. Uppermost in our minds was the murder four months back of two friends and comrades – Thomas Callaghan on February 16th, a brave Catholic private soldier who had defied IRA threats and refused to resign. He was seized on the bus he drove and bundled off to a chorus of screams from the passengers. His body was found later, shot in the back of head — It was a fate that any of us faced but this time it was poor Thomas whose number was up. The second casualty, on March 4th, 1972, Captain Marcus McCausland was another Catholic. He had served in the Irish Guards and he and I had frequently been shipmates on my old wooden cutter sailing to Scotland. His kindly happy-go-lucky manner and ready wit had made him perhaps the most popular officer in the battalion. As mentioned in Chapter Two he had attempted to resign but being doubly valued as Catholic was talked into staying on the books without doing any duties. Kidnapped as he returned from dining with friends at a hotel in Donegal he was taken into the Bogside. There he was first interrogated. His activities, which were characteristically careless, could conceivably have been interpreted as spying but to anyone who knew him a more unlikely agent than untidy easy-going Marcus it would be hard to imagine. Tried on a spying charge by a kangaroo court he was condemned by the casting vote of the president. Then he was horribly cut and beaten, hooded and shot. His poor body had been dumped on a roadside between the Creggan and the Border, a mile from our present post, near t a checkpoint he had often manned.

Thomas and Marcus had each accepted known risks coolly — higher risks than those faced by the rest of us Protestants. Each of the pair did his share of UDR duty with no outward show of bravado, just a determination not to see his country taken over by merciless terrorists — terrorists imbued with a fierce unreasoning hatred of all that democracy and the UDR stood for. Thomas Callaghan and Marcus McCausland died for their homeland as they knew it. Every man in the Battalion felt for them and their families. Of both it might be said

'He arranged his earthly life in such manner
that he set great store by his home and his country.'

Bulking even larger in our minds were two bombs exploded with no warning. They were in Claudy village, five miles back on the main road towards Fort Garry. Among those killed had been Kathryn, the six year old daughter of an officer of our battalion, and eight other innocents. Words are inadequate in referring to an attack on a village that could in no way be described as a military or economic target. It was not words we wanted but action ---- to catch the man that laid those bombs. God may forgive him. The UDR never did.[2]

This foul deed took place after the Security Forces had been forced to endure more than two weeks of inaction, while the Government dickered with killers – a truce aptly nicknamed in the Belfast Newsletter The Peace Which Passeth All Understanding.

The IRA meanwhile got on with their murdering. As one example Greenjacket Rifleman James Meredith age 19 had been killed by two shots from a Tommy Gun on 26th June at a VCP in Peppercorn Road just beside the main Foyle Bridge, 500 yards from where we stood. During the Truce ministers had made concessions to terrorists without any response in return. On July 21 the IRA marked the end of the Truce with Bloody Friday. On that day their bombs killed 11 civilians and wounded 13, not rioters, not soldiers, just passers by on their peaceful occasions in Belfast. The deeds of that day never seem to have been fully and publicly investigated.

The thought of these horrors kept us on our toes as we eyed passers-by and kept lookout. There were more and more indications, from increasing military road traffic and signals, of a re-occupation. Army Pigs full of soldiers went to and fro. Packed RUC Land Rovers sallied forth from police Headquarters beside us. They were painted naval grey with strongly armoured bodies, had steel cages round all lights, and long flaps between the wheels to prevent bombs being rolled underneath. But after so much Government backsliding and pussy footing we had learned to count on nothing in the way of positive action until it happened.

Checking Traffic

Platoon Sergeant Steve and I assisted by Major Sammy Hudson checked the cars for the next half hour. We were still regularly lit up by car headlights and I experienced an uneasy feeling in the kidneys at some moments while standing with back towards the sniper site. Our cumbersome flak jackets would be unlikely to stop a high velocity bullet. Major Robin Allers-Hankey RGJ had died after being shot through his flak jacket some months earlier. Not that we discussed private fears or needed counselling. Soldiers at that time had never heard of such a thing.

Our platoon base was on the mile-long Strand Road, normally a busy route north from the city centre to Donegal. Because of the risk of car bombs all traffic except military was prohibited from using its inner end. Civilian vehicles had been re-directed along the River Foyle quay, past No 4 shed and piles of steel scrap to rejoin the main route about half a mile north of Waterloo Place, where Boating Club Lane leads up from the river. The handsome Edwardian boathouse after which the lane is called hadn't seen a boat for a generation. It was cob-webbed and securely locked, as were the garages and workshops beside it. Only a niche where a gable projected three feet onto the pavement gave any protection from stray bullets. A stool in there had been warmed by army bums for several days. Now one of them was that of our signaller.

Traffic grew lighter as the evening wore on, and between vehicle arrivals we were able to dodge into doorways on the main road for cover. The best porch, to our right as we faced the City, was that of a tall Georgian building, part of Foyle College.

I felt at home there because through it my grandfather Wallace must have passed daily as a school boy a hundred years earlier.

The Strand Road as we viewed it looking towards the city from the sangar was then an undistinguished street of middling size shops and terrace houses.

On a normal summer evening corner boys would have been propping up their favourite walls, 'eedyuting about' as one soldier put it and drinking lemonade on the footpaths. Now it was deserted, bordered by coils of rusty Dannert wire and concrete dragons teeth.

A butcher's shop sign had the only touch of wit--

'PLEASED TO MEET YOU---
MEAT TO PLEASE YOU' .

Further off where the street was still lit we could see patrolling soldiers dashing across openings. Sudden bursts of brilliance as a flare went up made the dark figures freeze. The refection of a few lit windows made the scene reminiscent of a diascuro by Rembrandt. But even that great man could have included a helicopter nattering overhead and turning it' s Nightsun light on the river to investigate what might have been a small boat. It turned out to be a discarded mattress. The river in those days was so polluted that Derry citizens would tell you that the fish had to swim backwards to keep the dirt out of their eyes. Water skiing was referred to as 'going through the motions'. The Scots Guards Tactical Headquarters was about 400 yard south of us. We'd heard them on the radio a few hours back when we took over. 'Green friends have arrived'. But they'd been too busy since to pay us a visit. The UDR was still clad in plain khaki at that time rather than the disruptive pattern worn by regulars. I hoped that the 'green' referred to the colour of our coats rather than our state of training.

Some regular battalions treated us at first as moss troopers, maybe even Dad's Army. But few did so once we got acquainted . We knew and they soon learned that, although nothing like as skilled as trained soldiers in battle tactics, we were at least five times as effective as them in identifying baddies at checkpoints. By midnight 26 Platoon had stopped some 300 cars and breathed enough petrol fumes, stale perspiration and exhaled alcohol to fill a Zeppelin. That was since taking post at 7 o'clock. We'd sent five drivers and several cars under escort to Battalion HQ for detailed examination. One driver had 'sunk his boot', as the saying goes, and sped right through, narrowly missing a soldier as he went. In days gone by we'd have fired at his back tyre. The second or third shot would have brought the car to halt, and the inmates been arrested unhurt. For some reason which I have never heard satisfactorily explained the army disapproved of this; if they fired it was at head level and thereby joy riders and sometime innocent people got killed. Lengthy legal proceedings and imprisonment of soldiers ensued. In 1972 we were not allowed to shoot unless fired on by the escaping car.   Nuff' said.

Ninety nine percent of times the check went like this:

'Where are you going, sir?'

Or more directly, 'Whar' ye goin'?

If asked, 'Why do you want to know?, our orders were to reply. 'This a security check and I can give no details'.

Most drivers had kindly faces and were only too anxious to get on with their own business. 'Good on ye, boys!', came from a few or encouraging words like,

'I'll throw you in a few apples next time I'm passing', spoken sotto voce . It didn't do to be seen to be too friendly with soldiers just then. 'Keep the buggers heads down', was another supportive aside. A reply from pedestrians as to their intentions was sometimes,

'I'm out on my *ceilidhe.*' That meant the pleasant Irish custom of calling on neighbours to catch up on local news.

Ceilidhe (pronounced kaily) implied visiting friends for an evening's craic', (Anglice crack) – an exchange of gossip, jokes and story-telling. English still lacks an equivalent word. Craic has since been commercialised on pub posters with the laudable object of luring tourists in to buy drinks for local blethers. But I haven't heard anyone talk about being on his ceilidhe for some years.

Our powers of search were strictly limited. Occasionally we would frisk a man if his answers seemed unsatisfactory. In the case of females this was virtually impossible : the Women's UDR was not to be formed for another year. To summon a policewoman would take such a long time as to be impractical unless suspicion was very strong. Terrorists passing through were generally well groomed and ultra-polite. All that we could be sure of doing was to prevent them passing with faces blackened and weapons across their knees. We made lists of car number and owners and these were submitted to HQ — whether they were binned, spot checked or thoroughly analysed was rarely revealed.

'I'll fook you first', was the reply from one man to a polite request to open his car boot for examination. He'd carefully donned his most truculent sneer and was looking for trouble. Luckily it was Stuarty, the section's funny man, who received this one.

'Is that a threat or a promise ?' his calm riposte, was enough to make the driver pause.

'What'll you do if I don't open?' he next snarled.

Operation Motorman
Strand Road Sanger

Operation Motorman
Check Point on Boatling Club Lane, looking towards the river.

Now it happened that we had been approached by an amiable drunk an hour earlier. He could scarcely stand, let alone walk and been laid out on the pavement on a blanket to sleep it off. Stuarty jerked his hand back and pointed at what looked just like a stiff.

'Well, er ,all right, if I have to', and swiftly the boot was opened. Empty as expected.

One inviting looking girl with auburn hair brushed over her left ear, freckled nose and a slash of red lips, got out to display a pink micro-skirt. Showing the contents of her handbag she said , 'I wish it had enough gelignite in it to blow you all to hell!' .

'Catch yourself on, Mam,' might have been the local reply or something a lot ruder. But Soldier X just had to bite his lip and bleed inwardly. We got to know that lady quite well later and nicknamed her the Donegal Spitfire. When it came to 'verbal', the female of the species in Ireland then was far more deadly than the male.

Regular Army and UDR work together

The Spitfire was clearly out to provoke from a soldier a response about which she could formally complain. What counter measures could we devise? No bright ideas until a private nicknamed Wallop came up and said something in a low voice.

I heard the response from the Corporal.

'Wee man, you've got my brains woke up'.

The private had a pocket tape recorder and next time the lady came round we got her comments on disc — only to be used if she tried to wrong-foot us.

Funnily enough after that we never saw or heard of her again.

'Wallace, have you nothing better to do than this?' had come earlier from an immaculately groomed lady of my acquaintance, irritated at being held up time after time while shopping. I couldn't blame her, so gave the soft answer: but indeed I could think of many pleasanter ways of spending a weekend. Time mainly with my young family.   The Catholic Bishop of Derry drove by and motioned his driver to turn up hill towards one of his churches. "I think I ought to tell you, sir, that we believe we've been sniped at from the spire". said   Malachi, our colour-sergeant, in the politest tones. The bishop pursed his lips and drove on. Even the tactful Malachi couldn't frisk a bishop but three recent escapees from Maze prison were believed to have been smuggled over the Border dressed as priests. So we had to try to be at once thorough and yet remain within the bounds of civility.

Patrols in my hearing never asked a person their religion, although regular soldiers lacking local perception did it often enough. As a Northern Ireland resident one usually knew within the first sentence. Even if I didn't know I could not have made myself mouth the words. The question, other than as an odd exception, was unnecessary, intrusive and ill mannered. Almost all of us had friends or relations both sides of the religious divide and almost all of us tried to do the job we'd volunteered for with minimum provocation.

MEANWHILE BACK AT THE RANCH

It had been a long day. In the morning it had been in the Factory Office struggling with a problem as why some linen yarn hadn't arrived. I was never destined to find out. The phone rang. 'O Group, Magherafelt, in half an hour' (O group stood for orders by a commander). A quick two miles home to change into combat uniform, and collect mapcase, web equipment, Verey pistol, torch, poof kit and small pack.

The magazines for my 9 mm pistol had been so well hidden (from children as well as intruders) that they were not to be found. Never mind - a jumper pulled well down over the butt would cover the deficiency and I'd borrow one at HQ later.

Was this the summons we'd been awaiting for? Had the craven men in Government turned at last? Months spent negotiating a truce and trying to buy off the IRA had failed and left the enemy stronger than ever, with areas in Belfast and Derry where security forces could only enter in company strength. With these thoughts I drove twelve miles to Fort William, the Magherafelt base. In the Company Commander's Office I found round-faced rubicund Major Sammy in conference with the adjutant who'd come 40 miles from Battalion HQ in Derry with important orders. Tim, a WWII Para Captain, was hairless, skinny, efficient and helpful . . 'Forty men for three weeks,' he told us, 'are required to be maintained resident at Battalion HQ.' There would be patrolling and a number of checkpoints to be manned continuously.

'Which of yous can go ?' asked Sam. We had five officers in the company now -- , Jim, Willie and Eakin plus the OC and me, but missed the dashing Esmond who had dropped out a few months earlier. I began to calculate which period to bid for.

'I can see what you're at, Wallace ', said Tim, ' You don't want to miss the action'.

'Too right,' I replied.

The chance of an enemy contact after weeks of frustration put a gleam into the eyes of all. Sammy, seeing the problem, solved it with characteristic decision. 'All officers must go for as long as they can be away from their jobs. We'll need three or four of yous on duty there all the time.'

For one-man farmers, key executives or technicians, to be away from work for more than a few hours at a time was an on-going problem. Locally near Magherafelt there would be patrolling at double the normal rate to protect civilians and guard our bases against expected retaliation by the terrorists. That meant 24 hour foot patrols in villages and duty every other night on duty for those unable to be away for a continuous spell in Derry. We soon sorted it out among ourselves and I managed to bag first stag that very evening. Within an hour the Fiery Cross had been sent out and men were coming in. A rumour that pay would be at full regular army rates for the period of the mobilisation (almost double the UDR norm) helped to encourage any waverers. We had our rifles at home at that time so could be armed and off quickly. A wink to the storeman supplied the missing pistol magazine. We piled into our Land Rovers and set off through Bomb Alley, as Glenshane Pass had become known. It was usually banned to military transport at this period but was reported to have been swept for mines. I wondered; it takes only minutes to set up a claymore, filled with shipyard confetti as the soldiers called shrapnel. And there was no way the whole ten miles could be watched.

We had one helpful officer who used to say on these occasions,
'Put me in front. I'll never die from a road mine'.

Well, he never did. Joe, a rather solemn man, tall and heavily built, was a believer in signs and the unnatural; he had curious convictions about unlucky numbers and BBC weather forecasts. After service in the RAF and Colonial Service he had become an Income Tax Inspector. Goodness knows how — I'd tried him on company accounts for three short weeks; it took as many months to sort out the mess he made but his faith in his fortune teller was justified. His vehicle was mined once that I remember but only part of the charge exploded. No one was hurt. Years later good old Joe died in bed.

We checked in at Battalion HQ at about 6.30 pm. The building was in vaguely Raj style with shady verandahs fronting each floor. It might have been designed by a nostalgic Indian Army sapper. Inside were small shabby offices daubed with scratched brown paint. 5 UDR was low down in the pecking order in this vast establishment that showed evidence of years of organic growth.

Ebrington Barracks sprawled over a thirty acre site sloping down to the east bank of the River Foyle. Accommodation blocks, mess rooms, cookhouses, training areas, stores, magazines, gymnasiums and canteens filled every corner. Conspicuous among them were Brigade HQ and Ops Room. The building they occupied had been not long ago a Maritime HQ, used to plot the movements of Russian nuclear submarines. That evening Ebrington was hotching with soldiers and full of the delightful bustle of war. Ugly troop carriers, hauled in by the MOD rake from far-flung outposts, filled the roadways; their colours varied from desert yellow through jungle green to Arctic white. The new arrivals made an odd contrast with experienced local Pigs whose bonnets bore the rubble of half bricks and the oily leavings of petrol bombs.

Around them soldiers in shirt sleeves sat on steps cleaning weapons and clipping up ammunition belts. Others were busy netting in radio sets, filling ration packs and fuel tanks, attending O Groups and studying maps. Still more soldiers could be heard zeroing rifles in a tunnel range A fine demonstration it was of all the jobs which produce battle readiness. Saracen armoured cars, Samson recovery vehicles and Samaritan ambulances blocked the roadways. Red-capped military policemen directed traffic. We were just in time to see a newly arrived battalion falling in by companies on the big parade square. This lies open to the west overlooked by the high ground of the No-Go area which we were hoping they'd soon clear. From that direction came short bursts of rapid rifle fire aimed at this large and tempting target.

A screaming sergeant-major command made the parade disperse in a most un-Guards like manner. That must have made him worse tempered than usual. Minutes later I heard him telling off a sheepish soldier, 'Yer beret's all covered with shite. Ye might as well come on parade with yer cock hangin' out'.

Within an hour we were briefed, fed and on our way to man check points on the bridge and Strand Road as described above. Other companies from 5 UDR were allocated sectors to form a cordon round the city.

Much anticipation but no action

Apart from that bit of sniping before dusk it was a quiet night.

Saturday Morning July 29th 1972

We came off stag at six am and hoisted in a huge Catering Corps breakfast in an improvised cafeteria.   Then we slept hard in an untidy store room above Battalion HQ on sagging camp beds. Private Robbie, my next door neighbour farmer, in Upperlands was missing in the morning. A search revealed him comfortably asleep on straw in his private apartment — a kennel — the dog not to be seen. And so started our 12 hours off duty.

At midday I bummed a lift home to Maghera. Had an hour with the family and came back in my own Mini van so as to be more mobile for the next busy days.

Back at Ebrington I peeped into the ante-room of the big Victorian officer's mess. Fifty feet wide by a hundred long, it brought back memories of Battle of the Atlantic Dinners when this was a joint Naval and Royal Air Force base. Now the room was hushed, stripped of furniture and furnishings, dimly lit, and laid out as a hospital with fifty beds. In one corner was an operating theatre, with accompanying blood banks and a pile of body bags.

Thereafter it was a day of briefings by HQ, arranging soldier accommodation and bedding, letting some men with urgent commitments go home and getting others to take their place, making up deficiencies in kit, drawing up duty rosters for days ahead and laying in some personal supplies.

Saturday night must have been uneventful for I can remember nothing of it.

Sunday July 30 1972

On Sunday morning I looked into the small Garrison Chapel at the hour advertised for Communion. Out of several hundred soldiers, Pat the Brigadier of 8 Brigade and I seemed to be the only two communicants. He didn't want to be drawn into conversation but looked at the sky as we emerged and ventured, 'It should be an interesting weekend'. I still felt it probable that the whole show would be called off by some political fudge.

We took post again on Sunday afternoon. Derry repartee continued at an even better pace than usual. Perhaps because there was an air of tension that misty August evening. Everyone in town sensed that something big was afoot. By 8 o'clock traffic was thinning out. A lady who had been asked to open her car boot stepped out stiffly and was given a steadying hand as she walked round to do so. Then she was helped back into the car by our oldest soldier, a retired postman. Seeing me observe his good manners, he said with a smile, ' There's room still for a little chivalry. I recall His exact words, as though it was yesterday. He'd been on his feet for hours and I replied, 'Well done, Tommy, but it's time you took an hour's rest inside'.

'Right, sir, but I'd rather be in the sangar and lie dogma'.

Then I spoke to a Scots Guards sergeant from the Isle of Mull, a fine big man with a stiff jaw and flashing brown eyes, who'd just joined us.

'Watch those guys moving around at the top of Asylum Road', he warned. I told him I'd been doing so for hours, assuming for lack of info. that they were IRA.

'Worse than that. That's the line mob; they're Budgies!'

This was the libellous name for a distinguished county regiment, from the cockade they wore in their berets. Goodness know what the Jocks called us.

"The only training the Budgies get is that anyone not wearing a hackle's an enemy".

The Foot Guards, out of their hearing, are called Wooden Tops and their cavalry Tin Bellies. You could be collecting the names that the trade call each other like cigarette cards! What we didn't hear was that at 8.30 that evening the BBC broadcast a warning to all concerned that the army was about to move into the No Go areas. Even if we had, we'd probably thought it was bluff.[4]*

About midnight I handed the post over to Steve and relaxed for half an hour. A door in the Commission Legal Office beside our post was open and we'd been using its staff room for shelter, shaves, showers and shampoos. Whether this was open by accident or design never became apparent but it was damned handy. Those of us off duty laid aside rifles, pistols, web equipment, torches and other impedimenta. Just as I'd settled down the man beside took his boots off. The resulting hum made repose almost impossible. Old soldiers say that if you can smell yourself its time to change your clothes but this player had never heard the adage. An occasion for RHIP (rank has its privileges), thinks me. So I moved to a small office upstairs and lay down on the carpet with my flak jacket for a pillow. Utter bliss to ease all the muscles of my back and legs.

Soon after midnight I was up again. A runner from Scot Guards had come to give the codeword *Ratweek* which meant, 'Let no traffic through.' We put stop boards out and watched. This looked like action. The only remaining arrivals now came on foot from the US Signal Base across the river.

'Can you guys find me a broad?'

This in the accents of the Middle West from a tall lean youngster in jeans. Garry, our rear lookout man, signed to him the house a hundred yards up the road where there had been a fairly steady inflow of gentlemen all evening.

'The lust for grumble and grunt is terrible.' came from soldier Joe beside me in the dark. Thirty years back the little old whore house that these men were patronizing must have done a brisk trade with sailors off ships in from the Battle of the Atlantic for repairs and bunkers. More recently news of Nato ships coming in after an Exercise would spread as far afield as Cork and Limerick. Bus loads would arrive of sportive ladies ready to leave their doors ajar. Now the only ship alongside was a Polish merchantman, in to pick up steel scrap. One of her foredeck hands was the next arrival. Knowing minimum English he said, 'Koorva?' (Whore in Polish; one of the words I'll never forget after serving with Polish sailors.) Just in case we didn't get the message he made a ring with his left middle finger and thumb and put his right forefinger through it. So we sent him along too.

'We ought to be getting ten per cent commission for all this, or one on the house.' said Joe.

US Aid

Next loomed a big burly fellow with a New Orleans accent and an air of authority. He introduced himself as a Master Sergeant, and we fell into conversation. He was checking that his men were not getting involved in any fracas that might be about to occur — or worse. At the mention of the whorehouse he drew from his pocket a cautionary sheet.

'FLIES SPREAD DISEASE.'
'KEEP YOURS ZIPPED!
If she wants it, she's had it'
If she's had it, she's got it.
If she's got it, you'll get it.
If you get the rip,
You'll miss the ship.'

'Thanks' said Malachi, 'I'll put that up in the sangar. Might keep our lads out of trouble.'

Our evening rations had failed to arrive from across the river and our radio didn't seem to be functioning.

'Anything I can do for you guys? said the Master Sergeant'

'If you could get us some chow from your base on the other side of the river it would be swell. '

'Cap'n', he said, 'The US Army has more planes than the US Air Force and more ships the American Navy. I'll sure see you're fed'

Big thermos flasks and a box packed with doughnuts, cookies and pots of peanut butter, arrived swiftly and mysteriously. We felt very pro-American. Having mislaid my mess tin I ate out of a hubcap from the Mini, much to the amusement of the Yanks.[5]

Old days on Derry Quays

Warmed by excellent coffee there was time for a reverie, recalling other days in these historic surroundings. Sharp contrasts came to mind to the events of the last 48 hours.

From here a hundred years ago eigrant ships like the swift Minnehaha of the McCorkell Line had carried thousands of emigrants to America. Pathetic scenes multiplied as relatives waved them off. During the Battle of Atlantic destroyers, frigates and corvettes of the Royal Navy lay in trots three or four deep alongside this quay — convoy escorts, they were, in for rest, and to land desperately burned and shocked survivors. Later, in 1945 the same berths were packed with surrendered German U-boats, their anti-aircraft towers bristling with guns, their tubes full of chase-me fuck-me torpedoes.

A burst of machine gun fire from God knows where soon ended my reverie. A shout came from the sentry at the river end of road.

'Looksee!. Something funny here. Keep me covered hi!'

A half man topped by a woolly cap had arisen over the edge of the quay, like Proteus from the waves. When the rest of him appeared the sentry realized it was a red-eyed marine. His high speed rubber boat had come quietly alongside under paddles. The Bootnecks had been patrolling the river for hours and needed a respite.There was enough left of the US Aid to provide them with a snack. At around 0100 I walked half a mile with Willie, my driver. up the river bank past the carapace of a burned out bus to visit the section working on the main Craigavon bridge. 'Let's get the gunners out of their shells' said Willie. We found White, their captain, up a rickety set of RE steps in a sangar overlooking the traffic.

'Expect action in an hour or so', was the word. 'You won't be relieved until 0800.

I countered with, 'Don't be nicking our rations next time the tea boat comes round.'

Beside us on the river were steel floats, writhing as if alive in the powerful tide They supported the barrages which the Navy had anchored each side of the bridge. This was in case the terrorists should try floating mines to blow up the piers.

"You know the Provos are supposed to have got some of those German jumping mines from WWI; they can lep over the barrage and then hit the bridge', I advised the section leader.

'Yessir. If I see anything like a big football coming I'll shoot at it before it gets to the net.' But I don't think he took me too seriously. I'd seen a German jumper or two stripped at the end of the War but if the IRA ever got hold of any we never heard of them being used. This possibility led to the tale of a sentry reporting 'Small round object approaching the bridge, possibly mine.'

'Certainly not mine', was the reply from the watchkeeper in the Ops Room.

But the story is naval and of WWII vintage. Back at Sierra 6 all was quiet except for an occasional shot from among the houses north of us. One Shot Willie might be back. Better do a prowler patrol and keep his head down. I briefed Billy, Jack and Jim to accompany me. Hughie checked that their magazines were full and the cam cream dark enough on their faces. 'Diamond formation. You'll be rear lookout, Jack'.

'I'll not can walk backwards. Never could get the lease of it'.

'Nay bother,' said Hughie, 'I'll do it'. It was the most exposed job in a city by night. In the country we rarely needed a TAC (tail arse charlie). But in Derry one battalion had suffered two men killed in this position. The platoon they belonged to was on the way to losing its nerve until Johnny, the Company Commander did TAC himself for the next three patrols. But their risk from snipers was at its worst as they patrolled in the heart of the Bogside. Our area was still Protestant and relatively a doddle.

Off we went with rifles at the Derry Port. That meant barrel skyward, butt on your right hip, finger on the trigger guard. For twenty minutes we traversed silent darkened streets Our eyes were mainly on the roof tops where an agile sniper might be in hiding. At street level a lady pulled up a blind and stared out.

'I shouldn't put your head up, love, if I was you. You might get it shot off', was a friendly warning from the guardsman who'd joined us. A scuffle in a backyard seemed worth investigating. 'Just where the cats have crept in and crapped,' reported Jimmy after he'd looked in.

'What'd you find ?'

'Not much.' he said with a big grin, 'But the smell in the wee outhouse was so bad I had to fart to get a breath of fresh air'.

We were careful to return by a different route to our outward one. That and to keep still when a flare went up were the most practical lessons I'd absorbed in years of training. And to keep moving. 'Once a patrol is saw', a Belfast instructor had told us, 'its use is done.' We detained two men who didn't seem to have a good explanation for being abroad in the small hours, and brought them with us to Sierra 6. At 4am came by radio the code word SNAP UP meaning H Hour. The battalions really were going in. We cupped our ears in an effort to find out how they were getting on.

Footnotes

1: Intelligence briefing at the time gave First IRA Battalion in the Brandywell, Second on the heights in the Creggan. The favourite watering hole in the area known as the Bogside Inn was guarded by armed sentries. Third Battalion and at times PIRA Brigade HQ, was a mile or so north in Shantallow Housing Estate. Fourth Battalion territory was east of the River in the Waterside. Due to SF attrition Four was at times little more than a name.

Dispositions of this sort were subject to rapid change.

During the No Go period the IRA outer road blocks were on the Lone Moor Road, Lecky Road, and Bishops Street Without.

Similar No-Go areas operated in Belfast. An Ulster Defence Association No Go Area existed at times in East Derry on the Waterside

End of footnote One

2: The man who placed Claudy bomb is believed to have died in the year 2000. More shamefully comes to light in 2002 the probability that the commander of an Active Service Unit who directed the attack was a Roman Catholic priest. The information, long suspected in South Derry where the turbulent prelate (now reported to be deceased) also initiated attacks, was laid publicly by a fellow member of his Church.

3: The Foyle College building is now the Institute of Higher Education. Boating Club Lane remains much as it was but most of the Strand Road buildings in the area have in 30 years been replaced or changed out of recognition. The Commission's Legal Office where our off-duty men rested, and the Electricity Board Show room beside it, have been replaced by a Medical Centre.

4:   *Memoirs published years later, indicate was that it was the Bloody Friday*
     IRA bombs, killing 11 civilians and wounding more in Belfast on 22 July,
     that had determined Northern Ireland Secretary Willie Whitelaw himself a
     Scot Guardsman, to allow the troops to go in. The date had been planned
     long before but the Op. was indeed very much subject to cancellation .

5:   *Future generations might be interested in the kit.*
     My reminder list for Motorman was as follows:
     Combat kit (shower- proof lined cotton trousers and blouse)
     Jumper, Beret, cap badge. puttees, boots
     Flak Jacket and steel helmet
     Field dressing .
     9 MM automatic, Mags and ammo.
     Rifle, magazines and 762 ammo
     Verey Pistol and flares
     Jack knife, cord, whistle and lanyard
     Compass, pocket torch, batteries
     Map case, pencils, protractor, camera
     Note book, Yellow card. Phone numbers.
     Binoculars
     Mess tin,.knife fork and spoon.
     Small pack with change of underclothes and 'poof kit'
     (which for the benefit of the curious was a sponge bag).

CHAPTER FIVE

MOTORMAN, PART TWO
July, August 1972

A Brigadier, A Bus and A Brothel.

Soon after 4am on Monday 31 July flares over Derry became more frequent and the bursts of automatic fire longer. Nine battalions were stirring from their start lines. Most of the young soldiers, being human, had butterflies in their tummies. Almost all the inhabitants of the city expected a bloody battle. The terrain at the south east end of Derry is steep and favours defence. As we on the east perimeter tried to read the battle it was clear that most of the firing came from that direction. Few maps succeed in showing the way the City is situated on an isolated two hundred foot ridge. In bygone days this ridge was virtually islanded by a split in the River Foyle. The main stream ran as at present while another passed west into the flat area now known as the Bogside. West of the Bogside the ground again rises steeply 500 feet to the housing estates of the Creggan. After that it extends west for a couple of miles over bumpy open ground to the lateral road, nicknamed Bomb Alley and the Border.

A 'tribal map' produced by the army showed new chums the score – Protestant areas in orange and Catholic ones in green, Mixed in yellow and Business in pink. It is large in scale – 1:5000 – but has no more than the odd spot height to indicate the features like the drop of 200 feet, vertical in places, west of St. Columba's School to the Lecky Road. The soldiers had to learn the terrain by hard experience.

While the soldiers crept forward let us recall that in a mini-Motorman operation a year earlier, 18th August 1971 to be precise, Lt Colonel Mostyn (later General Sir David Mostyn) led 2 RGJ into the Bogside and Creggan almost unsupported. A stealthy approach during the short summer night to hidden start lines achieved complete surprise.

Three companies entered at dawn and found minimal resistance. The Sappers, imperturbable under fire, cleared over thirty road blocks and what was more important removed the material from which they were made. Later the riflemen were tasked to destroy an inner barricade in

Westland Street while watched by 200 irate Bogsiders. Firstly this meant manhandling a troop of teenage girls sitting on top, ready to spit, scratch and scream. One false move could have caused a major riot. But with firm hands and some Cockney banter the even-tempered riflemen literally pulled it off.

In the follow up pioneer platoons began to build sangars and consolidate. The First Battalion The Royal Anglians and two Gunner regiments followed mid-afternoon and in the next 24 hours cleared the Creggan. Casualties amounted to one enemy gunman killed,his rifle being recovered, one captured and two almost certainly wounded. There were only half a dozen minor security force injuries. A single battalion had lived up its motto *Swift and Bold* to achieve by exquisite timing and tactics what nine were now about to undertake.[1] A footnote lists the positions of the main barricades cleared that 1971 day.

Then — Wait For It — Before the end of August 1971 all the troops were ordered to withdraw. If they'd stayed put the subsequent history of Derry could have been much less unhappy. Bloody Sunday might never had happened and the vast cost of Motorman avoided.

Let us now tick off some of the 1972 Motorman regiments – anti-clockwise. The First Battalion the Kings Own Border Regiment had passed us earlier on the way to their forming up point behind Foyle College. They were to move from north west with a start line on Artisan Street. Each of their four rifle companies were to take over a rectangular area some 500 yards by 300 in the outer Creggan, south east of the Reservoirs. Our friends Second Battalion The Scots Guards would be approaching from a start line in Ballymagowan, moving due west to take over the west end of Creggan. On their left was the start point for the Royal Scots On their right the Second Battalion The Royal Regiment of Fusiliers advanced from the heap of rubble which had earlier been the Mex Filling Station on the Letterkenny road, half a mile south of Craigavon Bridge. They were tasked to move up Lone Moor Road to meet the Jocks at the top of the steeply rising cemetery. Now we come to the Royal Green Jackets who had pulled off the coup a year earlier. I'd written about them the previous spring in Defence, the UDR Magazine.

'A few months ago we used to think that a Greenjacket was a form of locust or one of Robin Hood's merry men. Now we know them as 2RGJ who provide the Derry County Company beside us and have co-operated

in the closest way.

Our first impressions were not so far wrong. Like locusts they'll consume all your food and drink with incredible rapidity. But they'll give you a skinful of theirs at the next opportunity. They are just as merry as Robin Hood's men and will tackle an astounding variety of jobs with enthusiasm, fix your car, build a sangar, show you how to operate a radio set, mind your baby; mind your wife too, if you're not careful. Being keen to learn, F Company have acquired most of their habits. With them we have been stoned on a number of occasions.'

For Motorman A Company of 2 RGJ were attached to The First Battalion The Royal Scots to approach from the river and secure a large school on the outskirts of the Creggan. C Company of 2RGJ were given the expert's role of securing one hour before H hour some vital high ground in the Brandywell This meant a silent advance uphill from the river abreast the Craigavon Bridge. Dangerous going, ascending a maze of narrow streets to reach flatter ground south west of the old stone city walls. But unlike the newly arrived battalions they knew every hole and alley. Thereabouts the riflemen had in past months done much hard fighting, mostly by night. The Leeson Street Patrol by war artist Cuneo (painted in Belfast) gets the atmosphere of those Derry days exactly.

The lead platoon of C Company crawling over open ground near St Columba's Wells found it mined so closely that section leaders had to probe with bayonets for buried charges. Once dogs were brought up the mines were quickly located and neutralized, allowing a patrol to overlook the low ground of the Moss.

The Blues and Royals filled in another bit of perimeter in cavalry fashion with patrols on the north east. On sudden arrival by night three days earlier they had laagered as per Staff instructions at Ballyarnett, to find themselves in the middle of a Pony Club camp. At first the pony owners were horrified as they woke up to find soldiers shaving in their feed buckets, then pleased as the same soldiers gave expert help with grooming and tack cleaning. Mutual admiration was fine, but soon amid the roar of heavy vehicles, 24 hours a day movements, and the risk of accidents the ponies and children had to go. The Royal Artillery held the Craigavon bridge and acted as reserve. There were of course members of several other regiments present with the assault force on attachment or by normal cross postings.

You may deduce from the above that the shortest route north to

Donegal was guarded lightly, if at all. The army were adopting the maxim of a Chinese General who lived a thousand years ago and knew that men fight their best when trapped. Perhaps there was a bit of Irish blood in him because he said he aimed to surround his enemies on three sides, always leaving one way out open.

Meanwhile about 5am beside our humble abode on the Strand Road a short sturdy character dismounted from a parked car by the river, took a deep breath and lit a cigarette. He had the hot eyes and tired face of a man who'd been making love all night. We'd seen arms and legs flailing in car windows for the last two hours. Soon he got back and the car springs began to gently see-saw again. We had to admire his stamina and *sangfroid*.

A mighty rumble in the road heralded the approach of a pair of armoured bulldozers (Assault Vehicles Royal Engineer, or AVRE's). They had been landed under cover of darkness a few minutes earlier. A figure hunched behind the turret of the leader was guiding with hand taps the driver whose view was limited by a closed visor. I learned later that it was General Robert Ford, who had dined at our home not long before. He was using his cavalryman's eye and local knowledge to make sure they cleared the right road. The Bogsiders had built barriers based on steel beams cemented deep into the approach routes. A prolonged clearing job and worse still media photos of tanks in use against innocent civilians would have made quite the wrong image.

The Northern Ireland Office seemed to believe in their naivety that a Hearts and Minds policy could succeed even with hard core terrorists. Just this once however NIO got its image right. The AVRE's cleared the barricades like a scythe cutting corn. They passed us again at about 7am and were re-embarked before the journalist knew they'd ever been ashore.

'Operation successful: Minimum resistance; Casualties IRA one; Army nil,' came the bulletins in the morning. Official figures were slightly modified later but overall the bloodshed had been tiny in relation to numbers involved.   I never met a man that could give a full account of that night. Each unit had its own problems and victories. Doubtless there was a report with that label so derogatory to us natives – 'UK Eyes Only'. It never reached mine. To us, the night looked different. We'd seen ambulances rolling by with occupied stretchers and heard groans and cries from inside. Armoured cars had to be used with hospital markings, because some factions of the insurgents continued to fire on army ambulances. Intermittent rifle fire and the odd grenade explosion had gone on steadily for four hours. For the regular battalions it was no picnic. We were content at least to have had a ringside seat.

Stories filtered back. A Greenjacket platoon commander worked himself head first through a hole in a wall while trying to outflank an enemy position. Making an awkward landing he found himself attacked by stone throwing thugs. It looked like a lethal situation until two elderly ladies came to his aid, clearing the crowd by heavy play with umbrellas![2]

General Robert who had lead a troop of swimming tanks ashore on D Day 25 years earlier as a young lieutenant told us how the secret of the use of the tank-like vehicles had almost been blown. They were observed being loaded onto a landing craft on Clydebank by a Glasgow Herald reporter who had become curious while out dinghy sailing. There was only just time to convince him that it was a routine exercise.

Our support was the biggest operation the UDR ever mounted. 'We couldn't have managed it without you,' said the General Officer Commanding Northern Ireland, dining in our Mess after the dust had settled. We knew that but it was nice to have it confirmed from on high.

Visitations

At 7am a colonel from Ebrington decided to bless us with his presence. That brought all hands to the alert. To my relief our regalia of civilian scarves and gloves passed muster. I remembered another colonel expressing consternation on a callout in the spring at the sight of Marcus, a D Coy Captain, carrying a shooting stick and wearing civvy trousers and red scarf. 'Oh, the Guards always fight in corduroys,' was the unabashed reply.

'Keep a good look out for snipers,' the visitor said. I could see the expressions on the faces of the soldiers as he spoke. The second most important rule in war, one is told, is to refrain from giving unnecessary orders. I couldn't remember the most important one but assumed that the colonel didn't know either. He soon hurried away to inspect the Company up near the Dog Kennels and Bomb Alley. There on the border side of Derry were three official and thirty unapproved crossings to be guarded – a near impossible task. Most of the minor ones were blocked with Dragon's Teeth. But it had been reported that terrorist arms and ammo. were coming through them on motor scooters which could pass between. Some crossings couldn't be physically blocked because of farmers who owned land on both sides. They were supposed to keep the gates padlocked but naturally were reluctant to do so. It would have been more important, but no one did it that night, to stop traffic going the other way --- IRA policemen, IRA warriors, IRA godfathers, the IRA justices who had sentenced Marcus, scuttling away to safety in Donegal. Their exit was known as the Londonderry Races. At least that's what I heard the UDR call the stream of gunmen whose leaders had sworn to fight last man last round, disappearing at the trot over the Border.

Wise heads on both sides had allowed it to happen. Operation Motorman produced no martyrs. For 8 Brigade it was a bloodless victory.

The boring thing for the Volunteers was the inconvenience of returning shortly to collect the Invalidity (often referred to as the Infidelity) Allowance and the Boru (that's the local name for the Unemployment Benefits).

'It's a wonder them Westminster officials didn't arrange to have the cash paid out to the boys in Buncrana to save them bother. ' said one G company soldier as he watched them go. For a few days in Donegal there were too many Bogside warriors to be given beds and meals. A retired naval officer living in Fahan on the shores of Lough Swilly found his outhouses and hayloft full of hungry strangers on the first morning; being non-political he provided what food he could. In due course the Garda arrived, threatened arrest and told the refugees to move on. The naval officer was next accused of reporting the arrivals. This he most certainly had not. Threats later grew so persistent that he had to move off to Scotland. Relieved at 0800 we drove tired and hungry south along the river under the grinning muzzles of a dozen 17th Century cannon on the city walls. Opposite them were the blackened gables of the Guildhall, ringed by the carcases of smouldering cars, empty cartridge cases and broken glass. Then over the bridge to the comforting security of the army barracks. The Indian charwallah, on call 24 hours a day from his bunk under the counter of a dark tearoom, jumped into view to sell hot drinks and 'wads', cokes and smokes to all comers.It was handier to buy from him than queue in the overworked canteen where the tea was the colour of a long dead mouse and the main food hard boiled chicken. As I crossed the big barrack square after breakfast a bank of white fog came rolling up to enhance the blue gleam of the river and emphasise the stillness. A low sun was highlighting a speckled mountain side in Donegal, the one that inspired the *'Green Hill far away'* in the famous hymn by Mrs. Alexander, wife of a Bishop of Derry. The sun picked out too the grey spires of Protestant and Catholic Cathedrals and copper green church cupolas rising over the maiden city. Earth had not anything to show more fair that perfect summer morning. Man seemed particularly vile.

We filled in patrol forms, reported to Battalion HQ, then tried to sleep. But minds remained astir, so most of those off duty foregathered over coffee to exchange experiences. One platoon had had been sniped on the Strabane Road but no casualties. Private Bobby Linton on the Check Point on the Letterkenny Road heard a bullet smack into a wall just above his head. Another platoon up north had come under long range machine gun fire near Ballyarnett and fired a hundred shots of suppressive fire in reply. No hits claimed. They'd arrested two suspects and handed them over to the RUC. Others had found weapons, masks and ammo discarded by fleeing Volunteers.

But the attack really had gone in and had been ninety per cent successful'.

Sic Transit Gloria Monday.

For the whole day of that day the No-Go area and much of the city was held within a tight cordon while searches took place. No person was allowed to move in or out. Hundreds of IRA weapons, thousands of rounds of ammunition and tons of explosives were found. But for searchers and searched it was a most distasteful job; the innocent along with the guilty suffered the indignity of having their houses ransacked and in some cases damaged. The airless room above our colonel's office was full of exhausted soldiers snoring in hot bunks, emptied by those who'd gone on duty. Obtaining leave at midday I drove home for an hour or so to sign some letters.

There were more wonders to come. No sooner had we settled down at 5pm that evening at our now familiar checkpoints than a summons came to an O group. It was The Scots Guards, still in their nearby Tac HQ. The agenda was to re-locate checkpoints when the Guards moved into another base. This was being built at the top of the Creggan. The structure was to grow like Alice until it was reported to consist of a million sandbags. Meanwhile the army units lodged in school buildings, unused during summer holidays. Lieutenant Colonel Tony was complimentary about our help; saying that he felt his men were very thin on the ground without us. Next item was counter-measures against sniping. This is a form of enemy activity which annoys soldiers most. Locating the sniper and shooting back was, we knew, the best cure but often impossible under the restriction of the Yellow Card. The IRA were free to shoot at us any time, any place, while we could only reply if life was positively endangered. ie one of us killed or seriously wounded. But bold action was planned and duly flushed the killers out .

'Wont' you stay and eat?' was an invitation hard to resist.

The Jocks had, in common with most roulment units, established a Senior Ranks Mess where officers, warrant officers and sergeants lived together. The atmosphere round a scratched table, decorated with gallon jars of ketchup and brown jollop was convivial. Lots of laughs over a mixture of jokes and shop. The battalion had been recalled from general leave at 12 hours notice only a week before. Many members had been away from home on family holidays, some in cars en route to France and Spain; others in the Scottish hills. Most inconvenient it had been, but all seemed to be taking the disruption in good part. An additional problem was being under strength with several subalterns only weeks out of Sandhurst. One of these showed me his trophy -- a page from a school book in childish writing.

'I spat on a wounded soldier lying crying in the street.'

The Scots at the table were excellent company, an elite battalion out of a picked Division. Diners came in with faces showing traces of camouflage cream, just off patrol, others sat down fully accoutred, snatching food as they were about to go out.

'Woolly pulley' jumpers were the trade mark of Ops. Room staff and signallers.

Food was good and lots of it, big steaks and choice of veg. Chips with everything, ice cream, and vast hunks of orange cheese.

Red Cross Meals

I told them the background to the Red Cross meals. For many years hot food had been delivered four times a week to a hundred pensioners in the city and the No-Go areas. Despite barricades, highjacking of cars, bullets and bombs a mixed team of Derry ladies with backgrounds from all over Ireland, Scotland, England, Wales and the USA had carried out this service throughout the Trouble. On the day of Motorman with the city ringed and no one allowed to pass, it took the Red Cross President and her deputy hours of telephone calling to get to the right authority to request clearance to deliver as usual.

NO ONE had ever stopped this Red Cross service. The IRA and UDA had let them through. So they were determined to persuade the army to do the same. The President and her deputy succeeded. These two ladies unaided delivered all the meals that day. Besides taking along 'the dinners', they negotiated the delivery of milk. Ironically, after all that effort, they were accused by some pensioners of being late!.

'The Red Cross makes no distinction as to nationality, race, religion, class or political opinion.' was the ladies' watchword. I had felt very humble seeing them at work that day. And needless to say the Jocks at their own check points had been most courteous and helpful.

Then it was the Ops Room to see the latest Sitreps, Intreps and Mug Shots (details of wanted men).

'Have a dram,' the Colonel said as I was leaving.

'What? In the Ops Room?', queried Angus, his second in Command, perhaps a bit of a stickler.

'Sure, right here', said the Colonel

I looked forward to that drink but never got it. A signaller handed me a message marked Urgent. 'Return to Sierra Six at once'.

The Battle of the Box.

Some two hundred yards north of Platoon HQ two busses stood strangely stationary in the middle of a T-junction. A small crowd stood by one passenger door.

Johno must be doing a thorough search, I thought. Jumping up on the step I found him glaring across the aisle at a bus conductor who was clutching his large tin cash box.

We'd been told to look into these as they were sometimes used to smuggle in small arms or ammo. The Lough Swilly Bus Company served east Donegal and this bus had come from across the Border. Usually the opening of the box was a routine request and a quick glance sufficient. But this time the conductor, making allegations about cash having been stolen, had refused access. Johno was insisting. He'd said

'You'll sit there until you open !'

He and I put on stony expressions; the remaining passengers got out.

Suddenly it seemed that there were a lot of buses around and growing crowds anxious to get on home after work. We realized that a strike of all bus crews had been organized.

Perhaps the whole thing had been a set-up. I was in a quandary, not wishing to back down on Johno's word. The second in command of the Scots Guards arrived with a posse, looking cross.

'What sort of mess have the bloody UDR provoked?' I heard him ask a policeman.

The crowd thickened and the road became grid-locked with vehicles of all sorts. A scowling shop steward climbed on board. Local politician followed. Newsmen with TV cameras snapped open their tripods. It had been a quiet day and a riot just now would make some good copy. How the hell could we save face and get out? We kept talking, hoping for a break.

Then a Daily Mirror staffer to whom I had unknowingly given a tip some weeks earlier, came up the steps .

'What's it about?', John White asked. I explained.

'Would it help if I opened the box?'

'It sure would!'

He did so. It contained, as expected, nothing but a few pounds worth of coins. Honour was satisfied.

The buses started up, the crowd dispersed and the storm in a teacup was over.

Boy, was I grateful to that newsman?

The Raid on the Brothel

I can't remember if it was the night after Motorman or a day or two later that Angus, an eager-beaver Jock Platoon Commander, arrived at our sangar. A familiar figure by now he'd brought along a Saracen armoured car with a telescopic ladder tied on top

'Goin' t'raid the knocker shop, he shouted . 'Like to come?'.

'Sure'.

'All right for some', came from an Ulster voice in the background.

'Got to enter from the roof , in case its booby trapped.' said Angus,

We tried to manoeuvre the ladder inside the trees on the footpath. Why we couldn't get it up at the correct angle and what sort of trees grew in Strand Road I've long forgotten. So instead we knocked quietly on the door. It was opened by a weary unshaven man who was clearly expecting clients. He eyed the hefty Jocks.

'Can't manage you all at once.'

Perhaps he thought, like Kipling, that it would take a troop sergeant's widow for big lads like these.

'Tut, Tut. We haven't come here for a jump', said Angus,

'Just like to look around'

We clattered up narrow carpetless stairs that reeked of unwashed body, flat beer and stale sex. There had been so many surprises in the last few days that I hadn't quite worked out what to expect-- .

Half clad ladies, perhaps discarding tinselly bras and licking their lips as they peeped from curtained doors. But it wasn't the Sea Dyke in Amsterdam. Far from it.

Empty bottles, unwashed dishes, rubbish piled in corners, met our gaze. Grey sheets on unmade beds, and a couple of listless lasses in jeans and T-shirts sitting on rickety chairs. A shamefaced youth was plucked to his feet out of a corner .

'You needn't bother with this kid. He's just come in his pants', said the doorman cruelly.

The only girl in bed looked with hollow eyes from a white face.

' That's Concepta ; she's sick', said our guide .

'Where's the lady of the house ?' I asked cautiously '

'She's upstairs puttin' on her.'

Down the stairs she thumped - a stout lady, heavily busted, with the fierce expression required of a Madam.

'Concepta's vomitin' steady', she volunteered. The contents of a bowl beside the bed confirmed the story. We moved on.

'Please get everyone in the house into one room', said Angus.

That's what the drill book on house searches says, I recalled, as I tried to think if there were any special orders about brothels.

A search disclosed dismal empty bedrooms on the top floor; nothing vaguely suspicious. A cap that might have been a sailor's, a pair of filthy underpants; a few tattered girlie magazines. Angus seemed relieved. He'd been half expecting to find one or two errant Jocks on the job.

'Will you sign the Search Warrant, Wallace? We couldn't get a policeman to come with us', he asked me'

Knowing lads, the Derry police, thinks me, as I put my name on a form to certify no damage. It was no place to hang around.

But none the less as we left I took the chance of shooting out the street light above the door. It was white, not red so I wasn't spoiling their trade mark and it had been bothering our section for the last week.

'What was it like?,' said Joe when I got back. I had to make good story

'Dancing girls. Free beer. Big eats.'

'Did you search 'em thoroughly, Jock? said a UDR voice behind me, addressing a soldier who' d been with us.

'Sure, Paddy. Just smell my fingers!'

More Visitations

The next order reached us in the chill of the following dawn.

'A message by hand from B Company, Sir', said signals Corporal Shortarse.

The runner with a beret askew over short grey hair, his amiable country face flushed from activity, slowed to a walk and started to give Shortarse a Ballymena nod.

Then spotting me he turned it into a Ballymena salute.

'Message from Ops Room, Sir. Big Sunray due in an hour.'

Then he thought hard to remember the rest.

'Re-Me will be down shortly to check your 41 Set.'

Sunray means 'Commander at any level', so we didn't know what to expect.

In due course a strange brigadier arrived. complete with bodyguard.

Tall, erect, soldier-like, brave ,and merciless, he had a reputation for liking to eat a couple of platoon commanders for breakfast. So I was on my guard. But he was in good form because Motorman had gone smoothly.

'Hello, Wallace, you young buggah,' was his greeting.

'What's all this about brothels and bus strikes ?'

I explained as well as I could how the bus problem had started and suddenly been solved. 'You were quite right to back up your sergeant. I'll see that your pressman friend gets in early on the next good story'.

'Did you think the girls might have tried to get some young soldiers drunk and lured them into that kip shop?

'Well, sir, my men are all married. Anyway they'd have had to be pretty drunk to enjoy that joint.'

Then a major jumped out of a Land Rover, shooting his cuffs, dusting well pressed pants and stroking new-reaped chin; as bright eyed and bushy-tailed, as the staff officer in Henry V. He checked that his equipment was on straight, looked round at our dispositions and said, 'Good show, chaps.'

The radio was still not working but no one was very keen to admit that to the Brig.

'How are your communications ?'

'Had some problems, sir, but the set's on top line now .'

' Well then tell Red 4 I'll be up there in ten minutes. '

'Put it in code', said the major, 'and I'll see if they manage to de-cypher'.

Shortarse tapped away, thinking hard . He'd just have time to send a secret runner to Red 4 with the message on a signal pad and get it there ahead of the Brass. UDR privates, like Greenjacket rifleman, have lots of loyalty to their company officers but love taking the micky out of non-regimental ones. We heard no more, so the bluff must have held. Perhaps the brigadier never got to Red 4, as a big bomb went off somewhere south of us a minute or two afterwards to divert his attention.

A bit later I was with the Jocks again and asked about a Mess Bill.

'Forget it! Treat this Mess as your own'. I was told 'Come in for any meals you like'.

I didn't take that offer up often but it was heart warming to be made so welcome .

A helpful training major came to see if we were happy. He quickly got spare batteries for the radios and gave us a run down on Int. A good 'un he was but training majors were at that time a mixed bag; often seemed to be chuck outs from their parent battalion. We had already heard of a mild alcoholic, a pair of nervous breakdowns, and a bankrupt: all nice guys but we didn't take them too seriously on first acquaintance.

'What have you done?', or, 'Why did your own battalion decide to send you off to us?' my wife June, with her twinkling Dublin wit, used to say to new arrivals.

Later the standard improved. And the remit was widened. The title was changed to TISO, 'training, intelligence and security officer'. Now hand-picked, several of them followed on as first class UDR commanding officers.

The Regimental Sergeant-Major came round next with stalwart form, slight swagger and an occasional twirl of his stick as befitted a Green

Howard and a Yorkshireman. He chatted amiably but his eye was
searching the while for any irregularity. It fell on one of our older men
Robby aged about 60, of proven bravery and reliability, leaning
momentarily on his rifle.

'What sort of a soldier are you?' he barked,

'Your rifle's not for use as a walking stick'.

'Well, sir,' said Robby with respect and dignity, 'I never get a chance
to use it for anything else'. That was true but didn't satisfy the RSM who
put him on a charge next day. But I was happy later to be able to dismiss
it .

It was the same RSM who later rebuked Private Thomas McCaughey
when on sentry duty. Tom was the key man in our rifle team and had won
a BEM in action. He was affectionately known as Fangs from his
irregular teeth, a valued member of the company but not noted for tidy
appearance. Out of character he saluted the WO smartly on arrival.

' You don't have to salute me', he was told.

'Aye, but ye'll dae rightly tae practice on'.

To fry or not to fry —A stag in The Rossville.

Another day we did a stag in the Rossville flats.   It was a curious
business. The Rossville is a high-rise block built to re-house dwellers
from much older back-to-back accomodation.   Said at the time to be Le
dernier cri in urban housing it was populated entirely by nationalists. It
would have been quite impossible to mix political groups in this location.
Even the most determined do-gooders had by this time realized that
aggro was less likely in segregated groups than deliberately mixed
ones.

Our Pig backed in to a side entrance. At a signal two soldiers opened
the portals from inside. The steel doors of the Pig clanged open,
touching the walls each side to give cover from snipers. We hunkered
in between them and hastened onto a stone staircase. It stank of urine.
Further up there were pools of it, brown besmeared walls and piles of
stale turds.

Multi-floors up and a bit breathless we knocked a code on an
armoured door and were let into a penthouse sangar. Sounds quite
romantic and it had a splendid view all round. But that lost a lot when
examined through sandbagged slits. My concentration as an observer
was spoiled by the uneasy feeling that the inhabitants below could at any

moment smoke or burn us out. Why they hadn't already put the heat on to previous watch keepers was hard to work out. Since terrorists tended to dislike the UDR even more than regulars now might be the time for them to have a go — that is if we'd been identified on arrival. If we started to fry, a helicopter would presumably try to pluck us out. But it might be shot down en route. As a leader I had to be prepared for a crisis but after running over some possible situations I decided there were no easy solutions and put them all out of my mind. No one attacked us. So we passed a tedious six hours watching the antics of courting couples, betting on the outcome of a prolonged dog fight, and noting car numbers, while the two trained spotters we were guarding identified old and new faces. At last we climbed down those steps again, wiped our boots, and climbed thankfully back into a Pig

And that is my last memory of Operation Motorman.

If I had known then what I later learned from personal contact of the ability and dedication of Willie Whitelaw, then Secretary of State for Northern Ireland, the launching and success of Motorman would never have seemed in doubt. His experience with the Scots Guards in Normandy where he won a Military Cross and peace keeping on the streets of Palestine meant that the top direction from Hillsborough was in the best of hands at that time.

Back to Base

A week later the callout was over. Fatigue seems to hit 24 hours or so after the event. Many of us found the need to tear off a lot of sleep in the days that followed We then returned to the routine of civilian jobs and part- time country patrolling. There were follow-up parties, good ones, in the succeeding weeks with the Jocks in their sandbagged villas, and some of them came to our homes in Upperlands.

In due course the Scots Guards left, returning to their Depot and the round of ceremonial guards and palace duties. Which was the better part?

Some of us envied their return to a world at peace but that had its own problems and frustrations. It was to get more tedious when the IRA started bombing bits of Britain and local authorities demanded guards on the most unlikely targets. That spoiled a lot of weekends which should have been spent on Rest and Recreation.

In 1972 we still liked our war and felt we were going to win it. The UDR up until Motorman had been adolescent. After that it was adult. But learning remained essential to keep up with the IRA advances in technology we were to meet in the months ahead.

Footnotes

1: Some barricade positions. August 1971
Lone Moor Road - (each end) 9, Kildrum Gardens, Brandywell Road 2, Bishop Street, Lecky Road, Foyle Road 2, Rossville Street 2, Fahan Street,. Little Diamond, Westland Street 2 Northland Road. Full tally: about 50.

2: A story, maybe apocryphal, of pre-Motorman days was of a marksman who'd just won the Thousand Metres at Bisley and was ensconced on the old city walls. From there he was able to pick off para-military snipers in the City Cemetery while they were firing at armoured cars on the road by the river. This was at such a range that his targets had great difficulty in finding where the shots were coming from.

CHAPTER SIX
MOONLIGHTING – UDR STYLE

G Company is Born

'Ulster trails have their secret tales
That would make your blood run cold.'

Soon after Motorman in September 1972 a general UDR expansion was authorised. HQ decided to form a new company in Maghera ten miles north of Fort William. The main street of this ancient town is nearly a mile long, narrow and curving. That demonstrates antiquity. Maghera is a market town eight hundred years old and its layout is in clear contrast to neighbouring Plantation towns like Magherafelt and Kilrea whose streets form a rectangular pattern.

Maghera has today about 5,000 inhabitants, half Catholic, half Protestant, all sorts of shops, expanding housing estates and lots of good pubs. Its Mid-Ulster Garden Centre is famous all over Ireland. The Twelfth Century stone church of St Lurach with a unique relief of the Last Supper is the oldest thing in town. The houses stand on relatively flat ground below the harmonic ridges of the Carntogher and Slieve Gallion mountains which form the backdrop to western and southern outlooks. For the meaning of the name you can take your choice — the *Town of the Plain or of the Ring Forts.*

The new Company, labelled G, was to take over the north half of the area described in Chapter Three –about a hundred and fifty square miles. Ireland has more roads relatively than any other part of the British Isles so that gave us plenty of routes to patrol and keep clear of culvert mines. We called our base Fort Garry. Picture the RUC Station on the Garvagh road where we were located as a rectangular white building with hipped slate roof of pleasant 1960 design. It incorporates a house where the Sergeant in charge in peaceful times lived with his family. Our quarters were to be a pair of portacabins in the wired-in yard.

Jumped up to Major once again I was offered the job of Company Commander. This was welcome, not least because it shortened my drive to and from duty from twelve miles to three. Many other members of F Company found the same and were allowed to transfer. So we started off

END OF CALL-OUT FOR ULSTER DEFENCE REGIMENT

All eleven battalions of the Ulster Defence Regiment were back on normal duties this week after fourteen days on full-time call-out. It was the biggest operation of its kind for the Regiment since operation Motorman in 1972.

The very high number of men and women who answered the call made a deep impression on many observers, particularly those who were aware that in a lot of cases the part-time members of the UDR were making a considerable financial sacrifice.

Though the attitude of employers generally was extremely helpful a large number were not in a position to make up the wages of employees on call-out.

All battalions found themselves actively engaged in operations. Incidents included a terrorist attack on the Letterkenny Road permanent VCP in Londonderry when a number of high velocity rounds were fired at soldiers of 5 UDR; a similar attempt to shoot up Magherafelt UDR Centre; and sniping at a patrol of 10 UDR in Belfast.

Finds were made by a number of battalions and 4 UDR did so well that the Commander 3 Brigade referred to them in a congratulatory message as the "4th Fermanagh (Finds) Battalion".

Both 7 and 10 UDR were involved in the arrest of men held later on charges in connection with serious robberies.

The following messages of congratulations have been sent to the UDR:

From the Colonel Commandant;
"I wish to thank you all for your splendid response to the recent Call-out and for your excellent work. Please accept my warmest congratulations. The Regiment can indeed feel proud of itself"

General Sir John Anderson

From Commander Land Forces
"My thanks to you ALL for your sterling work during this recent emergency. I fully appreciate the enormous upset that a Call-out of this nature creates, and the unstinting and selfless reaction from you all deserves the highest appreciation".

Major General RB Trant

Personal message from Commander UDR:
"I am extremely proud and honoured to have commanded the Regiment during the magnificent response that you have all given to the Call-out and which led to many compliments on the efficiency and enthusiasm of all the men and women in the Regiment. Thank you for all your efforts".

with a cadre of tried friends Others from close around who had been put off joining by the drive to Magherafelt came forward and recruiting was good. For all our scanty accommodation,we soondeveloped that feeling of self-sufficiency that comes with an independent command and an excellent team of sergeants and corporals. The Guard soon found that they could keep track of time by the Upperlands linen factory horn; it sounded three times in the morning – one toot at 6.30 am, two at 7.00 and one at 7.30. After the middle blast the guard would witness the Maghera workers heading north on bicycle, scooter, Mini, Morris Minor, Ford Cortina or Austin Cambridge. Other blasts helped at the lunch break and tea time. And it wasn't long before we had plenty of outside jobs for the soldiers.

Our first casualty came all too quickly. On November 22 Private Sammy Porter, aged 30, a plasterer by trade, left his section at 3 am to drive a mile home. He was red faced and stocky and usually wore his beret a bit askew. A fearless chap but rather shy, his conversation to me was usually confined to, 'Yes', 'No', and 'Aye surely'. He kept a reliable Alsatian watchdog but that night it failed to give its usual greeting. The silence must have made him suspicious but he started to turn into the gate of his cottage. A gunman in waiting opened fire. Perhaps Sammy never heard the shot, for a half-spent bullet from a .45 revolver hit him in the head. His wife with two young children didn't hear the shot either. The dog had earlier been poisoned. Poor Sammy was found next morning by a neighbour, dead on the road, fallen half out of the door of the car. The pistol which he didn't have a chance to draw was still in his pocket. It was conjectured that he had 'seen too much' and been silenced.   But the killer was never found.

A fallen comrade was a new experience to most of us at that time. The death hit hard. Sam was a popular man and each member of G and F Companies contributed a day's pay to a fund to help care for his children. He was given a full military funeral with the RUC Band in the lead and many senior officers following attending.

Learning to be a Company Commander

I soon began to re-learn the problems facing an OC. These had become a lot more complicated since early days with F Coy. The OC was now on call all the time. There was in his life, as it says at the beginning of the Bible, 'no day and no night'.

We got through the first few months while I was the sole commissioned officer by virtue of great support from sergeants and corporals, and indeed everyone. We were lucky later to acquire the meticulous Captain Sammy, ex-North Irish Horse, as a second-in-command, and by promotion three tough platoon commanders. Non-commissioned officer courses soon produced additional section leaders. Between us we shared the main task of planning and conducting operations amid the increasing chores and administration. Signing 'Ten Twenty Threes' and fifty seven other types of Army Form, checking security of weapons, updating Standing Orders and weapon training, vetting and swearing in recruits, not to mention audits, study days, officer's mess meetings and lengthy Battalion O groups. Often the most time consuming activity was the greeting of visiting dignitaries.

You learned to allow a time lag of so many hours per star - a four star general would be three hours late, a three star two hours late and so on. Politicians were more predictable but usually convivial; most liked whiskey.

Our self invited guests varied from top to bottom of the scale. Chief of the General Staff Sir Peter Hunt, the most charming and considerate of men arrived at predicted ETA and took a deep interest. At the other end were long winded small-time officials. A company commander dealt with daytime visitors by leaving his civilian job and dashing in to the Fort, hoping to lose minimum working time in the process. No way could he avoid a loss of efficiency in his civilian role but this applied to all ranks in varying degree.

Pay was still not a prime motive of most soldiers but it was important to all and to some members a major source of income. The manner of making up pays was an irritant — both to those who sometimes thought they had been underpaid and those who strove to make up pay sheets in a fair manner. I was lucky again to have in succession two charming civilian lady clerks who took a lot of the load. The Army pay system was so inflexible that only a full eight hour duty could be paid for. This applied to all ranks of part-timers. A ten hour gap was stipulated between duties which could be accumulated for pay. Great in a Pay Corps office. But if a man came in and worked a consecutive sixteen hours he could only be paid for eight. Long spells are often required of soldiers in war conditions. If guards and patrols were to be maintained, ways round the rules had to be found.

Company commanders who dropped in to work for a few minutes or a couple of hours almost daily were told verbally by the CO to lump several short duties together to make up the eight hours and put in the total in as if it had been on one of the dates.

All very well, — it's no crime to break the law in Ireland — but military law is tougher. Soon some awkward Brass Hat forgot about the verbal orders and started a hard nosed inquiry. One heard of company commanders getting quite unfairly into trouble. I think that the system was improved later on. In the case of private soldiers a man might send a message to the Guard Commander to say he'd be late coming in because a cow was calving. He was not supposed, officially, to add up duties in the way just described. On one of these occasions I telephoned a wife, asking if her good man could do a short replacement stint.

'Willie's out on the moss', she replied. 'I'll go and shriek him'.

Willie was the sort of obliging soldier one really valued and said,

'I'll gie ye a wheen of hours'. He appeared promptly, did the short spell that was needed and went home. A good PSI would credit the time to him and make up a full eight hour pay later on. We had to bend most of the rules, except the ones that mattered. In G Company we were not only the best company in the best battalion we were blood brothers; all ranks hung together. The RUC was a good example of how to support each other. It wasn't as bad as a merchant navy ship I served on in the past. One of the foc'sle hands commented, 'There couldn't be a mutiny in this ship – the old man would join it'. But at times it might have seemed like it .

I must add — and George Lapsley, OC of the redoubtable E Coy in Coleraine — would be first to agree — that each company in the battalion was as convinced as we were that it was the best. It had to, because if it didn't, it was probably the worst!

The Vital Role of Company Wives

My trusty mate June like many UDR wives showed great courage in staying alone night after night, listening not infrequently to bomb blasts and small arms fire, as well as seeing lurid TV coverage. In praising her I pay a tribute to all G Company and all regimental wives. Other married UDR soldiers may not have put it into words but I am sure that each felt much the same. Some things are a bit too intimate to speak about. Without courageous wife support there would never have been a UDR. To June's bravery I owe the possibility of being in the UDR.

My life I owe perhaps to Sanda, a West Highland terrier, who would bark at any unusual night sound. We lived, still do, in a two hundred year old cottage up a long lane three hundred yards from the nearest house. It was a mile from my civilian place of work and three miles from Fort Garry. Early on I thought it a good idea to teach June how to use a .38 pistol. She was natural shot and always hit the target even though she tended to fire with both eyes tight shut. We put about a story that she could infallibly split a match box at forty paces! This bit of dis-information was so successful that hostile visitors probably thought twice before calling.

Other families dealt with the problem in their own diverse ways but let it never be forgotten that all and each of us did our soldiering only by dint of home courage and support.

A Moonlit Ambush

One memorable patrol three months after Sammy Porter's death took us up into the hills. We fell-in on a clear spring evening. There was a touch of frost and the agreeable prospect of two hours of daylight ahead and then a moon at near full. Shorter nights were making it a little more difficult for terrorists bombers to place their charges unseen. Hot intelligence indicated that Russian-made RPGs (rocket propelled grenades) and explosives were being brought in by night on an old pack horse route over the 1500 foot mountain which stood west of Fort Garry. A delivery was expected within 48 hours. This looked like the 'advance precise information' on which General Frank Kitson placed emphasis in his book that I thumbed so often, *'Low Intensity Operations'*. But it was not so precise as we would have wished. Hardly ever is. We decided not to hand this tip over to Rucsac or the Blankshires platoon up the road. We'd follow it up ourselves with an ambush. It was first ascertained that there were no other SF units in the area. The boys were warned to bring extra warm clothing on the excuse of a night shooting practice. We arranged to be dropped by CPC (civilian patrol cars). The whine of a Land Rover engine was at that time enough to shout *Army!* to any house within half a mile. If the Land Rover was heard to stop even briefly the insertion of a patrol would be assumed to have taken place.

At 9 pm in early dusk, faces darkened with camouflage cream, we disembarked silently about a mile and a half short of the selected ambush point. The moon would rise at eleven. Before that we had to climb some five hundred feet up the mountain face. The first half mile was on a narrow lane. When the lights of an oncoming car appeared each of us dived for cover into a thorn hedge.

'Maybe that's the IRA pick-up car, in early to meet the back-packers,' I optimistically guessed to myself.

'Would ye mind taking your boot away from my face, sir?, came in a whisper from the corporal who'd jumped in just before me.

'Sorry, Mac. You move first. I've got a thorn to get out of my ear'.

Mac was a cloth-packer by day, a familiar figure in working hours. A comrade and friend of many years standing, always reliable and even tempered. As the ground rose we moved slowly, trying not to sweat — a layer of clammy perspiration on the inside of one's underclothing is not the best thing for a long stake-out on frozen ground. The lights of Swatragh village astern in line with those of Kilrea gave us a good course, simpler and quicker than using a compass. An incandescent moon soon began to light the smooth slopes of the mountain. Black bars of tree trunks made a striking contrast to the silver of puddles and the pale pewter gleam of tangled grass stems at our feet. The boys with the possibility of an enemy contact moved quietly in exhilaration — every sense alert, and faces chilled by the night air. When one of them muttered, 'That's a quare night to be out on', I knew their blood, like mine, was up.

There had been a near miss from intercepting an RPG at a recent check-point and this just might be a chance to even the score. A patrol in Cloane Wood had seen two cars approaching on a minor road after midnight — most unusual.

'Stop the second one, Sir 'said our man Willie to Lt Charlie, the DWR officer in charge. Willie Currie had an idea that weapons were being brought in and it was normal practice to run a safe car in front of the one carrying the weapons. The Lieutenant ignored the advice. The front car seeing the stop signal gave three flashes of its headlights and several horn toots - clearly a signal. The rear vehicle one could be heard laboriously making a five point turn with trailer in tow. 'Lets chase it, sir' suggested Willie. All the reply he got was, 'It might be a come-on', and a refusal. An INT report came in afterwards confirming that a cargo had been missed.

Once clear of the trees we climbed making no sound louder than the squelch of a boot in mud, an occasional dislodged pebble and the puffing of Private Joey just behind me, one of the strongest men in the section but tubed like a horse We had allowed an hour for the ascent. There were delays as the last man lagged behind – the rear file by some curious rule always does. And in bandit country he's the one most likely to get shot at. We'd just skirted a level patch where a burn debouched into soggy sphagnum moss when muted curses us told that Private Jack had gone through the surface and fallen almost waist deep into liquid mud.

'Fook this for a game of soldiers!', said the man who hauled him out and got nearly as wet himself while doing so. A long drawn out, 'Augh!!' from the victim conveyed many things in that single syllable. Thanks — irritation at the prospect of wet trousers for several cold hours — determination to carry on in spite of all. The short puttees we wore would keep feet dry from momentary immersion but not this lot. We got our breath while he squeezed some of the moisture out of his clothing.

'That's the shooter's wages. At least falling into a sweel hole's better'n gettin' a shock on your private parts; like on real dark night when you hit an electric fence,' whispered Roy beside me.

'You mind that night yon big E Company officer they didn't like fell into a sheugh at Lisnacree? And one of the boys whispered, "Jump on his shoulders when you have him down"'.

Carntogher mountain is a 1200 foot ridge running north and south. The old trail zig-zags up the eastern face. Rushes merged into heather as we made our way direct uphill, half a mile north of the intended interception point. Once on the correct level about 200 feet below the crest we contoured left. At last a bluff with a low cliff on its south face appeared, marking the edge of the track. Here we'd see the rocket bearers, if any, between us and the moon. Rusty the section leader organised our planned dispositions.

'Go you on down that way!' was enough to put two men as lookouts and snatchers some yards west, along the probable enemy approach. 'Houl' where you are, Jo', to my runner.

'Get down that madder', placed another pair in a meadow below us on an escape route.

No one was to fire until I gave a verbal order or blew my whistle.

The Gimpy gunner and his Number Two lay on top of the bluff, and myself by the roadside below them. Rusty with parachute flares a bit to the rear. Radio silence was the rule. Only to be broken if a definite contact was made. We settled down looking to our front for a long motionless wait. The wind was getting up now and the moon hanging by its teeth to the bottom of ragged clouds. When it was hidden I used the old wildfowler's trick of fixing my eyes on a bush about thirty yards off. If you just stare into the distance your eyes will be out of focus for close objects, and inclined to miss them. It's curious how the mind can work on two planes at once. Without detracting from the essential vigilance one could muse on our surroundings;

The silence that is in the starry sky,
The peace that is in the lonely hills

Only the exigencies of war would get you lying out on a night like this.

I recalled Major Johnson who had been grouse shooting on this mountain with my grandfather. He was being shaved by his valet one morning in his Donegal home about 1922 when two gunmen broke in and told him he was to be executed .

'Why me ?', he asked, 'I've been kind to my tenants, sold out nearly all my acres under the Land Acts. I've never been involved in politics'.

'Don't know why', said the nervous terrorists. 'But we've been ordered to shoot you and if we don't we'll be shot ourselves'.

He was allowed to say his prayers, write a letter to his wife and was then led out and executed. The pattern hadn't changed. It was evil things that we were fighting.

Then a blood-chilling wail came up the hill. The sound reminded me of Oona a professional keener I'd heard on Tory Island at a funeral. High it went, then low, followed by gurgles and ending in a hellish chuckle. I had to remind myself that was not the Banshee but just a vixen wanting cubs. A few minute later came a chink of tin from near the crest of the mountain to our right. Cold fingers moved along icy steel barrels towards triggers. John Biggs-Davidson's parliamentary effort to get gloves issued to UDR had not yet matured. But we knew that if the IRA were running arms they'd probably send a scout up first to see if all was clear. The vital thing was to not be seen by the advance party. An ear to the ground brought a patter of slow hoof beats. Then appeared the sharp silhouette - two beasts with bundles on their backs, stakes sticking out and shiny cans glinting in the moonlight hanging off their cruppers. It all looked familiar.

Roy whispered, 'That's Paddy, the gipsy tinker'.

I lay still but Paddy knew he was being observed — an eye glinting bright in the moonlight had been enough. He reacted calmly. Living in the wild he must have had a sixth sense of human presence. When I spoke the donkey, with no blinkers, shied wildly but the load stayed on and Paddy soon calmed her.

'Augh, Major, is it you? I'm just doin' a midnight flit. The young cubs is got very bad to me the far side o' the hill.'

First time I'd met Paddy, years before he and his family were encamped on a night far colder than this one by a mountain roadside. They were lying on the bare ground in a tent less than four feet high under a strip of worn canvas supported by withies hooped into the ground. At one end stood the hearth in a slightly higher tent, about six feet square.

As I and Murdoch, an RUC sergeant, looked in through the smoke hole at its apex and shone a pocket torch at the embers Paddy's shaggy head and bare torso appeared out of the crawl tent. He blinked up, trying to guess who we were. The sergeant made himself known while gradually the tinker's wife's face emerged and later three unkempt naked children — a family as hardy as wild ducks. The ring of five upturned heads with wildly tousled hair would have made Medusa-like creation to win prizes in the Tate Gallery. I wish I could have made a record but it was long before the day of pocket flash cameras. We became friends after that and Paddy occasionally called at my house to earn a small fee for soldering Primus stoves and repairing hurricane lamps. His father had been a swagman walking round houses selling trinkets from a back-pack. I quietly checked his loads as all clear. The only mildly suspicious item was a bottle. I sniffed at its contents. It was poteen.

'That's a nagon of mountain dew. Good stuff. Have it, Major. Ye'll hae need o' it lyin' out there by yourself.'

'Thanks. Don't be talking about this, and make no noise till you're off the hill'.

It was still just possible that Paddy was a being used as a blind. More interesting traffic could still appear. I gave the poteen to our two wet-footers to pour into their boots. That really does work. We stayed a couple more hours without seeing or hearing a thing.

A couple of donkeys for our night's work. Bathos, you may say. But was it really? Worth it, we concluded, as nineteen out of twenty IRA planned operations were believed at that time to be cancelled. And we'd upset one more. Perhaps a similar proportion of UDR ops failed to achieve their direct object. We just kept on trying and at least that supply route would be looked on as potentially dangerous in future.

'We cannot tell, but Allah knows
How much the other side was hurt'

It's that sort of war. 'Keep on trying and at least you'll make the enemy jumpy'

The SAS could, and did, stay in ambush for up to ten weeks. A regular Battalion's Rupert Bear or reconnaissance patrol could lie up for three days Four hours or so was the longest we as part-timers could maintain an ambush. But on other occasions that produced some excellent results.

Getting back to base was next priority. Where possible we never retraced our steps. And as a result, while we were ambushed quite often in vehicles, we were never in my time surprised while on foot.

Now it was a matter of climbing over the ridge, then a traverse 300 feet down the west slope of the hill to an RV with our pick-up vehicles in the Whitred Wood (that's the local name for the weasel. But we saw none that night.)

We were a bit early, so Rusty posted a sentry. Away from habitation we could relax and get out Thermos flasks and sandwiches among thick nettles in the shelter of the ruined walls of a gamekeeper's cottage .

'Try that, major,' said Leslie handing over a piece, 'It'll keep the wind out of your stomach' . 'Don't.' said another voice. 'He's having you on — that's army bully beef and you'd need the heart of a lion to eat it'. But it went down OK. There was time to talk

'Augh, man, my father told me of some quare days here afore the War, so he did.'

'That was when Colonel Chichester used to come and stay in the Lodge a mile up the road for a week at a time o' sport, and wild parties, women and whiskey. All finished when the Lodge was burned by the Shinners in the twenties'.

'I know rightly', I replied, 'and there were plenty of grouse long after that. The colonel had a couple of Scottish gamekeepers looking after it. There was one day on the face of Benbradagh my grandfather - they called him Hellfire Hal in those days — shot 25 grouse to his own gun.'

'I did beater one of them big days and mind the game cart and four cribs full o' birds. Now you'd be lucky if four guns shot five brace in a day's walking.'

Everyone was getting chilled now as we cooled off after the exercise

I handed my flask round. Sometimes it was just for sippers. Tonight justified gulpers and it came back empty.

'Did you not have some, Tommy ?

'Nah! The wife's vast agin' drink.'

But for the others the spirit was enough to get the crack going.

Private Bill, the machine gunner, had been married about two years and had unwisely admitted disappointment at not yet having started baby

'Will you face Ina when you get home?'

'Aye, I suppose I'll gie her a volley'

'But she'll not houl?'

' Dunno I' m sure puttin' plenty of the stuff intil her '.

'What about Marianne? said another voice

This was a lady well known for her attractions and obliging ways.

'Augh, I never see her these days. Is she getting much of it?

'I'll tell you there's such a confusion of cocks about her arse I don't think she's getting it at all! '

We were interrupted by one of the sentries.

'Something to show you. I just ta'en a notion to look under the road'.

He led me to a concrete culvert, wide enough to hunker along, beneath the main highway to Derry from Toome Bridge. His torch showed a neat hole recently excavated in the eastern wall, big enough to hold 80 kilos of explosive. The soil was still moist. It was recent work. We withdrew, careful not to leave any trace of our visit. It was too late to do more than note the location and best approach, with a view to getting it staked out later. That culvert was indeed watched by other members of SF and an arrest made. Of that it is still too soon to give details.

The CPC cars arrived and it was time to be off, get home and sleep hard.

Lorries and a Bus

Main road stake-outs were usually a bore and to be avoided whenever possible. But doing them could sometimes be amusing. In Glenshane Pass one night the mobile patrol came on four hi-jacked vehicles abandoned in the usual style — mid-road — a bus, a car and two lorries. It was a bitter night. Remarkable how a matter of 500 feet additional elevation above our base always made the wind so much sharper. All four vehicles had keys in their ignition. An invitation? A box with wires leading out of it sat on the bus driver's seat. A bomb? Perhaps; but maybe a shade too obvious. Then we spotted on the rear bench of the bus a courting couple. They were having a good time. If there had been a trembler switch in the box their activities would long since have set it off. Their presence seemed to make a booby trap less likely. They'd been dandering up the road, the man said, and taken advantage of this warm spot to rest in. We politely suggested that they should carry on their activities elsewhere. They left behind a half empty bottle of poteen, excellent stuff which it seemed only right to take into protective custody. Then once again it was a matter of deal with the situation ourselves or stand around for many hours.

A simple device, recommended to section leaders, came into its own that night. An insulated hook on a hundred feet of tenter's twine (ex local weaving factory) plucked the box off the seat by a pull from a safe distance. It fell onto the road and burst open showing a stuffing of newspaper. We checked each vehicle over for more wires or boxes. Big Willie, a bus driver by trade, jumped up and started her. Lexy manned one lorry and Shortarse another. Soon we had our convoy parked in a neat row outside Maghera Police Station.

I got a rollocking from the CO in the morning for having disturbed possible evidence and... and.... and .... *Semper in Excreta* we seemed to be — *Always in the Shit*. But that time it was well worth it! And after some Ops like this G Company became known as the Hill Billies.

A Concrete Story

Many a story came out of patrols among the mountainy men. Willie, a civilian neighbour, was driving a lorry load of cement to a mountain farm along a minor road near the Pass. He told me the story wide-eyed some time later.

'I was held up by a man in camouflage wi' long hair and a sweat rag round his head. He was carrying some sort of Sten gun. "Come out, ye fooker", he said, and dragged me from the cab and laid me out on my back like a paddy frog. He stood on my hands, prodded me with a rifle muzzle and asked a lot of questions. I'd a lot of money on me, the week's pay for a dozen men I'd collected from the bank. I thought they were IRA and going to rob and shoot me. But after nearly an hour he let me go'.

They were in fact regular soldiers and covering an arrest taking place a mile or so away See page 215-217.

Mines and Minesweeping

Picture a Greenjacket patrol, working under dim moonlight in bounds from field to field in open order beside the Maghera-Dungiven road, on the lookout for claymore mines. The corporal counts his section -- seemed to be one extra man, a figure bent over something in the long grass . 'Who's that?' he challenges. Up stood a man in dirty civvies with the T-Bar of a dynamo exploder in his hand. The wires were traced to a culvert bomb under the road. It was a fair cop -- a red-handed cop --and many an army would have shot the man or roughed him up. But the good natured riflemen put him under guard in the LR , and gave him a fag and a cup of tea while the fingerprint boys got to work on his kit . Later he was handed over to Rucsac. One more bomb attack foiled.

One, all too recently, had not failed.

Lance Corporal David Moon was with 664 Aviation Squad when they drove east along Glenshane Pass very slowly on June 24 1972, escorting a low loader on which was a damaged Sioux helicopter. He had volunteered for the recovery as his last job before leaving the army and joining the family law business. 120 pounds of explosive were detonated, killing David, also Sergeant Stuart Reid and Private Chris Stevenson. David's father, a country solicitor, later wrote an open letter to the people of Dungiven asking why they had killed his son, a non-combatant fitter. Several sympathetic replies were received.

G company kept in touch with Mr Moon afterwards and tried to explain that we as residents felt deep sympathy, also gratitude to his son who had died to preserve democracy, law and order.

After these incidents Glenshane Pass was banned to military traffic for months.

Flying to an Explosion

The next memorable patrol was an Eagle (ie by helicopter) and produced a surprising result. We'd had a report of a possible bomb factory 16 miles away. It was described as in a shack in the tall trees surrounding a manor at the north edge of our patch. Three armoured cars were based with us at the time. They'd relieved The Duke of Wellingtons who'd got to know the people and the country well. Patrick, who commanded the troop, knew neither the men or the country but always behaved with perfect cavalry dash.

'Let's take a couple of my Scorpions over there and clean it out', he urged.

I reckoned that the noise of armoured cars would give the game away. A visit by helicopter might catch the makers flagrante delicto. Patrick's disappointment was so clear that I got out the whiskey which lived in my locker for moments like this and poured him a stiff 'un'.

'Arn't you going to have one?' he said after downing it in a gulp.

'Not just now. I don't like to go out on patrol smelling of whiskey'.

'Good Lord. My men would think something was wrong if I didn't smell of whiskey', was his memorable reply. We got ourselves an RAF Wessex, approached low over the top of the big house and landed about 200 yards on where the spacious lawn ended under mature beeches. The minute wc disembarked the soldiers dispersed to search the wood. I halted briefly on seeing a tall lean female figure emerge from the stately portals and approach at a half trot. All unsuspecting I 'Advanced One', as the drill book says, to explain why we were there .

'What the hell do you mean flying over my roof? — We've just spent ten thousand pounds on repairing it — now you've probably blown half the slates off. Get off my ground quick or I'll put the dogs onto you!!! Haven't you bloody soldiers any thing better to do?'

All this before I could get my mouth open. Lady Beltup was in better than good form that day. We'd met round a tea table a week earlier.

She drew breath for a second volley. 'Bombs here? Bollox more likely! They wouldn't dare to ...'

But I never discovered what they wouldn't dare...Suddenly she stopped in mid sentence....went white-faced and totally silent .... then finished limply, 'Wallace , I'd no idea it was you'. It was like a collapse of stout party scene in repertory sketch! I did my best to disembarrass the poor lady. Had a good look at the roof with binoculars and to my great relief was able to assure her of no visible damage. We carefully flew off without going near the house. A red ring with exclamation marks round the manor was entered on the Ops Room map. The incident was never referred to again.

We'd had an explosion all right but found no bomb factory. They wouldn't have dared to set up shop on that demesne!

Down by the Riverside

In 1974 a UDR checkpoint captured ingenious plans to take over the pilot boat in Lough Foyle and use her to put explosives in the bow of a coaster. Said coaster would then be rammed into the side of HMS Rame Head which provided power for Fort George in Derry. So a heavy protective boom was built.

Rame head was commanded by Lt. Commander David Ogilvy who used the Navy's non-combatant position and his skill as a host and poet to arrange from time to time meetings which reduced tension and averted bloodshed.

A haul of home-made explosives

CHAPTER SEVEN

Gruelling Years
1973 to 1975

*'We are governed by a set of drivellers whose folly takes
away all dignity from distress and makes even
calamity ridiculous'*
Sir Richard Steele. Sixteenth Century. Quoted by Junius

The Coming of the Greenfinches

Nineteen Seventy Three was a dull year — just steady guard duties
and suppressive patrolling. In spite of suffering a succession of casualties
we were never allowed to get up and at 'em. Events started true to form.
The New Year had its familiar activating effect on the assassins.

On January 3rd Captain Jim Hood, second in command of D
Company, Limavady was returning from duty at about 11 pm to his home
in Straidarran, ten miles east of Derry. His son, a UDR private, was
putting the car away when he heard a loud report His father lay dead,
killed by shot in the back of the head by a gunman with a twelve bore
shot gun. A kindly and wise man of proven bravery, a distinguished USC
officer and father of three fine sons. Jim was sadly missed in many
circles.

Ten days later Constables Dorsett and Wilson RUC were killed in
their car by a bomb near the Guildhall in Derry. On March 2 we heard
with horror that Sergeant David Deacon of B Company in Derry was
missing. He was last seen offering an acquaintance a lift home from
Cassidy's Bar and appeared to have been abducted.

A day later the gallant Deacon's poor body was found near Molenan
— hands tied behind the back, hooded and shot in head. Why him? I
never found out.

Yeates, the poet, wrote of the 1922 Troubles
'A man is shot, a house is burned,
But no clear fact can be discerned.'
I used to wonder what he meant. Now it rang horribly true and was

happening again.   Against this fearful background UDR Headqurters were launching a major effort to recruit up to our full establishment.

On April 3rd, the regiment's third anniversary, a centre-spread appeared in the Belfast Telegraph. The left page asked for recruits for training. Pay offered was, '£ 2.79 a night (8 hours or more)' That was hardly generous, even by 1973 standards. But multiplied by twenty or so nights on duty it could make up a useful month's spending money.
The right hand page appealed for experienced officers.

'COULD YOU LEAD THE MEN WHO WORK FOR PEACE?' it asked .. *The UDR particularly want men with previous military experience and who would therefore have the right sort of qualities. As a newly commissioned officer you would receive £ 4.79 a day'.*

This advertisement plus frequent personal appeals from senior officers produced a substantial improvement in our numbers.The trend was in direct defiance of increasing casualties. At the same time the IRA were celebrating, in blood as usual, the anniversary of the 1916 Easter Rising. A Derry sniper killed four men between April 11th and May 3rd. This was in the City, near where G Company did its share of patrolling. The dead men were Gunners Idwal Evans and John Venn and Sergeant Thomas Crump from the 22 Welsh Light Air Defence Regiment, also Royal Anglian Private Anthony Goodfellow. After Crump's death the sniper was not heard of again. Perhaps he tried once too often. The 8 Brigade Commander himself David Mostyn had a narrow escape. He was out for some exercise on a Saturday afternoon by the edge of Lough Foyle and walked on a bit ahead of his wife and young son. A villainous looking man approached Mrs Mostyn and pointedly asked,
'Who's yon walker ahead?'
She cleverly put him off with a false name.

Bombers were active too. On June 3 a bomb killed six civilians in Railway Road, Coleraine a university town where patrolling by E Company had so far managed to keep the peace. My cousin Heather Simpson greatly distinguished herself in aiding the wounded. A Bellaghy man later admitted to placing the charge.

The loss that hurt us in G Company most deeply came when on June 5th. Two policemen were on a routine patrol in Enniskillen A long burst of Thompson machine gun fire from a passing car knocked one constable bleeding to the ground. He was David Purvis, beloved son of a G company sergeant who lived within two hundred yards of Fort Garry.

Poor David died in a helicopter en route to hospital.

Two weeks later a Bomb Disposal Officer Captain Griffen was examining an IRA arms dump on the Lecky Road when killed by an explosion. On June 26 Robert McGuiness a former Irish Army reservist was shot in the Brandywell - probably a tit-for-tat for Barry Griffen. Shortly afterwards it was a luckless civilian, a popular charwallah with a counter in Ebrington Barracks. Noor Baz Khan, father of five children, was pistolled to death at short range in a car in a Derry street.

It just seemed an endless stream of pitiless slaughter.

A New Boss

A diversion on 30 June 1973 was a new Commanding Officer to be broken in to our ways of going. This was Derek Woolstencroft the Queens Regiment, a Richard Attenborough look-alike. His initiation mainly took place at Ballykelly but Derek soon became a frequent and helpful visitor to G Company. He had a lot of NI experience. One memorable incident he related was in the Ardoyne. When a Protestant crowd was making trouble Ian Paisley arrived and helped cool the agitators. He was good at that. Afterwards he took tea in the sangar and Derek heard a young officer ask

'Dr Paisley, how do you see the future in Ulster ?'

The great voice boomed out a surprising reply.

'I see myself as the leader of a Protestant community in a United Ireland'.

The Lassies

Following the sadness of so many losses now came a great boost to UDR effectiveness. Credit for it is largely due to the persevering efforts of Brigadier Harry Baxter, our third Regimental Commander. An Irishman with a twinkle in his single eye, a fund of good stories and a personality that appealed to all ranks, he visited us often. At length his efforts succeeded in persuading the authorities to allow the UDR to recruit women.

Applications were invited in August. The response was most gratifying. 350 of the 500 places allocated were taken up within four months. What an enormous help and ornament the girls were—signals, intelligence, searching and catering all rapidly improved. Greenfinch, starting as a signals acronym, was soon adopted as the official title for this regiment of women. The girls were full of guts and enterprise. At first they were not allowed to bear weapons. General Peter Leng, then CLF, who had had backed the introduction, told the story of being asked for arms by a blue eyed blondie.

'Could you kill a man?' he asked

'Sure. Just give me twenty four hours!' she replied.

Joke or no, they soon were allowed out on patrol and some given personal protection pistols. Their skill in recognition of suspects was far above that of the average man. Polite conversation in the back of a Land Rover had been usually neither. Now Greenfinch presence in all sorts of roles kept the party cleaner and added a certain piquancy to the work. Females in the Battalion Ops Room were witty as well as efficient A bold notice on our Greenfinch plotter's desk bore the winged words

We know where to draw the line !

In G Coy we soon collected, as one of the male privates remarked, 'a wheen of real good Greenfinches.' That amounted to about ten. UDR wives could now solve the problem of being left too much on their own at home by joining up. Lots did. Included were a number of Commanding Officer's ladies. Of course some speculation arose as to the domestic occasions on which they were required to salute the boss. To my relief a senior officer known as a Goldfinch, or just 'Ma', was appointed to visit companies to look after their welfare and discipline. I still had to have a hand in promotions which required more tact than in the case of males. There was a tendency among females to act like sergeant-major on the strength of a single stripe.

Male recruiting

Male recruiting had now settled into a pattern. In early days, as mentioned, the Fifth Battalion had recruited some 70 Catholics, about 20% of the total. Now all except one had been intimidated to the point of resignation. Three who did not resign had been shot dead by the IRA — *'pour encourager les autres'*.

It was in a follow-up to the Easter advertisement that Brigadier Denis Ormerod, our then respected Regimental Commander, pointed out that only three per cent of Ulster people of military age were joining up. He asked the question why.

By now many of the answers were known. Of those residents who supported the security forces some 50% were not sufficiently concerned about terrorism to do anything about it. So easy it was, as one of them remarked to me, 'to get into a rut, pull the lid over your head and forget about the troubles'. You could live for years in many parts of Northern Ireland and never see a shot fired or hear a bomb. More deaths were occurring year by year on the roads than by political violence. Perhaps another ten per cent occupied themselves politically. That did not mix easily with UDR duty, although Major Ken McGinnis MP (now Lord McGinnis) managed to do both well. A country school headmaster,

an active Aughnacloy company commander and a shrewd political commentator Ken has, as I write in 2001, been justly elevated to the House of Lords.

Some people for business or family reasons just couldn't put in the twenty hours a week often needed. An unforeseen hindrance for those with links south of the Border was the fact that for the ten years or so when the trouble was at its height it was unsafe for a UDR man to be recognised in the Irish Republic. Many of us in normal times would have spent weekends in Dublin or holidays in Donegal. But that had to be given up 'for the duration'. So you cut yourself off from southern friends and two thirds of your native country. June and I sometimes went south under assumed names.

Other sympathisers with no military tradition in the family found it hard to submit voluntarily to the perceived harshness of army discipline. Assassination and intimidation risks to UDR members were now facts, not as at first, hypothesis. For the owner of a one man business and father of a young family the risk of sudden death or kidnap was a fully understandable reason not to join. It should have affected recruiting but the numbers now joining showed that it didn't. Warn an Ulster girl or man not to do something risky and it makes them all the more determined to go ahead. On the plus side sport was starting to play an important part and attracted lots of recruits. Soccer, rugger, golf, sailing, darts, go-karting and parascending all became organised UDR recreations.

G Company now had almost as many trades as soldiers --, Architects, Bleachers, Building Contractors, Concrete Block makers, Bus Drivers, Civil Servants, Council Workers, Dyers, Electricians, Farmers, Firemen, Garage owners, Joiners, Linen manufacturers, Quantity Surveyors, Shop Keepers, Salesmen, Schoolmasters, a. Sailor, and a Weaver or two. Some came from the ranks of the 10% unemployed and almost every one of these became fine soldiers.

The arrival of a few oddballs of extreme political views didn't bother the rest; we quietly got rid of them.

In the regiment as a whole Commanding Officers came from nearly as varied a background — Household Brigade, Cavalry, Gunners, Sappers and Paras as well as Light Infantry. It was soon found best for each UDR battalion to draw, wherever possible, all its full time staff from one Division. Our best ones came from Scottish Regiments, close to Ulster by tradition and temperament.

For career officers a UDR command was now recognized to be as important as that of a regular battalion. A CO could vary in methods and temperament as much as did his men. Some had their faces blackened four nights a week. I recall Nick of 8 UDR making quite an entry on his own birthday. A contact had been made and after it he came in to sit at the head of the table for a six course dinner — his wife was a famous cook — wearing a combat jacket with his face covered in cam. cream. And of course the party flourished.

Paddy Liddell, 1 UDR, (Ex Skins) was tops on OPS. One of his men told me in admiration 'If ever a patrol was in trouble Paddy had a knack of climbing out of a near by ditch, on hand and ready to help'. (He died about 1995). At least one CO hardly ever visited his outlying companies. Mike Campbell - Lammerton, a Scottish rugger international, was able to go round various sporting clubs and be listened to when saying bluntly,

'The regiment needs officers. Give me two years of your time and I'll make a man of you'. That worked. It was widely felt that his two year period in command of Nine UDR was not half long enough for Mike.

G Company arms were now In. That meant that each evening we had to go through the lengthy business of drawing rifles from the Armoury, a box-like Portacabin with thick steel walls and heavy cruciform locks — an unpleasant windowless cave, smelling of gun oil and cordite which made me feel claustrophobic. In another company we'd heard how a rifleman, careless from exhaustion, had brought his rifle in with a round 'up the spout'. He discharged the bullet which ricocheted off the walls of the armoury some ten times. With almost unbelievable luck no one was hit. Accidental discharges meant a heavy fine for the culprit and dismissal if repeated.

It was about this time that we were issued with the Shorland – a light armoured car built on a Land Rover chassis. It had a turret with an aperture for a machine gun and out of it the gunner could stick his head up like a gopher. Us country boys were not allowed to have the right weapon for the mounting, so manufactured a dummy barrel which was just about as good as the real thing and took a lot less form filling and cleaning. Shorlands were a bit top heavy. If one fell over on a sharp bend it was never the same again. Nor was the gunner if underneath. So we didn't mind too much when they were withdrawn. That was probably on political grounds as looking too aggressive.

There were a number of minor incidents. At one period we were bothered by a sniper. He was a good shot too and liked firing into the back of Land Rovers where the armour wasn't. Luckily he didn't have one of those US Army Barrett Light 50 rifles, now in use on the Border with an effective range of 1,000 yards and the punch to go through any body armour. But an Armalite was good enough against lightly armoured vehicles.

TOOME ROAD AMBUSH

At periods when enemy movements were expected checkpoints on the six Lower Bann bridges — Toome, Portglenone, Kilrea, Agadowey and Coleraine — could control on all traffic passing across the north half of the Province. On one such occasion in 1973 a G Coy Section spent the day at Toome. About 5 PM we got an American style signal,

'Get your arses to Castledawson at the rush. Investigate malicious fire and shooting.' A relief from the boredom of a long static job, it seemed. We came under low velocity fire a mile north just short of the Creagh Road turn off. Both Land Rover crews debussed a hundred yards on. One round appeared to have hit the rear vehicle. It must have been very low velocity as it was stopped by the armour. An advance of a hundred and fifty yards on foot over a rising field took us up to the apparent firing point which was on a by-road parallel to the main one. Long before we got there the enemy scarpered. As expected. It was a feeble ambush. The incident in Castledawson had been planned to bring us to the target zone —perhaps to blood some IRA recruits. Whoever did the firing had little stomach. In the autumn more killings occurred.

On Oct 3 an RAOC soldier called Dobie was killed by parcel bomb delivered by hand to Bligh's Lane army post. Then on Nov 25: Gunners Pizarek and Brookes, were shot dead by a sniper in Derry City in the Bogside. By the end of that year in addition to the two UDR men the IRA had killed eight regular soldiers in Derry including one ATO, as well as the Indian charwallah, and to make up the dozen two of their own volunteers who were alleged to be informers. Times were bad as the UDR reached a peak strength of 9000, with just 4% Catholics.

About this time a land mine was buried by PIRA in a bank beside the Old Kilrea Road out of Swatragh at the Lismoyle fork. Several attempts to lure a vehicle past it failed: or maybe the detonator was a dud. At last they asked the army to deal with it, a not unusual end to road mines. It was swiftly dismantled by ATO. I must have driven by it half a dozen times myself as it was beside a snipe bog we visited every winter month.

On Dec 22 1973 the Company lost two rifles in a cleverly planned stick-up and snatch at a crowded moment among Christmas shoppers in Hall St, Maghera. The raid was annoying and the loss should not have happened. The same could be said of the Inquiry that followed, evidence taken down in longhand over a period of two days in the Christmas holiday period.

Nineteen Seventy Four - The Year of Building

Twenty six new UDR Bases were constructed in 1974. Not that we ever saw much of them. Battalions rarely interchanged staff at that time. Once again there were New Year killings.

On Jan 21 1974 Sergeant John Haughey of 94 Locating Regiment RA was killed by a booby trap in the Bogside. Jan 25 saw the death of Lt Howard Fawley, Duke of Wellington's Regiment with whose commanding officer Peter Mitchell we had established great friendship. Poor Howard was killed by booby trap in a Ballymaguigan field near Toomebridge. The owner took no more notice of his shattered body than if he'd been a dog. A UDR patrol cautiously searching the area later found a boot with a foot still in it.

The Police Station in Magherafelt was badly damaged in March by a 500 pound bomb in hijacked lorry. One civilian Mr Johnson, who appeared to have ignored police warnings, was the only fatal casualty.

That month saw the first Greenfinch killed. Private Eva Martin was fatally wounded by a splinter while descending a stairway close to her husband during a set piece attack on the Clogher UDR base close to the Border.

May brought the Ulster Worker's Council strike. There had been much talk among nationalists of an imminent British pull out. The NIO denials seemed weak.

This dismayed and infuriated the most moderate unionists. So the strike had wide support and brought business to a halt in many parts of the country. G Coy was not much involved. We doubled guards and patrols in case the IRA should take advantage of the regular army's pre-occupation to pull off a coup. As far as possible we avoided UDA-controlled areas. One evening a feeble block of branches on a narrow road known from its arch of trees as the Tulnagee Pipe demanded attention. It was near Desertmartin but I can't now remember why the block needed to be removed. Perhaps it was cutting off some householders from necessities. I decided to clear it. This took all of five minutes but brought a notable remark from a soldier.

'Only time I saw the UDR scared'.

It was not literally true but indicated an understandable distaste with having to confront splinter political factions. The strike brought by May 30th the end of the power-sharing convention. It had enjoyed a life of only five months. Continuation of talks between the IRA and the British Government were strongly denied by the Northern Ireland Office. But clearly direct contacts went on. Rather sadly UK politicians, specially those connected with NI, came after this to be regarded as habitual liars. We could never afterwards believe anything they said. Their efforts at this period led indirectly to the so called IRA Truce of December 1974.

G Company's turn for new quarters came on October 5th. General Sir Frank King, GCB, MBE, GOC and Director of Operations, flew himself in by helicopter to open the new U-shaped red brick building. A paratrooper who had fought at Arnhem, he looked every inch the practical man who had little use for small talk or superficial entertainment. His tour became recognised later as the most successful period of the campaign.

In three years from '73 to '76 King, well supported by CLF Peter Leng, reduced bombing and shooting incidents from 12,000 to 2,000 per annum. It looked as if we had just the right man at the top and he made us feel we were winning. The jovial Colour Sergeant Roy Moore commanded a guard of honour, trained for occasion by RSM Thornton. Roy did everything well and it was not surprising that he was complimented by the general

I had been ordered in advance to write the general's speech. It was an occasion, the only one as it turned out, to draw public attention to our status as the direct descendants of the Londonderry Light Infantry, a distinguished 19th Century yeomanry unit, commanded by my forbear Colonel Clark of Largantogher. I would love to have borrowed for the occasion some of the Light Infantry silver which can be seen today at Spring Hill House, Moneymore, in care of The National Trust.

The general declaimed my words faultlessly but referred to me as Major Jones for the entire evening. I knew enough by now not to correct

Lieutenant Colonel Ian McBain hands out some prizes. Major Peter Hill at rear left. CSM Malachi Conway with back to camera.

him, so I suppose the accolade he might have intended for me as speech writer went to some undistinguished and surprised Jonesy in another unit. Dad's Army fans said it was lucky that he didn't call me Captain Mainwaring. Then, during the bunfight afterwards I had to introduce him to some ten groups of people and laugh as he told the same joke to each. To an extent his success against urban guerillas had made things more difficult for us by forcing terrorists to seek softer targets in the country. But it was a burden we shouldered gladly. All G Company hungered for was the post of honour nearest the risk and a chance to get to grips with the enemy.

Mrs Alfred, Sergeant of Greenfinches, was given a Certificate of Bravery by the general for defending her Post Office in Rasharkin. She had driven off a pistol - packing raider with her handbag!

All in Fort Garry was now luxury — an office (which I didn't want) for me, another for the PSI. Stores for the QM, a Guardroom, Junior Ranks Club, and a private perch for our Greenfinches. So a more spacious time was had by all. But somehow the crack was not as good as it had been in the old portacabins where we all mucked in together.

Battalion Drum at the opening of new 5 UDR Headquarters

On July 23 in Garvagh Corporal John Conley, E Coy, whose home was in Ballylintagh near Coleraine was in charge of clearing residents from their houses at 3.45 am after a bomb alert. No warning had been given. It was local unarmed vigilantes who had spotted a suspicious car in Bridge Street. As John was making a final check for an elderly lady believed to be still in her house the 300 pound bomb went off. John Conley, killed by the blast, gave his life for others.

That year Land Rover Number 77, the pride of driver Corporal (later Sergeant) Willie Currie, renewed its fame as the luckiest in the company. Early in the troubles a patrol commander had taken his vehicles through Swatragh in the dark and carried out an hour long VCP a mile beyond. Then disregarding Company procedures and some advice from his 2 I/C about the risk of retracing steps, he headed back towards Swatragh. Not surprisingly he was fired on from two sides - the car park of Friel's pub and the cover of telephone junction box opposite Desmond's Factory. Bullets went through the petrol change-over switch of 77, cutting off both tanks, and punctured the bonnet and front wheel. All lights were off but the ignition still seemed to provide a spark. Willie Currie managed to drive clear, and no one was hurt. Afterwards Willie found his vehicle in his own words 'rather drafty'.

Then in 1974 she was blown over on her side by a mine at the bridge beside the Legavannon Pot, a deep re-entrant between Glenullin and Limavady. Currie crawled out smiling. And shortly afterwards she was shaken by another mine between Draperstown and Moneyneaney. Sergeant Eric was hurt on the head and suffered a severe gyre when thrown up to the roof. Patrols were ordered after this to wear tin hats on all occasions. But neither incident caused any fatalities and there were always volunteers to ride in Land Rover 77.

The Biters Bit

An IRA check point at Granaghan Chapel near Swatragh at this period provided one of our best contacts. One Saturday evening the IRA started to check traffic, army-style, beside a church on the Swatragh-Maghera Road. A corporal from Tobermore and his brother were returning from watching a football match in Coleraine when they approached the checkpoint, recognised it for IRA and drove through at speed without being identified. They carried on boot to the floor three miles and gathered weapons and five men from the Guard at Fort Garry.

Thus reinforced, they returned in two private cars to find to their great
satisfaction the enemy still in position. The G Company boys
disembarked and opened fire from fields on both sides of the road. The
IRA quickly gave up stopping cars and started to shoot back from behind
tombstones in the graveyard. Getting the worst of it they soon withdrew
over open country west of the church. Immediately on hearing the news
I rushed in to tell the boys how well they had done.

As a company we were afterwards rebuked by Battalion. HQ and told
that we should have called out Land Rovers, got the regular army in
support and done an elaborate encirclement. One of the silliest bits of
advice ever. This would have taken 45 minutes and enemy would have
dispersed long before it was in place. A decoration for the soldiers who
had turned the tables on the enemy would have been more appropriate.
Three unmarked graves were said to have been found later and a number
of bullet marks on tombstones. But no enemy casualties were admitted.
It was quite a while before the IRA tried any more VCPs in our area.

1974 ended on another note of success. On Dec 16 a much wanted
man was identified by a patrol at Lisnamuck. Dressed all tidy and with
the manners of a Sunday School teacher he gave a false name and
identity documents.

Held by the patrol commander he was locked up by the police and out
of the way for some time. Those of us who lived near Swatragh could
sleep a little easier.

1975 - Truce and Frustration

On January 2nd that year the IRA, believing the rumours of an
imminent British withdrawal extended the usual Christmas ceasefire by
fourteen days. But when no additional concessions had been granted by
mid-January lethal bombs were detonated in London and Manchester.
These so frightened the NIO that more secret approaches were made. On
Feb 9th the IRA renewed the ceasefire as 'indefinite'. A good term that
was, from their point of view; in real life there was no cease fire at all.
All truces are broken but few so often broken as this one. Appeasement
set in. G Coy patrolling was reduced and arrests were discouraged.
House searches were allowed only in extreme cases.

New Brooms

Early in 1975 Major James Anderson, a gifted after dinner speaker, convivial and kindly man joined as adjutant. Short, red-faced and jocular he was perhaps a living example of Clausewitch's dictum that clever and lazy men make better officers than stupid, energetic ones.

A change is as good as a rest and much as we liked Derek Woolstencroft it was good news when Lieutenant Colonel Ian McBain of the Kings Own Scottish Borderers took over as CO. Derek had been unaccompanied throughout his tour and as a generous entertainer was able to develop close relationships with members of staff. Under him F and G Companies had improved in training and equipment.

Ian, one of a famous pair of commanding officer brothers, was a short in stature but long on determination. His ready smile ironed out many a disagreement. Now Ian's wife June and their children played a most helpful part in getting the scattered battalion families wives to know and support each other. Ian's expertise in piping gave the Band a big boost and his personal leadership on the range improved our marksmanship. In

Commanding Officer Joe Hordern (left) addresses General Dick Trant CLF (centre) and Major Wallace Clark at Fort Garry

Border dug-out - rear entrance

Lough Neagh — Scaddy Island Raid.

terms of casualties he was to see us through our worst time. Later he was able to arrange one of the most memorable weekends ever — G Company ski training based on Fort George at Inverness. We took the company van and arrived at mid morning Saturday. Skis, sticks, boots, the lot, were provided and we were on the snow at Glenshee that afternoon. Our enthusiastic instructor was Private Jim of army champion standard.

I'd had a couple of ski holidays but only one of the rest had ever tried before. On day three Jim, in his unique accent of thick Geordie overlaid by army Scots, encouraged us all to try to 'hot dog', and then go over four foot jumps. I felt at nearly fifty I was too old but no bones were broken. It was a particular pleasure when my son Milo a newly fledged Greenjacket officer came up to join the fun. The Fort George Officer's Mess proved unfriendly — no one spoke to us — but evenings out with the boys in Ardessier village made up for that. Private Jim came along and gave a rendering of his native song Bladon Races. It was a near perfect weekend.

Back home month after month went by with no contacts. To jump ahead it should be remembered that eighteen months later the Truce had still had not been formally terminated. Ian McBain in his Directive of 27 July 1976 could only say — 'The Cease Fire has ended to all intents and purposes and we have been made well aware of this from our casualties' This revealed the slipshod way in which the Secretary of State for NI left such a deadly serious matter. Our local tragedies started in May 24 when a Police Constable Noel Davies was killed by a booby trap in a car abandoned near a skeet ground between Maghera and Tobermore. In clearing the car ATO had missed a pressure plate hidden under a front wheel. Noel was ordered to drive the car away for examination. It blew up before he'd gone three feet..

On May 10 Constable Paul Gray was killed by a sniper on Derry walls. On the plus side Keith Robson, OC 657 Squadron Army Air Corps, was very helpful. Six Sioux helicopters based at Ballykelly were available to support patrols. At times a flight of three of these were based at Fort William, Magherafelt and their surveillance frustrated many an enemy movement. This was particularly valuable when most of the company were away for our first overseas camp at Warcop in Cumbria in 1976 and only skeleton forces remained behind. By August the ceasefire was being so freely broken as to be over but was never, as I recall. declared as such.

On Oct 6th Detective Constable Love RUC was booby-trapped in a pub near Dungiven. On Nov 25th a member of our own battalion Robert Stott was killed with ten shots outside his home in Fountain St, Derry.

From that year of truce, appeasement and muddle in which the last internees were freed, seven UDR men were later to pay with their lives. In spite of political fudge and lies, G Company had some interesting evenings. Of one of these I wrote in Visor, the British Army NI Magazine.

A night in The Derry Enclave

"Are you a man or a woman?" said Sergeant Willie in the darkness beside us. The long-haired passenger in the car we had just stopped turned towards us with a grin. The sergeant 's voice had been genial as well as firm. If the answer was woman, our hands were tied, the lack of women searchers was a chronic difficulty. "Man", the creature squeaked. "All right, sir, get out please and put your hands on the roof of the car". We searched him; the driver, already examined, looked on in amusement. "What are you trying to do? Tweak his legs off?", he asked.
We checked the boot, engine, doors and upholstery and spaces under the mudguards.

Earlier still Corporal Jackie had entered a bus full of women returning from a game of bingo, and the driver looking for trouble had told him aggressively that he was improperly dressed as he was not wearing a tin hat. "Very sorry", he said "I got a bullet through it a few minutes ago and it's letting in the rain". A poor joke, but good enough to raise a laugh among the passengers.

It is odd bits of back chat which relieve both tension and monotony on endless stints on the road. Five hours earlier at 7pm a platoon of G Company had fallen in at Fort Garry. "Paddock tonight, boys", said the signaller in the portacabin which served as office. This operation would mean 10 hours on duty and a 50 mile drive over the mountains to hold a place in the ring of checkpoints surrounding the Border city of Derry. It poured as we set off. In the Land Rovers the unfortunate 'tail gunner' in the rear seat with the doors open was going to get considerably wetter than if riding outside, for all the rain comes down from the roof at neck level. Oilskins help a bit, but there was not much we could do to prevent a gradual soaking.

Arriving at Tac HQ for orders we had been instructed to report at

Creggan Camp, a new Army redoubt on a bare hilltop just outside the city. Thrown up in a month after Operation Motorman it looked like a Wild West fort. Four rows of prefabricated huts were surrounded by walls consisting of 250,000 sandbags, corrugated iron sheets for cover from view against snipers, with sangars on stilts at each corner and roads made of fist sized stones. Additional anti-rocket protection had grown up round each hut. Now overhead protection against mortar fire was being added. "The only way we haven't been attacked yet is with submarines", said one of the regular soldiers at the gate.

Sergeant Willie and I entered a crowded hot Ops Room. We blinked in the sudden light at a row of strange friendly faces, decided which face was the one to give us our orders, and then climbed into an armoured Saracen for the final leg of the journey. In the Saracen sitting in the seat farthest from the door I felt claustrophobic. The surroundings were the hunched shoulders of the driver, the legs of the man in the turret, the rifle of the next man on the bench seat, pipes and wires, flak jackets and ammunition boxes. I suppose everyone feels that if you are going to be shot you'd like to get one or two back at the enemy. In here you have about as much chance of retaliation as a sardine in a tin. The driver skilfully navigates without lights along narrow twisty roads, rutted by traffic they were never designed to bear. The Saracen drops us at a lonely windswept junction, and the men we are relieving climb thankfully in before it rumbles into the darkness. We spread out over 200 yards of road for protection well deployed to stop oncoming vehicles or foot traffic. The men with me are an electrician, an apprentice fitter, a farmer, a shop assistant and a school teacher, all of whom have done a normal day's work before setting out for this duty. With us are two regular soldiers of the Light Infantry. By the end of patrol I know every intonation of their voices, a great deal about their families, history and ambitions. We have exchanged our philosophies and developed a considerable fellow-feeling, but all in darkness, so that I still know so little of what they look like that if I met them in the street next day I would probably not recognize them. Regulars usually respect our local knowledge and appreciate something of the effort we are putting into helping them, but look on us perhaps as "friendly tribesmen". We respect their professional skill, their good nature and bravery, but realize they are only here for a very short time to assist in the guard which many of us have been maintaining against the IRA for all our adult lives. They perhaps envy us the quick return to home and family at the end of the patrol, but we feel the same in a greater degree when they talk of four weeks leave to come at the end of the month, and an appointment in some far off sunny clime to follow. It adds up to a good relationship, the regular and part time components of the party, each on their mettle. Joint patrols are good patrols.

Darkness is a pleasant shield. Last time here we spent eight hours in daylight with the uncomfortable feeling that a sniper could crawl up in perfect security behind that hill on the other side of the border 200 yards away and kill a member of the patrol with scarcely any personal risk. At night the exposure seems much less. For the first 2 hours it feels as if the time will never pass; then your mind seems to get benumbed and the rest of the stint passes quickly, as civilian life and cares slide into remoteness. We drink army tea from a plastic jerrican; it tastes of chewed cardboard and looks like water wrung out of a mop .

On a hundred such patrols no incident relieves the familiar routine, but this is the hundred and first. Just after we had settled down in our positions I heard the crack and thud of rifle. Then silence. 'I suppose that's One-Shot-Willie", said the man beside me referring to the expert sniper who has accounted for four soldiers recently. 'I wonder if he's hit anybody.' More silence, but it isn't One-Shot this time and three more shots shatter the stillness. We see the muzzle flashes; they come from near a dwelling house where the lights are still on, and decide not to fire back. More silence. It is a difficult decision; Do we follow up and charge at the muzzle flashes, maybe just what they want us to do, and get drawn into an ambush? Do we do nothing, thus encouraging a sniper to have a further attempt? This time we summon an armoured mobile patrol by radio. They drive their vehicles over the fields to where we had seen the flashes, fire Verey lights, give the tracker dogs a sniff, seem to find nothing, go away and leave us. Later as we swap over duties I meet a man at the other end of the check point who had seen the dust kick up on the road by his feet in the moonlight and just had time to wonder what it was before he realized he was under fire.

As the night wears on vehicles get fewer and fewer. Among the lights of the city behind us an odd flare shoots into the sky or a shot is heard. Sleet showers and lightning punctuate the night interspersed with periods of bright moonlight when there is a gap in the clouds. In turn we are allowed to fall out and relax in a small stone shed, and I experience the relative bliss of half an hour lying down to doze on a stone floor with a flak jacket for a pillow. Then it is 3am and the distinctive whine of a Saracen engine tells us that our relief is approaching. Back at the camp we are taken to the canteen for tea and food, good tea this time, hot as hell and strong as the devil, and a choice of steak or fish, which we eat in a half-built canteen sitting on packing cases. Then back into the Land Rovers and through the city. Derry at night becomes a soldier's town, muffled figures at road junctions lift barriers or pull aside barbed wire webs before waving us on; convoys of two or four vehicles speed past us up the deserted street; a foot patrol appears sprinting across a lighted gap. We cross the bridge and set out on the hour long drive home in the unheated Land Rover, swaying to the jolting springless motion, the rear man braced against the sudden acceleration or turn which might throw him out through the rear doors into the road. Back at our own HQ. chilled and sleepy, we check in our arms; and each of us sets off eight miles home in our own cars. This is the creepiest bit of all. If another car comes up from behind you feel like jinking to dodge the expected burst of fire, and relax only when it has passed. Next morning after four hours sleep I waddled into the office with the all too familiar feeling of a black barrier just behind my eyes and a brain haze of flashing lights, loaded rifles and aggressive drivers. My shoulders felt as if there was a twenty pound weigh slung on each. But somehow a little work gets done.

Scaddy Island Raid

It was on another January night that Lieutenant. Eddy Temple of the Kings Own Borderers detachment at RUC Magherafelt came to ask me if I could help out with a dinghy. It was a strange request. The army usually do small water born operations in their issue rubber boats. Eddy had the boats but was having trouble with the outboard engines.

'Sure, I could tow you in my ten foot yacht dinghy with the old Seagull.'

'We've got a buzz that Number Two on the wanted list lies up on Scaddy at the north end of Lough Neagh. C. O. wants us to raid it tonight and see if we can lift him'. That sounded interesting, so I set out at 8 pm with the dinghy on a trailer. I'd visited Scaddy years ago looking for duck and merganser eggs and recalled it as an island of shingle, small boulders and rushes, hardly more than three feet above water level and marked by half a dozen staldery trees. It seemed unlikely that the wanted man would choose to lie in such a comfortless place. But at least it would be an elimination exercise, and a pleasant variation on endless road patrols.

We launched the dinghy in a tree–ringed cove on the north west shore of Lough Neagh, a bit north of Moneymore. Eddy had brought two black rubber boats plus a spare. I was to lead with a machine gun in the bow and the two boats with three men in each on a line astern. That would stretch the 4 HP Seagull outboard but I reckoned she'd do it at about two knots.

Eddy must have been studying naval tactics or reading Captain Hornblower novels. He knew just how the assault should be planned. The man on the island could be expected to fight. So when we approached the dinghy was to lie off where the machine gunner could give supporting fire while the two rubber ducks went in abreast. It could be our first Combined Ops assault.

Nico, my crewman, was a young lad who had joined the KOB six months before. He couldn't swim so we tied a life jacket round him and put him in the bow with a bucket for bailing. The good old Seagull started at once and off we set in a pitch dark night for a three mile leg eastwards. Lough Neagh is some ten miles wide with low muddy shores, rectangular except at its north west end. There just north of our starting point a two mile wide bay leads off to where the lough empties via the Bann River. This meant a stretch of open water which we had to cross before regaining the coast near Scaddy. There had been neither wind or waves in the wee cove but soon after we got out it blew up to Force Three from the south. With the low surface tension of fresh water, that breeze created breaking wavelets which soon began to slurp over the gunwhale.

"Fook me", said Nico when he saw the dinghy begin to fill.

"The only boating I ever did was on the fookin' pond in Carlisle Town Park". But he bailed manfully with his bucket, and I was able to help with a saucepan in one hand. We kept her free of water and fairly comfortable but it was hell for the two little boats tailing astern. They were almost awash and only just discernable by a radio aerial and rifle muzzles pointing upwards against a light patch of sky.

Navigating by a pocket compass on the seat beside me was far from easy. The lights of Antrim town beyond our target island were a good guide, and the sodium glow of Toomebridge village at the head of the bay to our left gave a cross bearing. The main worry was being blown off course to the north, that is to our left. If we got onto the lee shore with the waves now building up we'd never get off again.

Scaddy island lies in shallows about half a mile off the north shore. We kept going for half an hour until I thought I could make out trees ahead. Stopped the engine, rafted up to the rubber ducks, took some bearings and had a whispered conference. In the silence we could hear what seemed like a boat engine to the south. An unpleasant possibility was that a Lough Neagh fisherman, his boat taken over by IRA, might be approaching. The encounter would have made a good subject for naval analysts. We would have the fire power and he would have the speed. If he'd read his Hornblower he could have circled and punctured the rubber boats and then finished off the dinghy before we got the machine gun to bear. Would Nico have got naval decoration if we managed to sink him as we went down? Might be a VC. They like to bury you first for that.

Thank God the engine noises died away and left no signs of any other boats. It was still very dark and getting rougher. Then came a little light in the eastern sky. With eyes close to the water a silhouette could be made out which might be Scaddy and the bushy shoreline to its left. But there were a lot of other reefs and tree clad points that it might be.

It was not the moment to disclose doubts to the Pongos but it did seem incredible when ten minutes later we got to the island at first try. It was like a hole-in-one. Any idea of lining up for an assault had to be abandoned; we were only to glad to scramble ashore on the lee side up to our knees in dark lough water, stumbling over boulders where sparkly little ringlets of waves seemed to wake from their sleep. It took about five minutes for the soldiers to establish that there was no human presence or indeed any shelter that would make it possible to keep dry on a winter's night. But there were remains of a recent fire, perforated tin cans and empty bullet cases. It was a matter of launching again and finding our way back. We punted out with paddles and just managed to get into deep enough water to get the outboard engine going. Luckily this part of the lough had no weed to choke the propellor.

After going south for a hundred yards we turned to starboard and headed back a little south (ie left) of the reciprocal of the course that we'd come out on — about 280 degrees magnetic. There were no shore lights to guide us. Half an hour later, wet as if we'd been swimming we sighted the low scrub of the western shore with nary a break in the skyline to act as a distinguishing mark. Where was the little cove? I'd aimed a bit south so we could be fairly sure that a starboard turn would take us in but it was too dark. We had eventually to abandon secrecy and

fire a Verey light to be sure. So at 3am, very cold and rather disappointed
we landed where we had embarked. The trucks were there to meet us.
Then a dram when we got back to the Mess. It had been one of the
luckiest bits of pilotage of my life. A memorable night but the chances
of our man being on Scaddy must have been based mostly on
imagination.

The Lough Neagh eel fishers are decent men, skilled boat handlers
men, fiercely independent and protective of their rights. They'd helped
me on lots of occasions when I was collecting bird's eggs as a youngster
or in later years shooting duck so I was glad there had been no
confrontation Later the UDR and at times the Royal Marines patrolled
Lough Neagh in high speed Dories, That made arms smuggling by water
hardly worth the game but I never heard of any more Combined Ops
landings. Ducks in the spring and wildfowlers in winter had Scaddy
Island to themselves once more.

Private Soldier's View

So the year rolled on. This book is in no way intended as a political
commentary but it would unrealistic not to include some mention of
UDR soldier's opinions of the antics of their elected leaders after three
exhausting years. Comments like 'The Northern Ireland Office – they're
far too laxative. They just want Ulster out of the UK'. Or in the words of
an ex-RN sailor who joined G Company, 'Those guys up in Stormont
Castle – they sit down to piss '.

Tough times it seemed but in retrospect this was the period when the
IRA began to realise that against the combined efforts of Regular Army
,UDR and RUC they could not deliver an unacceptable level of violence.
That later on caused them to enter the political field and the fragile, much
broken, truces of the nineties.

And that was, perhaps, the greatest success of the UDR.

It is as yet too early to say for sure that the dearly bought truce will
assist our long term objects My objects were clear enough: A united and
peaceful British Isles with democratic government in each area and
maximum devolvement consistent with protection from foreign invasion
and economic prosperity. I think that view might have been shared by
most of G Company. We didn't talk politics much. Our immediate
concern was the suppression of terrorism; without that no democratic
system could flourish. In the shorter run the Government's Police
Primacy policy turned terrorists to concentrate on the shooting in the
back of off duty soldiers and policemen.

Before going on to see how G Company suffered from this in 1976 let's have a look in the next chapter at some weekends spent playing away from home.

G. Coy covering a V.C.P. from a bridge parapet near the border

*Private Bertie Rainey receives Long Service Medal
from Brigade Commander*

CHAPTER EIGHT

BROODERS AND PROODERS

'Wide's the world to rest or roam
With change abroad and cheer at home
Fights and furlough, talk and tale,
Company and beef and ale'.

The continual overstretch of infantry gave rise to a pair of schemes which helped the regulars, and relieved the UDR of the monotony of patrolling the same patch year after year.

Each weekend **a Brigade Reserve UDR** (soon known as 'Brooder') was called up. It was of platoon strength, and took on tasks away from home but within their own brigade area.

Province Reserve UDR or 'Pruder' took an additional reserve further afield, often to the Border. In 5 UDR each company provided such a mobile force about once a month.

Here are some examples of tasks we were allocated.

A PROODER in MIDDLETOWN, COUNTY ARMAGH
Spring 1975.

'How are you enjoying it, sir?' said the Tank corporal as he approached out of the Saracen. 'Better than a weekend at Butlins's', I replied, although my legs ached from bottom downwards, and my head felt as if I would like to bury it in the drift of hailstones by the roadside. It was true. A change of surroundings was welcome, fifty miles away in another Brigade area after four years of patrolling our own patch. We had taken over a section of the Border from the Royal Tank Regiment thirty six hours earlier. But it seemed as if we'd been here for a week.

On Friday evening after work we had left our own Headquarters at Maghera and driven for two hours in a convoy of macrolon-protected trucks led by a Shorland. It was slow going, delayed by driving rain and by circumnavigating Ulster towns blocked off against car bombs. We unloaded our rifles in the charcoal blackness of Gough Barracks, stood around in the rain for a while and then were briefed by a squadron commander. He impressed us with his competence, and the way he broke off to dispatch a riot squad to one town and give orders about a proxy car bomb in another. In the brilliantly lit Ops. Room we studied maps, aerial photographs and details of the latest booby traps and road mines. The barracks by night was like the streets of some ancient city, sudden alleys, black tunnels, flights of steps, gratings to trip over and ankle-deep puddles gleaming in the lamplight. You returned to the 20th century in the open spaces full of helicopters, Ferrets and Pigs and Saracens. A few beers, then bed in a Portacabin.

At 6.00am there was breakfast in the high Victorian cookhouse - cornflakes shovelled from a box as big as a tea chest, huge piles of bacon served over stainless steel counters, two eggs and as much bread and butter as you could eat; tea from an urn with a press up tap, which foxed me at that hour of the morning. My tea went over the next mans trousers- -howls of derision! Load up the Land Rovers and a twenty minute drive, watching the map carefully the last couple of miles, anxious not to drive over the Border. We stopped at the bottom of a small valley of green fields and clumps of trees in autumn foliage. Beside the road was a river which formed the international boundary. The stone work of a bridge, blown up to block lateral traffic, provided cover from fire, a good point to check vehicles. A long take-over from the platoon we were relieving. We learned about Peggy and Doris, scanning devices to protect from stealthy approach. On the hillside north of us were two small trenches, referred to as the pits, sited to protect the men on the road. I took two would-be warriors up to each, and we hunkered down the slippery muddy steps to sit crouched on boards supported by angle iron stuck into the sides. There was a low parapet of sand bags and a corrugated iron roof. From inside you looked at the world over the butt of a machine gun. It projected over a pump for sucking the water from under the duckboards. You dodged your boots round a smoky paraffin heater. The sides were festooned with ammunition belts: the crevices were crammed with communication receivers, binoculars, parka overcoats, flares, solid fuel cookers. Loaves of bread and tins of half eaten rations lay under foot, the inevitable waste of war. It felt secure.

"Tank approach to an infantry problem", said the out-going sergeant with a tinge of regimental pride. It seemed as if we were part of an Old Bill 1916 cartoon, except that we wore berets instead of tin hats. We asked about the chances of being fired at. "They're cowboys", said the Tanks, "Shoot at you on Saturday afternoons when they stop work; but only if its fine. Not bad shots though". There was competition for the privilege of manning the General Purposes Machine Gun, referred to, as if we did this every day, as the 'Gimpy'. Down on the road the first cars began to come through, private motorists who we soon discovered to be a good deal more polite than those we were used to at home. "It's a cold day for you", they would say or some other pleasantry before producing their driving license with a smile. It made a nice change from the surly silence of at least half the drivers round Maghera, followed by slammed doors and over-revved engines to emphasise disapproval.

One lady was so vague about her movements that I asked for her occupation. "Protestant", she replied firmly. Then there were loads of pig guts in bulk, several days old, which no one felt like examining too closely. The Sappers come and do it every now and then. Attached to us was a Intelligence Spotter, trained in recognition of wanted men, and a trim military police girl. "She does knicker searches in the caravan", said the Tanks. Static Pigs, with Browning machine guns, guarded each end of the check point at night. We relieved the men in the pits periodically and carried out foot patrols, for protection and to catch cars, trying to dodge the road block. There were grisly visits to the Portaloo, an overflowing chemical lavatory on wheels. So the day passed. Dusk filled the hollows in the fields. Like the sailor at sea, the soldier on frontier duty carries on doing the same jobs by day and by night. I found myself looking forward to dawn as much as I ever have when making landfall on some wild coastline. Those who had a stag off returned to the barracks and raised a party with imported beer in the empty canteen. On the road cars continued to pass through at a faster rate than during the day, bound to and from dances in the Republic. By night you have the added difficulty of juggling with a torch, as well as millboard, pencil, and rifle, while recording details. Illuminated by headlights, or the flash of torches , as you search car boots and undersides, the checkpoint is a ideal target for gunmen or mortars from over the Border. To indicate the position of the caravans to drivers we placed amber flashing lights. Some lorry drivers seemed to delight in running over them, so we put caltrops, spiked chains, in front of the lights. The next lorry that tried it carried on down the road with a tyre going pssst..... whee-oo..... I reckoned he would just about make the Border crossing half a mile away before it went flat. He didn't come back. Dawn came up at 7am, striped pinks and blues over the treetops.

In the middle of Sunday morning, when the world was at Armistice Service, one of the traffic controllers fifty yards away calls out, "We're under fire". "Catch yourself on!", somebody shouts, back, "It's only a man chopping wood". In the Binner or control van the telephone rings; it's the top pit. A rifleman had been out moving a cow away from the trip flares and several bullets had whistled over his head. We really are under fire! I sprint 150 yards up hill, arrive breathless. "What's ..... happening .....?",I puff. "Muzzle flashes at the base of those trees beside the hill, sir", the sergeant said. "Watch my tracer". I thought I could see figures, in a fold in the ground, about 800 yards away. "Short bursts", I ordered, then "Check", for the enemy seemed to have gone to ground. There is no more heartening sound than a machine gun opening up from your side in a small arms fight. Another shot from the enemy. Ronald, a determined ex regular, swung the machine gun on its bipod and raked the position. I watched the red arcs of the tracers, moving incredibly slowly across the fields and ricochets shooting sharply skywards. Cows careered wildly across the grass, but there was no more sniping. "Close, were they?", I asked Jim, the Private. "You don't walk too tall when they start singing over your head", he replied. He had been firing his rifle at the enemy through the other aperture. Sand bags on the parapet were blackened and torn by the blast. We had fired over a hundred rounds, and the empties added to the clutter in the pit. We watched the quiet landscape.

Twenty minutes later a blue car with a Garda sign drew up on the other side of the border. Two figures got out, examined the house which we had been told was used as an OP and set off across the fields to where the fire had come from. More Gardai appeared and walked slowly around the area. We changed the machine gun belt, swung the binoculars and started to brew tea on the paraffin stove in a trip flare tin. The Gardai had gone now - it was lunch time. We expected more sniping, but none came. No signs of the Irish Army. Some one knocked over the tea can just as it was boiling, and we started all over again. After an age it began to bubble, then a voice outside said, "Time to go, boys". This was part of a planned move to a new position half a mile down the road. We abandoned the tea, and took up positions in the hedge while a group of sappers emptied the sandbags and filled in the pit. They kicked off the trip flares which erupted in puffs of white smoke. Down on the road other parties were heaving round the caravans and water carrier, hitching them to Land Rovers, grinding the engines of the Pigs into life and taking down the radio mast. By the time another three hours had passed, five o'clock on Sunday, we had moved the checkpoint and handed over the kit to the Tanks again. They would be carrying on with the same job ten hours on, ten hours off, until the end of their four month tour. We had at least given them one full night in bed.

A muddy G Company drove home in rain and darkness, checked in their rifles and scattered homewards. Next morning back at my office desk it all seemed a bit of a dream. Ron, the machine gunner, would be back at his cloth-laminating machine, Jim studying architecture at the Polytechnic, others farming, driving lorries, building or teaching. We would each have something to say at coffee break to those people, too busy to join the Ulster Defence Regiment, who keep telling you that there is no proper check on the Border.

PRISON GUARD AT MAGILLIGAN
Autumn 1975

This was a weekend job. It turned out to be more informative than most. Such was the army manpower problem that the Prison Guard Force at that time was made up of ten-man detachments from a number of regular units. After a short period of training they took over for four months. It could have been a high risk deployment, as the prison stands on a sandy point separated from the Irish Republic by only a mile of sheltered water. A well-led amphibious raiding party could have shot up the guard and sprung the prisoners any dark night when tidal conditions were suitable. But in the Seventies the IRA were not trained for Combined Operations. Our job was to give the PGF a break, putting twelve men on duty in the sangars on the outer perimeter. On arrival we were told what it was all about.

The prison we learned contained 250 IRA and 120 Loyalists; all convicted prisoners, not internees. PIRA ran a strictly disciplined battalion organization in two compounds with a company in each one under an OC, Training Officer and Adjutant. They drilled regularly and held parades on occasions like Easter in uniform with black berets. There was one compound each for UDA and UVF. In spaces between were sports facilities – badminton, deck tennis and football Prisoners wore their own clothes, usually jeans and track suits. They appeared to do no work apart from a little drill and some had a lay-about life, sunbathing and watching TV. Others volunteered for education courses up to degree level. Sex, we were told, was arranged once a month with girls sent in by the prisoner's aid committees. The ladies would ask to see Bobbie or Seamus, claiming to be a sister. The give-aways came if the lady walked straight past the alleged brother unless he was pointed out to her. They then grunted happily away in front of a warder. Liquor too, we were told came in regularly in cans marked coke or lemonade. Scrumpy or jungle juice was made by inmates to eke out supply drops.

The prison was surrounded by 20 foot high fences—an outer one with sangars; inside it a ten yard strip containing rubbish; another fence then a space filled with sawtooth barbed wire; a third fence followed by 20 yards of dog - patrolled grass. After that came the fourth and inner fence which fronts the main tarmac compound

On guard duty one climbed three flights of vertical ladders carrying rifle, rubber bullet projector and gas gun. At the top the entrance was through a hinged hatch about thirty feet above the ground. The sangar had Perspex sliding windows all round; on the walls were photos and diagrams naming each inner yard and building. In a corner a hole covered with perforated tin served as a urinal. A radio, telephone and Tannoy loud hailer connected the sentries with PGF Ops Room. A blue joke about an actress came across by Tannoy for the whole townland to hear until the comedian was told to belt up At night sodium lights shed a sickly overall glare. The scene below was varied enough by day to be amusing. One experienced a God-like over-view of the pattern of prison life. On the road outside at any time of day walked the civilian staff, smug, well fed and obliging. Why shouldn't they be? Never had it so good. Quite a lot of them by their tongue came from Donegal just across the channel. Other components were a bunch of UDR recruits in brand new suits under training, harassed by a plump, Belfast-voiced Sergeant yelling, ' Left right, Left right. At the double'.

A Para officer from Prison Guard Force swaggering by in a carefully faded jump jacket, with conspicuous blue sewn on wings, talking to a senior Prison Officer in a cool white jacket, blue woolly pulley and striped trousers. An ordinary Prison Guard making for a break at the charwallah's, with club swinging at waist, crash helmet, visor, gas mask and flack jacket. Another guard showing off a blue and silvereen uniform, peaked cap and grim expression. The charwallah himself, black lustrous hair over a yellow nylon shirt and green trousers, with guts hanging out over his belt. In the UDA compound a man in a towel and nothing else sauntering up from the ablutions block .A dog handler with a cheerful grin and friendly manner propelled by an Alsatian tugging on a rope. Few others were on view; 'They'll all be watching Grandstand on telly. Its Saturday' said the old hand beside me. But not the RSM, ultra smart with whitened shirt collar out over combat kit, twisting his moustaches as he strode out checking everything in sight for the smallest irregularity.

Off stag after tea I put on civvies and walked down towards Magilligan Point There fell into conversation with a Donegal man also off duty. He took me for English by my tongue and told me he'd worked on a salmon fishing vessel out of Greencastle all summer but now was the close season.

'Of course ye can always get a fish or two splash-netting off a river mouth when the bailiffs aren't looking. It's no disgrace to break the law'. Then he pointed out some fine big houses, beautifully situated, on the Donegal shore. 'Landlord families still in 'em', he said. But we'll have 'em all out in a few year's time'

I had plenty of friends over there in lovely Inishowen so it seemed like a good idea to change the subject. When we came to hand over the kit we'd drawn for the weekend several rubber bullets were missing. They make good, 'I was there', style souvenirs.

The officer said, 'Right. I'll leave the room for five minutes. If all the bullets aren't back on the table when I re-appear, your kit will be searched. There will be charges'. There was much groping in the bottom of small packs. As the Irish policeman said in court, 'After a frootless sarch all de stolen objects were recovered'.

It'd been an instructive weekend as a one-off but not what we'd joined for.

Later on some of our Conrate (Full Time UDR soldiers) did four week stints with the PGF and seemed to find it a congenial variant to life in the battalion

Ways to make UDR Manpower go Further

Talking of infantry overstretch we in the UDR suffered from the same problem as regulars. A thoughtful letter in the Belfast News letter at this time shows how the public saw the restrictions placed on the UDR.

'In a small country, where the majority abhor violence and only hope for a return to peace, is it not a travesty that these same people are not mobilized alongside our regular soldiers in an all-out and determined

drive to defeat the obvious minority of murderers at large in our country?

Some will argue that the UDR was formed in an effort to mobilise the people against the terrorists and that RUC and UDR are under-manned from lack of suitable volunteers.

In all honesty no person having examined the military situation today could accept that the UDR is being used today in any real effort to destroy the enemy.

The guarding of installations and power stations is of course one aspect of \Ulster's defence which is subject to attack by the IRA but to restrict the brave citizens in their tasks to guard duties and the occasional search of vehicles in selected areas is just as insane as the when the regulars are parading themselves as targets for the IRA . .

Following the IRA Ceasefire in 1972 the Government ordered a low key attitude to be adopted by troops All photographs of wanted men were pulled in . Mr Whitelaw ordered the destruction of very necessary files of known Republican terrorists. These Dossiers held by all police stations were an asset to police and army in gaining information and background but were destroyed because they were thought to lead to be harassment or interfer ence in people's lives'.

And much more on same theme

Signed: John S Baillie ex Sgt. in British Army

He might have added that a force of older men specially recruited for static guards was an obvious recourse. It would have allowed the UDR to give a much wider cover in patrolling and intelligence gathering .

In 1921 it was C Specials, a hundred thousand strong, with a static role who turned the scales against terrorists.

A PRUDR at LISNASKEA, COUNTY FERMANAGH

Another weekend in 1975 took us to a combined police and army base at Lisnaskea. Two of us did a recce by chopper to St Angelo a few days earlier to get radio frequencies and an outline of tasks. There were bunk rooms and a recreation room but we didn't expect to use either much. We'd be coming for Ops, not rest.

Food in the bare room the army used as a canteen was plentiful but the style grotty, collapsed loaves of sliced bread drooped over the side table amid plastic bubbles streaked with tomato and ketchup. Butter was in a well scraped bulk container. Tea came from a plastic mug dipped into to a tin cylinder. Hot food at specified hours was slung through a shabby hatch. I noted the need to bring as much of our own grub as possible.

Our first night function was to look out for boats smuggling arms across Upper Lough Erne. The lookout position on the north edge of the multi-islanded waterway was shown to us on the Ops Room map by a slightly bored 16/5 th Squadron Commander. He'd been busy making a return of men with venereal disease as we came in — a problem in Omagh that year! I was surprised they had time to get infected, and assured him that we had no current cases.

Forgetting the pox for a moment, he introduced us a local UDR man who would be our guide. This was a big rangy chap with a nutcracker face, a black moustache and a continually drooping cigarette. When I asked his name he said,' Call me Bob', so Call me Bob he became. As we approached the lough I asked him , 'Why's our location called Rabbit Point?

'Don't know a damn,' he said, 'Unless it could be because there's always thousands of rabbits there'. Ask a silly question and you get a silly answer.

'Those Fermanagh boys think they can take a hand out of a Derry man', said Corporal Willy beside me. But it was soon obvious that Call Me knew every slap in the hedge and sheugh in the area and was out to be really helpful.

We crept over grass sward to a hide in a strip of trees on the shoreline. The lovely shimmering waters of the lough turned from blue to pink as the sun set. Later they gleamed faint silver in starlight. We took turns to listen, heads bent like thrushes locating worms, and peer at the gap between two islands to our front. About midnight the dark silhouette of fast runabout appeared and stopped its engine.

'He's listening for us listening to him listening for us.' whispered Roy. Just as he seemed to be coming in a flare went up to our rear behind us. That seemed to scare him off. Then later still a boatload of sheep appeared and came in to a pier to our left. Decent ordinary smugglers could turn a few quid smuggling lifestock across the Border to collect a subsidy each side on the same beast; that and many similar dodges.

They varied as regulations and prices changed. Two of us checked the cargo for arms and let the crew proceed.

At dawn we marched back. There wasn't a rabbit in sight of course.

No comment but Call Me Bob regaled us with chilling tales of the ethnic cleansing along the Border. Landowners were at special risk. If a farmer was on his own, or was elderly with an only son, the successor would be picked by the Provos to be shot. Then the land would come on the market so that a republican could buy it at a discount. Case after case of this sort was quoted. And one heard similar tales from Armagh and Tyrone. This is high risk area for resident UDR. Many had been forced to move their homes further back from the border.

Billy Dixon an old USC friend visited us next day in his capacity as Lt. Colonel West and wised us up more. Weather-beaten and wary, smiling and helpful, his advice delivered in a pleasant Fermanagh voice was a tonic. His own survival while farming so close to the border was a near miracle. Billy's manner, in spite of the crowns and pips on his shoulders, was just the same as when he'd been a junior USC officer.

The next evening we were dropped in the dark by a Ferret scout car near a point where a river formed the border. I got out, looked around to get my bearings and talked to the driver through a slit in the armour The gunner kept his machine gun trained south with the barrel still in its black cardboard cover to keep off the Irish mist. After the Ferret left we could follow its movements for several minutes by the high whine of the fly wheel drive. Call me Bob hadn't been able to come but had said he'd join later. So we had to navigate cross-country in December dark. Getting six UDR soldiers through a tall bullfinch thorn hedge with a sheugh beyond it is a slow business. I went first over a high strand of rusty barbed wire. Is it best to slither down the far side into the sheugh and risk it being two foot deep? Wet feet meant misery later or just take a 'lep' from hedge level at an unknown landing on the far side and maybe twist an ankle. Mostly I sploshed down and found fairly shallow water. A small difficulty for me that was — hell for the signaler with an radio man pack, antennae and a rifle to unbalance him. We managed somehow. Now to skirt round a farm. Will those bloody dogs never stop barking? Bob said it's a spy house. Where's that rattle coming from? Ah! Two Verey cartridges in a tin box made for three in my pack Where's my left glove — couldn't find it on setting out. We'd like to label our kit but it is forbidden for security reasons, so its easy to have stuff 'borrowed'. We reach our hide overlooking a little known ford — check it for hidden mines or pressure plates, observe the approaches by turns for hours. It was dam' cold. I wished I'd had time to put on long johns before we set out. Our rear party on a lateral road 400 yards astern checks out half a dozen cyclists and three cars; little enough for the effort involved. But we'd kept up the guard for a couple of stags and given some hard worked regulars a night in.

One Stop Shopping

On another visit, in summer, to this area we did a daylight foot patrol for spot checks on small roads close to the Border. Careful navigation was again essential. On some roads the actual division was marked by a white line, a post or a notice, on others there seemed to be nothing. It was hot in combat kit and flak jackets.

'T'sweat's runnin' down off me shoulders between the cheeks of me arse', one plump private groused. Just as he said it what should we find but a convenient shop by the road side. Some ice cream, cold coke and smokes would go down well. We posted sentries and took it in turns to go in. The shopkeeper was most obliging and disappeared into the back for a minute or two to get a special brand of cigarette from his store.

'Smack it about.' the corporal said to the boys. 'Don't hang around'

The last man was only just out and ten yards north along the road when our tail gunner cried 'Look out!.

In the words of the ballad

' *We turned around to find*
   that a couple of stout policemen
had surrounded us behind'

Or tried to.

A Garda car had screeched to a stop, baffled at the vestiges of a line we now saw between us and the shop — close in beside the ditch. The rest of the mark had been excised, deliberately I'd fancy.

Mine Host had obviously telephoned them and deliberately delayed us to create a complaint, maybe even an arrest. A good trick to play on dumb chums from up north.

The Gardai, decent men, I'm sure, with a job to do, shouted at us. A little deaf from past gunfire, I found it hard to make what they wanted. We gave friendly wave and made a watchful retreat.

There's a sweet little angel that sits up aloft
         Looks after the life of poor Jack.

She did well for us that weekend.

And we got home safe, with no stragglers left behind in a Monaghan lock-up.

THIRTY SIX HOURS ROUND THE HUMP

It was a cold spring Saturday in 1976 when 30 G Coy soldiers checked in to the base between Derry and Strabane.

'**Welcome to Colditz**', was spelled out in white figures on a school blackboard just inside the gate. Someone had added '**Use a Featherlite, not an Armalite!**'. There didn't seem to be much hope of using either in this unprepossessing wire cage about the size of a double tennis court. It contained a single ridge stone farmhouse of 1930 vintage. Here dwelt the Recce. Platoon from the Coldstreams at Ebrington. Apart from the picket on the gate the place was deserted. Facing the house was a big farm shed fronted by a wide silage ramp.

'That's yours for the night', the Guard Commander, a Coldstream Lance-Sergeant, gloomily informed us. Poking round we found a mess room and mini-gym. This was a steel erection invented by some India-rubber-man for use by soldiers in cramped quarters. On it every muscle could be tortured in turn.

'Each bloke does 45 minutes on the fitness machine every other day. Married men like me get a big deal - one day a month back with their families', said the Lance.

The boys unloaded their small packs from the Land Rovers then erected camp beds four abreast in the barn.

While they were settling in Billy, Jim, Willis and I drove three miles to Strabane RUC Station for a briefing. We had the luxury of being four officer strong this trip.

Miles Disby, the Recce Platoon commander, made us welcome. The white stuccoed Police Station had high anti-rocket wire on all sides as well as overhead. There was an inner wall of corrugated iron embracing nissen huts portacabins and much transport, lined up to an inch with Guards precision. Spotless Pigs, shining Saracens, gleaming Land Rovers stood wheel to wheel beside an Armoured Car ambulance, conspicuous by its Red Cross on white ground. The former Police day room had become an OPS Room hung with maps from which Miles gave a textbook briefing.

'Information.

Enemy

A treacherous triangle protrudes 3 miles as a salient into Irish Republican territory.

It has seen a good deal of infantry fighting over the last three years. After one firefight a Greenjacket battalion used the classic tactic of a feigned withdrawal. They fell back leaving behind pairs of snipers who made good practice when the enemy followed up.

IRA units now regularly cross the Border to snipe or lay mines.

Own Troops: *None except G company will be in area.*

Intention: *G Coy to clear two routes, man two observation points plus a patrol base and provide a Quick Reaction Force.*

Signals: *A dozen code names for locations, call signs and frequency to take down'.*

Gin and omelettes in the Coldstream Mess followed. We tucked in wondering when we'd have time to eat again. 'Sounds pretty complicated', I said with my mouth full to Billy, 'specially the signals.'

'Well, in 24 hours, it'll all be over', was the comforting reply.

Next move was a familiarisation run with Miles. The Land Rover had so much electronic gear in the back that there was room for only one seat and that situated just where the rain came down through the hatch.

We saw the Hump itself, a strong post at the east end of the bridge over the River Foyle. Its task was checking trans-Border road traffic. Commanding it was James, a stocky subaltern who I'd last met on the Scottish island of Gigha, owned by his grandfather.

We hear en route that the Police want an escort to check out an assault case.

'Why,' I said, 'can't they go themselves. Are they scared ?

'They've good reason to be in this area', said Miles

It turned out be a murder. A blood soaked body was being wrapped up and carried out of the 'corp house' to an ambulance. Miles, prepared for aggro., had collected six Land Rovers in the street in front of the house. Big quiet guardsmen stood beside them with rifles levelled. Our Captain Billy, recalled from patrol, appeared in support, with face blackened, leading his section.

Somehow it seemed like a game of Murders. But no Poirot appeared; we never heard who had been killed or why. After the RUC moved in to check the house we dispersed for the night's patrols. It poured as we moved into what appeared to be a disused churchyard. Tall tombstones in serried rows rose out of bramble thickets, some erect, others at drunken angles throwing long moon shadows.

Under the fitful glints it felt spooky. But we were more concerned with gunmen than ghosts. There was supposed to be an arms cache in here and the brethren might be arriving to collect rifles for a raid. Footfalls in a field over the wall had to be investigated. They turned out to be cows. Soaked and chilled we emerged four hours later and returned stiff-legged to base. Perhaps we'd foiled an enemy Op — perhaps we'd achieved nothing at all.

The Border guard had to kept up. Next day I met a golf club trio who complained bitterly of the tough Saturday they'd had fighting round 18 holes in an icy gale. Best to say nothing, but you can't be hanged for your thoughts.

Lots of other Prooders followed in varied Border areas — seen one, you've seen 'em all — but at least on such sorties we were full time soldiers and could concentrate on our role. It was when near home where each of us had his private responsibilities to think about and could be individually targeted that risks were greater and narrow shaves more common. The PRUDR system ended a few months later in 1978. Nobody told us why. It had added some useful variety to our military lives.

CHAPTER NINE

A Company Commander's Diary 1976

The Year of the Assassin

1976 was the year when three of the most wanted terrorists in Northern Ireland, were at their peak of activity in the vicinity of G and F Companies with bomb, bullet and booby trap. The events and feelings of this most disagreeable period seem to come alive best from words and jottings made at the time.

June in the following diary entries is my wife. Born in Dublin she was a model and an air hostess before I was lucky enough to meet her. She suffered with minimum complaint and considerable bravery my many absences on UDR duty.

DIARY 1976

Jan 5th; Merlyn Rees, NI Secretary of State, announced today the first official deployment of Special Forces. Why? We know they've been around for yonks.

One bold brick hid in the roof space of a house in Swatragh a while back to photograph a parade for identification. They were bubbled and a fire started to smoke them out. Their quick reaction force plucked them out by helicopter just in time.

Today the IRA Christmas truce ended --- abruptly for us-- with news of the murder of brave Cliff Evans, RUCR. He was shot dead in an ambush at the junction of the Bellaghy and Toome Road near the Elk Bar. A horrible start to the year Two regular RUC men in the patrol car with Cliff were lucky not to be hit.

He'd had a narrow escape two years earlier when a gunman burst into his house at Bellaghy and opened fire. Cliff managed to escape but his luck's run out.

Went on blackface patrol to check out suspicious farmhouse near Hedley's Corner on Plumbridge road where IRA Ops. are said to be

A page from 'Visor', the Northern Ireland army magazine,
picturing operations in the G Company area.

BOOBY TRAP

Pte William Adams (45) of 5 UDR who has been a part-time member of the Regiment since its formation, lost a leg when a booby-trap device exploded in his car as he was leaving home for work in a local bakery in Londonderry. He is married with a family of four, one of whom is a member of 5 Bn.

Two soldiers of G Coy 8 UDR and a member of the RUC received minor injuries when a culvert bomb attack was made on a two vehicle patrol south of Coagh. They were taken to Magherafelt Hospital but were not detained. One Land-Rover was damaged. A number of HV shots were fired into the killing area from the east immediately after the explosion and the members of the patrol returned fire but did not detect any hits.

The GOC talks to WO2 McLean before presenting him with the BEM

Brigadier Bryan Webster 8 Brigade, 1977

5 Bn soldier gets BEM

Pte Vincent Lindsay of B Coy, 5 UDR has recently been awarded the British Empire Medal for gallant conduct in Londonderry.

Pte Lindsay, who is a director of the family furniture business, happened to be in Carlisle Road, Londonderry on 2 June 1974 when a lorry containing between 350 and 400 lbs of explosives was parked near No 11 Carlisle Road, where two elderly people lived.

Being familiar with the layout of the premises, he offered his assistance to the RUC who were clearing the area. This offer was gladly accepted and Private Lindsay and Inspector Johnston were successful in evacuating a 79 year-old housewife who suffered from defective hearing and was unable to walk.

A second person in the house, who was working at the rear of the premises and was unaware of the danger, was also evacuated minutes before the bomb was scheduled to explode.

UDR SOLDIER KILLED

L/Cpl Gerald Cornelius Cloete, 46, of B Coy 5 (Co Londonderry) UDR, was murdered by gunmen outside his home last Wednesday.

He was buried with full military honours on Saturday at Altnagelvin.

L/Cpl Cloete leaves a widow and five children.

planned. Dogs barking at slightest footfall prevented close approach.,

Afterwards on foot we attracted some stone throwing and verbal aggro. in avillage.

' I wish those hoods would follow us out into the country; then we could give them a real hammering', said one of the regular soldiers with us that night.

'Not when I'm in command, you won't', from me put an end to that game.

G Company was never in the business of beating up civilians of any age, or whatever the provocation. G Company is kind to prisoners and to detainees. The lads know that I will tolerate no physical abuse.

Jan 10th; The Minister at Cliff's funeral warned strongly against retaliation. Not much wonder ---we had heard of six Catholics shot in UVF attacks on two households in Armagh three days ago -- followed by ten Protestant workmen at Kingsmill machine-gunned outside their works van in cold blood. Please God similar things won't happen here.

Jan 12 th; Sam's last day as our Sergeant Instructor in G Coy. and in the UDR. He retires with a BEM due to ill health caused by stress. Tall and burly Sam has borne himself like the regular soldier he was. All our men loved him .

'I'd have carried Sam on my back any time,' one told me.

Sam's methods of administration were often unconventional but he got men out on patrol, armed and accoutred whenever they were needed.' 'In this job,' he confided to me,' I have to be doctor, confessor, marriage guidance counsellor, lonely hearts club, tax adviser as well as wet nurse to young recruits'.

The Company had arranged various presentations including a handsome engraved cigarette lighter. Their party at Fort Garry was a good one -the Sergeant's Mess Farewell in Ballykelly that followed went on until dawn .

Jan 13; Tight feeling at back of eyeballs at breakfast but survived a lengthy battalion O Group, called to meet increased threat. Then three hours admin. in Fort Garry with Robert, our new PSI. He is an old and trusted friend but new to this job.
Some problems from the take-over. Sam kept a lot of things in his head.

Jan 21; June and I drove 20 miles to Ballykelly. We stopped on top of the pass in the Sperrins to admire the view. Before us in the clear late afternoon light lay a great green plain, with patches of trees, dark hedgerows, rough dry stone walls and white houses. We've seen it a lot of times, but today with a gorgeous pink winter sunset backlighting the Donegal hills it was worth a stop. The town of Limavady with spires and towers lay below four miles to our front. The chimneys of Ballykelly village stuck up on the near edge of the leg-of-mutton shape of Lough Foyle, silvered by the never-resting tide. Radio aerials, and runways marked the 300 acres of Shackelton Barracks which holds Battalion HQ where we are bound and the lines of a regular battalion. Before that it was a Coastal Command Royal Air Force base. After a call for mail at HQ we drove on fifteen miles to dine with Brigadier Bryan Webster and his wife Liz in Clooney Park beside Ebrington Barracks. Bryan is a Royal Fusilier, newly arrived. We'd had an introduction from his predecessor but it was hardly necessary. With the Websters our families clicked at once. They are expert observers of birds. An interest we share but not Bryan and son Julian's extraordinary ability to recognize a new species from the flick of a wing tip half a mile away. It is clear from chat with other guests that the Brigade is at once under firm management. Command of 8 Brigade means working from 0800 until 2130 daily including most weekends. The job is reckoned so stressful that two years are enough to wear a man out. It's political as much as military, so double pitfalls lie in wait. Entertaining the right people (eg us!) is an important part. Observers say that a new Brig. will play it cool for the first six months until he knows the form. Then in the final six months he plays it cool lest some clanger should spoil his career. So he only commands strongly in the middle period. Bryan isn't like that. A gallant figure, well groomed with strong jaw and laughing eyes Bryan is a go-in-and-get-'em, damn the torpedoes, man from the start.

Principal guest the Commander Land Forces General David Young arrived by helicopter from Lisburn. A tall lean Scotsman with an impressive fighting record, he was full of bonhomie, new tactics, and ways of winning hearts and minds. Over the port he told us that his main concern is stopping re-supply to the IRA active service units in this area. Rocket missiles are being delivered by air.

'Efficient patrolling by your boys is one of best ways of inhibiting it, Wallace', he said. A serious Sapper from Lisburn advocated building a Great Wall of China along the entire border. He'd clearly like to do the job himself. That started a brisk conversation. 'It's been done before,' a University Vice-Chancellor pointed out. 'The Black Pig's Dyke in pre-historic times was just such a barrier. In mediaeval times swamps and bogs made large areas near the present border impassable to armies.

A police superintendent reminded us that, other than in people's imagination, Ireland has never been united. Except briefly under the Brits. The four provinces were at continual warfare for a thousand years before that, as chronicled in various books of Annals. I approved the wall idea; it would make life a bit tougher for raiders now and be a splendid tourist walk after all these tedious troubles are over.

One personal advantage of the present anarchy is that you can drive home with some drink taken. The Sperrins are hotching with IRA so for an RUC breathaliser to set up shop on Glenshane Pass would be suicidal. However, we'd been asked to stay the night so could drink our fill, help wash up, and go to sleep to the comforting sound of sentries pacing the board walk outside.

Jan 23: Our new PSI came to tell me that Private John Arrell F Coy, a poultry manager, married just a year ago, from Castledawson had been shot dead, yesterday at Clady; probably by Bellaghy ASU.

Jan 25; Heard more details at the wake. Mourners were so packed that no conversation could be private. My father used to tell me about how much drink was consumed in his day on these sad occasions and of one wake where he saw the corpse propped up at the table with a pipe in his mouth, looking un-lifelike and ghastly.

Drinks are not so common now; tea with cakes and sandwiches is usual.

It's a kindly practice as friends come round to keep the bereaved family company in the awful period before the burial. A gunman had entered the works bus that gallant John drove, asked his name and said, 'I've somethin' for you'.

Then fired a machine gun at point blank range. Poor John fell dead with one eye still open across the lap of workmate beside him. Extra shots were fired as bravado by a cover man using a Garand rifle from outside the bus. This has the stamp of one Bellaghy man who is reputed to like killing close up. To me the long as well as the short term future of Ulster looks bleak and violent. Impossible not to feel depressed; nothing but mindless mayhem in prospect. Behind us is a Government of flab. Security forces are handcuffed. No Int. comes through to us. No house searches allowed locally. Some covert investigations but little else.

Their record might be taken as a textbook on how not to defeat terrorism.

We pay the price. That's two of our men down in first three weeks.

Jan 25: As a fresh piece of appeasement it is announced that all UDR patrols must be accompanied by a policeman. No great problem for we often take them out with us anyway. But on most patrols it is not practical. Police are not equipped for walking cross country through scrambly hedges, so don't like doing so, particularly in the dark where uniforms get soiled and torn. As most of our work involves foot work the police usually find an excuse not to come but they like urban patrols and searches. With us as cover they can personally examine places not normally accessible!

Jan 27th: Dined out Esmond Black, our well liked Training Major prior to his departure. In reply to our Toast he said:

'I'll always be a member the UDR in spirit..I've learned more from you than I have imparted and feel almost ashamed to be going back to safety in England while you soldier on.[1]

Feb 1: Big bang early am This time it turned out to be Draperstown RUC Station. A car bomb up against perimeter wire. No serious casualties. I visited the scene for a briefing from the local regular company commander. Sappers were dispassionately starting to clear up mess, search rubble, shore up walls and re-erect wire fence.

No angst displayed; to them it is just another job of work ; it's better that way. The splendid British Tommy has kept his temper to a remarkable degree in face of endless deliberate provocation. But the downside is at the top That sounds Irish. It is. No follow up. No arrests. No questioning. No visible reaction following shootings of Cliff Evans and John Arrell. Next victim probably picked already. Maybe me.

Call it the will of God, the Nornies who selected the next Viking to die, Atropos who sheared the life of the Greeks – the same under varying titles. I think a lot of us are fatalists just now. Statistically the chances of being the next victim are small enough for each of us to think , 'It won't happen to me'. So we carry on There is bravery – sure -- but it is mainly a matter of stolid insensitiveness to danger, an ingrained sense of humour; and perhaps as in my own case a switch-offable imagination--- that keeps the UDR going.

Almost the only occasion when UDR men look embarrassed is when someone praises their bravery. I feel more exposed personally than for years ; now carry a pistol all the time ; did so in '72 but stopped a year or so ago. It's difficult when travelling to England every week or two. We are forbidden to carry personal protection weapons outside NI but how can you obey that and drive to the airport and remain protected?.

In Leeds last week I was being fitted for new suit by one of our customers. Got a stunned look from a Maenson tailor as he measured my chest, and saw a pistol butt protruding from my inside breast pocket. I've tried wearing shoulder holster but found it too uncomfortable.

Are we facing Unilateral Declaration of Independence by Ulster which would probably mean economic ruin, annihilation, invasion from the South, or just continual increase in violence? More likely the death of a thousand cuts as doled out by the Foreign Office.

Feb 3: Woke early and couldn't get to sleep so drove to Maghera. Snow squeaking under my feet. Turned out the Guard at 0330 and was able to praise them for being fully alert.

Feb 6; A less pleasant visit. Had to replace two Junior Ranks Club barmen. Cash short. Goodbye call from Brigadier Harry Baxter, a well liked Commander UDR. Always conspicuous by the piratical black patch over one eye. Always good crack. His presence at a party guarantees success. A brave soldier too. Sixteen years ago he was awarded the George Medal for driving a vehicle containing a bomb out of Gough Barracks, Armagh. Today he would have to fine a soldier for doing same thing. Attitudes change and one life is now more highly valued than any amount of material. This applies apparently to all except the Bomb Disposal officers or ATOs who often face extreme danger to disarm a bomb and save a village.

Harry told me that a three months full time mobilisation of whole UDR is being considered. I told him that the wire round our Fort is needed to keep the Jocks of our Scottish regular detachment in more than keep the enemy out. Two of them stole the tools out of the Police Sergeant's car and cut their way out to go on a spree last week. The Jocks are the best soldiers that come here but each company has in it one or two hard cases. Harry replied with a story of two young Greenfinches returning to camp through a hole in the fence. They were met by a Greenfinch Corporal.

'We're just coming back after hours', they said. 'Mum's the word', she replied,' I'm just going out after mine!'.

Stories about Harry are legion. At a reception held in St Patrick's

Barracks a glamourous Greenfinch lance-corporal carried round a tray of drinks. Harry had been entertained in her house at a recent pheasant shoot so when she came to him he seized the tray and carried it on round himself!

We'll miss Harry. If any one man made UDR it is him.

Feb 11: This evening June and I, in by the fireside for once, felt windows vibrate on the south side of house and heard a dull boom at 9pm Who's got it this time? Phoned our Ops Room. 'Think its Magherafelt No details as yet'.

Must have been a big one. That's ten miles away. Gradually details come in -- 500 lb. Proxy bomb delivered to the RUC Station which now houses the regular Army Ops Room. PIRA used a council refuse lorry. Part of crew were held hostage; blast damage up to 600 yards, many houses destroyed but no one hurt, thank God . except for an aged lady who was cut by glass and had her spectacles cracked.

Feb 14; Constable Willie Hamer RUCR killed by shot in back while on patrol in Claudy near Derry at 9.45 pm. His comrade seriously wounded and has suffered an instant amputation of leg. Ordered to do dawn patrol near Toome to check parties allegedly en route to funeral of Frank Stagg. He died at Wakefield prison after a fourth hunger strike. Much controversy as to location of funeral and whether shots over his coffin would be allowed. We found no weapons and let mourners pass.

Feb 15; (Sunday): Attended UDR orienteering competition at Tollymore Park, County Down Lovely surroundings. Walked over the course through mature trees and some scrub. Our team only fifth; we've not had enough time for training in compass work.

Feb 16: called at Fort Garry on return from Belfast at 11.45pm to de-brief patrol which had been shot at and returned fire near Gulladuff.
'I seen the scad of the boy jeuking in behind a wall, just as I was on the aim. I'd say he was badly shook,' said a patrol member. No hits claimed

Feb 17: Good news for a change. Wooffer's Rupert Bear[2] caught four Glenullin ASU men yesterday. Bad news follows. Lynch, a Roman Catholic civilian, shot near Claudy in retaliation for Constable Hamer. Tit-for-tat killings are now as widespread as they are ineffective.

Feb 19: RUC men Gilliland and McConaghy wounded in gun attack near Draperstown. I changed numbers on my car for third time in last twelve months.

Feb 21: Saturday. June and I sneaked over border to have dinner at Birdstown, Donegal. Hid our car in our host's yard and stayed night. Great sense of relief to be out of ASU area and in a country which is at peace

Feb 22 Sunday: 2.30 Watched Battalion football final at Ballykelly. Captain Dougy from B Company issued loud streams of four-letter encouragement. He was really gunked when he suddenly saw the colonel beside him and dried up like a gramophone turned off!. G Coy won. 'The cream always comes to the top', said Ginger, our most jubilant supporter! 'You can stir and stir but it still happens.'
Company NCO Conference pm. Income tax on pay a sore point -- various politicians have tried to get it exempted but it's a difficult one. They have managed, I think, to get certain categories of

unemployed allowed to continue to draw their Boru money (ie not
to be disqualified) while in UDR.
'The taxman never asked me if 'e could 'ave it. Now he's fookin'
throwin' it away.' was one comment
Efforts to improve our Call Out times was next subject . We strive to
get arms issued from our armoury in under 15 minutes. This is
spurred by the very fast times that I hear are being achieved in 8
UDR, Dungannon .

Feb 23; Last stage of big clean up for company Fitness for Role
inspection. HQ team arrives and spent hours going round. We
came out with compliments but Ronnie our excellent vehicle
mechanic failed to sprint a hundred yards in the standard time. It
is hard to see the necessity in his job but he'll probably be
discharged. For the likes of us fitness regulations for base staff are
an ass. It comes from misguided efforts by senior officers to try
to make us equate with regular soldiers, trained to do any thing
in any corner of the globe at short notice.

Feb 24 : Belfast Newsletter says UDR strength only 6000. Nobody
else tells us.
This reveals one reason why we are overworked ; we were supposed to
have reached 9000 three years ago. A letter in the same paper from
a retired soldier argues well that the high proportion of static
guards on bridges, public buildings and our own bases as biggest
deterrent to recruiting. Only one in a hundred of people of right age
and fitness joins. The letter calls for much more aggressive use of
UDR in patrolling IRA-dominated areas, raids, and riot control.
That's what men give up their time for.
It is true that at times UDR men have to guard Police Stations full
of policemen sitting watching TV. But it doesn't happen much in

our area We know each other well
enough to go in and point out the irritation of what is happening.

FEB 25; Visited Royal Military College, Sandhurst, to encourage
Charlie and Jim, two potential officers for company. They are on a
two week course. Saw them for a quick coffee between parades.
They were enjoying it but found the constant activity and swift
changes of kit expected between one type of training to another
exhausting Then lunch with the Commandant, General Robert
Ford who became a friend when commanding the 4/7 Hussars here
years ago.

MARCH 8th: Regimental Dinner at Milltown House,
Ballynahinch I sat next to Gerry Plover from 'Pally Alley' (Palace
Barracks) east of Belfast Told me about some good shooting ---six
shots thro' headrest of car driven by armed terrorist trying to crash
past a VCP. Sounds a wee bit tall but I wish we could do the same.

MARCH 9th: Study day at Ballykinler All UDR field officers-
- majors and above present --Can't recall learning much in the
formal sessions but good for personal reunions and hearing how
other units cope.

April 1: I heard from the duty officer that the stout-hearted
William McCutcheon of Moneymore, F Company was shot as he
drove away from night shift in cement factory at Toome. His body
was found at 0500 by a patrol. He'd died game trying to draw his
pistol but Oh, what a terrible lonely fate --- Terrorist deliberately
picked the date -- The sixth anniversary of our formation for this
murder.

April 2nd Friday: New Horrors each returning day to misquote
the hymn. Had just got back to office and started get desk cleared

when Robert rang up 'Bad news, sir. Postman shot near Drumard. Think its one of ours'.

Later confirmed., 'It's Bobby Lennox'. This G Company man was killed today with 20 shots as he delivered mail to an isolated cottage A World War Two Gunner in Coleraine AA Battery whose kindness as a postman in civilian life went far beyond the call of duty; he regularly did messages for elderly people in course of mail deliveries. Robert and I drove out to reach the house at 12. 00. Scene of Crime Officer (SOCO) already there. We saw Bobby lying dead on the concrete patch in front of the cottage beside the riddled Post Office van. The driver's door peppered with bullet holes lay open. Half Bobby's face shot away. Six rounds in his back.

Each bullet case on ground had by now been circled in yellow chalk. 'Weapons all right hand ejecting.' Said SOCO. 'Gunman stood here.' 'Don't walk on mud. Might be footprints.'

'The boy who lives in the cottage can't tell us anything. He's a dummy'. (ie deaf and dumb). Our mobile patrol soon found the getaway car. ATO blew it up

Battalion HQ announced a voluntary callout. That in army terms means every one who can possibly come. The feeling of doing something at least helps defuse the situation and reduces chance of reprisals.

At 9pm Captain Sammy Furl, an aimiable businessman in private life, arrived in flack jacket and tin hat with pistol at his belt, looking fierce and ready for battle. He had twenty men from E Company at his back.

April 5th Monday; Funeral 1030 at the Lennox house in corner of square in Curran. Ina, Bobby's gallant widow, red nosed, tired-eyed, pale but composed stood with five children beside her.

'Bobby Lennox had 60 years of honourable life to look back on', she said. 'The man that shot him will never have any peace He'll pay for it before God.' 'What must that gunman's mother or girl friend think?'

That must make Bobby the oldest soldier to die for his country in recent years.

I tried to express sympathy, listened to by 20 onlookers. Ina continues to use the third person It made each remark more emphatic.

'Bobby Lennox said every one's entitled to think what they like, even say what they like, provided they leave it at that'. 'Bobby was young in heart. I have the document, major. You and Bobby Lennox were the first two members of F Coy --- six years ago. He'd passed his medical for another year last week. He was killed on the 21st birthday of our eldest son Gilbert.'

I was in tears by this time. One of most poignant of all the many funerals in last few months .

April 6th; Just finished three days intensive patrolling and searches Two rifles found and two hundred rounds; otherwise doubt if we achieved much against the terrorists But it lets people feel that something is being done . The irritation felt by house owners when having their premises rummaged for arms or explosives may make the terrorists a trifle less popular

April 7th : Attend Beating Retreat [3] with June at 8 Brigade HQ. Very fine band music, marching and counter-marching at Ebrington Barracks. Like a miniature Tattoo . This is a part of military life, probably essential for soldiers and families in administrative units. They are often cooped up month after month within the tin walls of this huge establishment with limited chances to shop, visit pubs or entertainments in safe areas.

Troops out patrolling don't need it so much

Received some compliments from regular officers about UDR support

April 25: PRUDR Training Ballykelly . We are due for weekends on Border soon .

May 1: Officer's Mess dance at Ballykelly   At such functions one hears news from other companies and neighbouring battalions. The dance was of course arranged months ago. Now after recent deaths it seems callous. But the show must go on. Social life is generally at a higher than usual pitch, because of rather than despite of troubles.

Private Archie, a leading piper and skilled dancer got on the floor with the Pipe Major's lady during supper! He got away with it, to general approval. until hunted by the RSM.

May 6th: I accompanied the patrol guarding   Altnaheglish, a lovely serpentine reservoir between heathery hills above Dungiven, then visited sentries on Derry City Water Works near Greysteel. Finished with power station on River Foyle; this involves providing security in a Control Room with more tits than the Aghagaskin Girl's Band, as well as watching the perimeter. Some education can be derived from identifying the varied species of seabirds feeding on the fish killed at the cooling water intake.

'What's that gull with silvery tips to its wings ?' I asked a maintenance man.

'Them's not gulls; them's shitehawks, ' was the illuminating reply. He was an Ex hostilites-only matelot in the Royal Navy.

MAY 7: Off to Camp at Warcop, Lancs .Taken across to Liverpool in Sir Perceval, a troop carrier. She is built to civilian, ie not warship, standards to save money. Feels tinny but sea calm and

there was good crack in bar. I bunked down early for the luxury of full night's sleep Then travel by bus two hours to camp, an isolated handful of hutments up in the hills. Visited pub in village where everyone friendly and beer excellent Not that there will be much time to enjoy it. A camp programme must be nicely balanced If there is not enough work the boys say, 'Why are we giving up holiday time to be here? Might as well be at home.
If there is not enough recreation time, they say, 'No way we're coming back again on this lark'. If we err this year,. it will be on side of work

May 9 : A visiting officer who'd been a Ghurkha came to watched field firing with a kukri on his belt. He looked slightly vexed when one of lads said, 'See you've brought your KFS (knife, fork, and spoon) with you , sir.' But he took it in good part

May 14th; Finished with an excellent 24 hour exercise over twenty miles of open country

May 15 Hear that while we are away RUC have had worst day of troubles so far. Three killed in an ambush on the Border at Belcoo in Fermanagh and one at Warrenpoint. At present three Saladin armoured cars of 4/7 Dragoons from Lisanelly Camp, Omagh. lager at Fort Garry to keep the enemy heads down while we are at camp . Interesting to think back to 1969, even 1970 when the 17 /21st Lancers based in Omagh kept grooms and ponies in Phoenix Park, Dublin and played polo there every weekend. A different and less picturesque world today.
Did Eagle Patrol to recce. A track near Sawel mountain, Sperrins, for later coverage of supply routes, on foot. Splendid cheerful and chatty chopper pilot. They are all great men. I asked him, 'What happens if the rotor shaft breaks?' He said nothing but disengaged

something and we fell like stone about 300 feet. Then he brought us up about 30 feet above ground! 'That's what its like'.

May 20: Terrific dinner party with Geoff Lee, Colonel of The Kings and his wife Joy, best for years. Specially convivial because they are near end of a successful two year tour.

'Today's problems are tomorrow's laughs.' said one of the company commanders. One immediate laugh had been a mysterious package found in the Ops Room the day before. It had just been blown up by ATO. Result - Black Magic chocolates spread all over the walls and ceiling! We knew almost everyone present as we have worked with Geoff's battalion at all levels. Maurice Johnson Divisional Head of RUC) there with his sparky wife Jean, He is a brilliant policeman, combining experience, tact and firmness. Much good shop over the port. Heard about a recent ambush on Foreglen Road.near Dungiven. IRA fired on the Land Rover of another regiment from 200 yards One soldier wounded but rest didn't charge the gunmen --- due to risk of it being a come-on. Advancing on foot could have lead them, they said , onto a trip wire and a mine. 'The Kings,' says Geoff, 'always counter attack if ambushed --- as a result are not ambushed.' Really alert units seldom are .

May 21: Our Land Rovers dropped a foot patrol on route traced from air last week .

Found safety fuse and traces of explosive in gables of an abandoned cottage, probably used for training.

May 26; Farewell party at Ebrington. A private dinner given by Capt James Parter RGJ and his brother; a rare gesture but most welcome! He's been a platoon commander in our area; more recently a watchkeeper in Bde Ops Room for some months Came to our house often for riding or snipe shooting or just to relax.

Nigel ,the senior policeman in the County was one of the guests and remarked on the extraordinary complication and fragmentation of the current intelligence set up. Six different committees sit within O Division alone . 'My heart's desire', he said,' is to see the army and the IRA out of the county and sometimes I'm not sure which I want out most.' He'd been a wartime Lancaster pilot, who after demob. had joined the RUC as a cadet. Now he sighed for a return to simpler police days when he had run the security in his own area quietly and successfully with no competing organisations.

N 10 people virtually never appear at Army social occasions like this. Only time I ever see one of them is when his name comes to the top of the Attend Funeral rota. Fairly frequent these days. They are under a non-fraternize-with-locals order, as was the army in Germany for several years after 1945. 'Don't get too friendly with the natives,' is the intention. 'Might weaken your resolve when you have to leave them in the lurch'. But individuals are of course reluctant to admit the ban. The policy is very shortsighted .

We've entertained NIO ministers often, some friends of my brother Henry from his MP days, but they don't or can't retaliate. Douglas Hurd was the rudest, perhaps unwittingly; never even replied to June's invitation. Even army officer can get hung up about fraternization. One training major refused repeated invitations to my house and when I taxed him with it he admitted he'd been told not to get too close to the likes of me! But he soon did.

May 27: Geoff Lee CO of Kings and his wife Joy to a farewell supper round the stone table by our wee lake - just the four of us. Feel we are losing true friends ; people you could say what you like to. Must keep in touch.

June 2 : Police woman Linda Baggly RUCR shot Derry. Three men convicted of her murder.

June 10: Spent morning with our standing VCP at Toome Bridge. When traffic was slack I offered my lunchtime apple to a pony in the field beside us.

'What's the poor brute done to deserve that?' said a voice behind me. It was George Phipps, our amiable training major, on his rounds. Our families had become friends and there was lots to talk about.

June 25: General David House dines with us at Battalion HQ, the only GOC that has done so. He has a pleasant round-faced appearance and is a soldier's general, who speaks on equal terms to individuals at all levels. He gave us all a needed boost .

June 30. Saw two minor defaulters in G Coy. Always distasteful I hate acting in judgement on my neighbours, or anyone else. Fortunately we get very few people on charges. But I know at least one officer who seems to relish it

Then dash to a plane for Harrogate Textile Exhibition

Heard on TV news on arrival -- Olly Eaton, Jimmy's brother, shot in Belfast. Colonel in North Irish Horse. member of Police Authority. Shot as he arrived at his office in Springfield Road, Belfast. Last time I saw him was in Eaton's Bakery Derry in 1975. We saw his name in a Top Businessman list in Fortnight Magazine lately. This may have lead to his death. Three others on the list have been shot. Glad I'm not counted as a successful entrepreneur!

July 2: Merlin Rees talks more and more of policy of police primacy. Army to step back..As a company we work so closely with police that it probably won't make much real difference.

July 6th Good-oh! Off on a sailing holiday with the family to Brittany and back.

July 24 Back from leave. Hear of several disasters while I was away. A staff sergeant was killed by a bomb placed on a stairway in an accommodation block in Ebrington Barracks. Two bombs wrecked centre of Castledawson. An 800 lb car bomb wrecked Main Street, Kilrea - - at this time Kilrea is the most bombed town in Ulster (eleven explosions in the current series) Ewart- Biggs British Ambassador in Dublin killed by mine under car. Merlin Rees, and good supporter of UDR was expected to be in that car too. Glad he wasn't

July 30 Two local casualties reported today Cpl William McLarnon, F Coy, seriously injured by bomb, placed under his car in his garage at The Loup near Draperstown. Later hear that kindly and brave Robert Scott, F Coy, killed by booby trap bomb on farm gate which he used regularly going to assist an elderly lady living on her own.

31 July: Sgt Ellington's's mobile patrol ambushed near Glenshane. Track of two bullets across roof of Land Rover found afterwards. Patrol men debussed and fired back in direction of flashes. Brigade Intrep recorded this as, 'Ten low velocity shots fired at UDR Mobile near Maghera . Six shots fired in reply. No hits claimed.' It was just one of a dozen such incidents in last 24 hours. Our patrol was closely questioned afterwards, almost like criminals, as to why they fired back and at what. An answer of 'suppressive fire' is not acceptable. We ,like policemen, have to account for every round. How can you fight terrorists with kid gloves and Queensbury Rules?

August 1 76: Nine Bombs explode between 2005 hrs and 2215 in Portrush. where many of us now go for golf or swimming. Very sad as it has been looked on as neutral territory and almost untouched so far by the troubles. UDR rifle range overlooking sea just west of Port Ballantrae was mined. Seventy pounds of home made explosive was buried in milk churn under gravel on firing point sometime earlier. It was primed and a pressure plate inserted night before a weekend practice. One soldier injured, luckily no worse.

August 3: Private Watkins Royal Hamps killed in Dungiven by single round from a shotgun. It was fired from an upper window and got the poor fellow in the back of his neck above his flak jacket. Search party came across a very clever booby trap—an empty cartridge case lying on a picture of a Page Three nude beside the window of the empty house from which shot was fired; nylon cord from the case to 5 lbs of Semtex. ATO, even more clever, disarmed device

August 7: Today we brace ourselves for the anniversary of relief of Siege of Derry and the second half of the marching season. After reporting to Magherafelt Ops Room I was sent with the mobile to investigate a bomb at Ballyscullion House, Bellaghy. This is a graceful Georgian building facing across broad meadows to Lough Beg. It has historic interest as one of the homes of the 18th Century high-living Lord Bristol, Bishop of Derry. He was a major art collector and bon viveur after whom many a Hotel Bristol in Europe is named. Arrived to find ATO at work on the bomb. It was tamped by being in a specially welded steel case and sat menacingly on the top front door step. No audible tick . Sheila, Lady Mulholland, aged eighty-plus, was standing at the back of the house shivering in an overcoat, wondering if she would be

allowed back to go to bed . She was worried mostly as to survival
of her unique set of porcelain figures of Kings and Queens of
England. I persuaded her plus her willowy niece Claire to be driven
eleven miles and spend night with us. June had the spare room
ready . On arrival Sheila was unshaken and sat up for almost an
hour sipping whiskey. She is a sister of Lord Brookeborough MC
,the Northern Ireland Prime Minister who kept us peaceful for
twenty years. They were a tough generation! Claire and I returned
to find ATO successful at last and house unharmed.

Aug 8 : AM As run up to Derry marches the Company is ordered to
double local patrols. Lots of volunteers to do extra duty In Ops
Room 0030 hours until 0300. Wave of bomb reports by radio,
mostly hoaxes ,but G Company treats all as real until proved
otherwise. This is longest I have ever sat in an Ops Room. Hate the
places Far better left to a watchkeeper. My job is to be out with the
boys.

As an experiment we have just been told to share our Ops Room with
RUC. This in our case is entirely amiable but the two forces methods
of dealing with incidents are so different that I don't think it will
work to any advantage. Police training is towards one constable
present on his own at an incident being able to take charge and act
as he thinks best The army expect junior commanders to report for
orders at an early stage .

Further if one constable is present beside a full army battalion
under a Lieutenant-Colonel, the constable is now, theoretically, in
charge. The Army status is ' in aid to the civil power'. In practice.
with us primacy rarely matters. Decisions are reached by
agreement. I recall once only being ordered brusquely away from
a suspect vehicle by a young constable just out of Training
College. A superintendant soon arrived and told him to mind his

manners. (I have written this diary page on a loose sheet during lulls in the Ops Room.)

Aug 8 ,Sunday: General callout; Hamps doing a full battalion search on banks of River Bann. Set up their TAC HQ in Claudy opposite St Mary's College. We joined them from 0900 until 1200. A 30 ft. radio mast topped a massive signals set up. Off duty signalers in flack jackets sunbathing on top of Pigs but no major finds.

1700: Took mobile to top of Bohilbreaga Mountain above Moneyneaney rocks. We could have driven vehicles on cross-country to A5 in Glenshane Pass, as going was so very dry and firm. But time was tight and we couldn't afford to get a vehicle bogged down. It might have taken an hour or two to get freed.

1930: Return to meet Maghera security foot patrol. Many hoaxes reported. Some house bombing. Continue patrolling; our Ops room allocated some grid squares to be covered by E Coy from Coleraine. The Kings are in Clady area as well as Hamps. Got a Gazelle helicopter to whirl down and drop patrols for ten minutes in one location, then off to another. Avoids risk of ambush and inhibits enemy movements.

Aug 10th: Search continues in huge boggy area in Ballynease and Ballymacpeake Man who killed Lennox is known and can be caught. This is quoted as the Search of Century, based on info gained on the early lifts. Battalion HQ are screaming for more men. The factory where half the company are employed is closed for annual break so it is very difficult to trace those on holiday. I have become bored and cynical ; our mobile was this morning sent back from Churchtown after waiting around for ages because there were too many men at that location. This was after our boys got there an hour ahead of rest. Another half day wasted at Black Loughs, hanging round for lack of orders. More time was dissipated on ridiculous searches of Orange Halls, Protestant housing estates and unlikely farm groups. I am reluctant to call men from vital employment or from well earned holidays to be jiggered around to no effect

August 31: Battalion O Group, Ballykelly. Sentries to prove identity of all visitors-- even Gods like CO --- and identify each passenger Stop all cars outside gates. Is this a sign of panic messages to NI HQ from NIO ?

Training, particularly .with personal protection weapons, to continue. Elaborate plans for Inter Company Competition during next three months .

No company parades will be allowed on Remembrance Sunday as in past; token parties of six men max only. Looks like another concession to terrorism, following Enniskillen Armistice Day bombing .

Sept 1 : John Biggs Davidson MP came to stay with us and visit G Company. A gentle caring man and a great supporter of the Ulster Unionist cause who has the ear of Mrs T, as he calls the Prime Minister Through him, he assures us, she does realise the effort we are putting in to defeat the terrorists

Sept 3 Monthly board meeting of our family business. I cannot remember ever struggling so hard to keep awake. Dozed off in spite of many coffees; this as a result of patrol followed by a long de-briefing last night.

There was no time after the meeting for lunchtime siesta which is so essential when living a double life. I had to rush to drive sons Bruce and Milo off to a dinner party in Donegal. Back and in office until 1700. Then my car wouldn't re-start; traced to worn points. Then a short zizz before a UDR 2100 Ops Conference until 2300. Then I struggled back home and flopped.

Sept 5th Fort Garry and Maghera police barracks shot at; twelve rounds HV rifle fire no casualities. Just bullet holes in wriggly tin. Police fired on three days ago in daylight near Magherafelt Courthouse. We now do anti-mortar bomb patrols each night dusk to dawn.

Sept 12 th: Lunch in Fort Garry with Dervla Murphy, the travel writer. Bruce Willink, Royal Hamps Company Commander, joined us. 'This is bomber country,' he said to her with certainty, 'It's all young men we're up against. Too old at 26.' She arrived on her famous bicycle yesterday, searching material for a book about Northern Ireland to be called A Place Apart. Bronzed, fit and self confident with a pleasant drawly Cork accent she proclaims atheism, has one love-child daughter and is above all a great friend of my round-the-Horn shipmate Miles Smeeton. It is through him we got acquainted. Dervla wanted to sleep out on our lawn. There was a gale blowing and rain but only with difficulty did we persuade her to doss on our sitting room carpet. I wonder if we'.ll appear in the book. The hang-up Dervla suffers from (a not uncommon one) is that she thinks it strange, almost incredible, that Orangemen and UDR soldiers can be kindly ordinary people. She initially assumes that we are all bigoted bloodstained gorillas as pictured in the Cork newspapers. I think we shifted her view a little and found her excellent company.[*]

Sept 19: Weekend camp in sandhills at Magilligan. Training for province reserve duties on Border next month. We ran good fieldcraft exercises showing the value of stalking out of the sun but against the moon. Private Bertie Rainey, war time Gunner, brought me with great civility an early morning cup of tea in my tent --

an unexpected luxury on a Sunday morning. Bryan Webster appeared and joined us for a bivouac meal and drinks; shows great enjoyment of whiskey, tho' it never seems to have slightest effect on him! Told us how he'd almost had his platoon taken away from him when in the front line fighting in Korea. He hadn't shaved one morning when General Joe Kendrew, DSO and three bars, arrived for an inspection.

'Take a grip, man', was Joe's great phrase. A good one .

Joe was married to Nora Harvey a Donegal cousin of my mother's. I fired 120 rounds on the range from SLR. Still l much prefer my good old Lee Enfield. Colonel Fergus McCame-Bremner , a genial bachelor, currently Deputy 8 Bde Commander, came to us for a field lunch.　We have two volunteer cooks – Private Hughie and a curious character from Ten UDR. He has wife trouble so lives on the boru, plus UDR pay, to avoid alimony. The screw you get for screw you got. He also gets what he calls Infidelity Allowance (AKA Invalidity!) If the beak asks him about his residence or earnings he replies ' Under Section 15 of Official Secrets Act I cannot give you any details of the movements of any member of Security Forces '

Must keep that one up my sleeve if questioned on my income tax return.

October 8:　A local man Arthur McKay, RUCR, Kilrea killed by car bomb Gortmacrane. He was at the wheel of a hi-jacked car which had been cleared by army and was being towed back to the RUC Station. Pressure release device, invisible under wheel, ignited charge.

OCT 9th: Roy Hamilton, prison officer. shot outside his home in Derry by IRA

OCT 28 : Another postman was reported shot in Tyrone today by IRA in same circumstances as Bobby Lennox. The IRA attempt to justify the killing by saying that a UDR postman can spy when off Army duty.

Nov 7: Heard my friend Captain Ronnie Bond, second in command of B Coy, died today, He had been 'awaitin' on', as they say around here, for a week . No other phrase in English sums up so closely the anxious vigil. Gunned down with twelve bullets from behind as he walked home from his job in the Housing Executive towards his home in Harding St, Derry. He had a distinguished career as a lieutenant Royal Naval Volunteer Reserve in Combined Ops including landing a commando for the invasion of Sicily in 1943. He and I used to talk Navy.

Nov 9: Ronnie's Funeral. Commander UDR . Brigadier 8 Bde and many senior officers walk in cortege. At 8 pm: Heard Lance Corporal Jim Speer shot in back of head outside his garage in Desertmartin about 6 pm. An IRA scoundrel asked Jim to come and look at his car and shot him as he was bending over examining an imaginary fault.

A most obliging and skilled friend Always willing for an extra duty or to come in and repair a Land Rover. Much, I'm sure, to the detriment of his own business

A few weeks ago he came into Fort Garry with a big bottle of Terquilla after a family trip to Mexico, passing it all round and telling funny stories about his trip. Now dead from multiple pistol bullets.

A second gunman went round to the side of the garage looking for Jack, also of G company who was working in the Spray Shop at the time and very luckily had the door shut. Jack had, unusually, no pistol with him. With the compressor running he heard nothing until getaway car moved.

Nov 11 : Jimmy Speer's funeral at Lecumpher Meeting-House. Full military honours. The family, indeed most of the crowd, seemed to physically shudder at the sound of shots. I am not sure that volleys are a good idea. They honour a soldier but add to his relatives' agony. Jim's wife returned to Stormont Castle the wreath sent by NIO. This was in accord with stated wish by Jimmy two weeks ago as to what to do if he should be shot. Did he have a premonition? For sure he was one of best men in the whole battalion. Napoleon's saying when one of his marshals was killed in the middle of a campaign, seems to summarise the feeling of many of us just now. 'Why do I not have time to mourn him?

Lance Corporal Winston McCaughey, 5 UDR, arrived home on Edenbann Road, Kilrea this evening and stood beside his car while his wife and little son went on into the house A gunman shot him in the back and he was dead on arrival in hospital.

He was fine soldier and a fine husband. That's three of ours in four days. Worst period ever. A dreadful week for Colonel Ian who had to dash back from leave in Edinburgh and cope with the funerals and the families. What's to come?

Nov 13 1976 McCaughey funeral. General John Anderson came and walked behind the coffin. Also a Foreign Office man from NIO. A foolish, vicious private of our company shot a Royal Hamps soldier dead while playing at Russian roulette in the guardroom. I previously spoke for him in the County Court when he was charged for a misdemeanour at a VCP. Oh! how wrong I was to give him a second chance. Severity pays. Should have sacked him on the spot months ago. Now a wasted life on my conscience.

Nov 15; Attended O group Ballykelly. Excellent address by Bryan Webster.

New Policy; Police lead the attack -- UDR, Army more in subsidiary role. Will get killers but will take time. Have recently doubled attrition rate -- 122 terrorists charged in O and P RUC Divisions in last three months. Seven charged with murder in Derry area. But godfathers lying very low; middle and lower rankers doing killing. Teenage gunmen do most jobs

Problems of manning: in England 270 CID men can be tasked onto one murder. Only 210 here for whole Province. Only two Divisional Crime squads working in 8 Brigade area

Well put over. It made encouraging stuff

Nov 16: Thank God no one shot last night.

I jump if telephone rings in case it is to announce another death.

Party at HQ for two retiring full time staff from Scottish Division - RSM and Quartermaster.

Nov 17: Another Ops meeting 0930 to 1630. Head splitting; feels as if circular saw running through it; first vertically, then horizontally. Sleepy later. Too much port last night. Now must get ready for FFR inspection

Nov 20: My fiftieth birthday. Never had a better one. What a full day. Search Operation Craigavole am (It is pronounced Craig-y-ole). Then some sport; Lieutenants Jim Smyth and Willis Hessin accompanied me to shoot pigeons from The Whaler, our family seventeen footer, in coastal sea caves. We made an exceptional bag of over 50; the crop of every one stuffed with corn so the farmers should thank us.

'My God,.do ye's never miss? said a small boy as we landed them. If only he knew! Shooting from a sitting position in a pitching boat doesn't make for easy shooting and it's better not to count the cartridges. Then back to an excellent dinner cooked by June. Malcolm Havergal, Lt. Colonel of the Coldstreams and his wife Fiona, the Websters and eight others. Lots to eat and lots to drink.

Nov 23 : Joe Glover, civilian, shot in Derry by IRA in retaliation for a civilian called Toland killed yesterday by UDA /UVF.

Nov 25 Brigade Intrep records 'James Loughrey, civilian, Greysteel shot by UFF'. This was considered to be in retaliation for the murder of Captain Ronnie Bond..

Dec 11 Howard Edwards, Sapper, killed by sniper in Bogside. A 19 year old assistant quartermaster of 1st Battalion PIRA in Derry is said to be the gunman.[5]

Dec 5 June and I, en route to a Trade Textile Exhibition in Cologne visited Derek Woolstencroft our previous CO in his new role at a NATO Base on Dutch-Belgian border. A good man and kindly host. Known, I was told, in own regiment as 'cotton socks'

DEC 12 '76. Peter Mitchell, CO of the Duke of Wellingtons, called to tell me to be careful on mountain patrols. He and his vivacious wife Di are skilled entertainers with whom a close friendship has quickly grown up in these stressful days. Two of his Land Rovers carrying a patrol commanded by his godson Charlie Greaves, were blown clean off the road by twin culvert bombs on Drumlane Road just north of Glenullin. The pair of mined culverts were spaced exactly right about a hundred yards apart to get both vehicles. If ambushers had followed up they could easily have wiped out whole patrol. Instead the Duke's sergeant returned their fire at once, then and gathered ammunition from injured soldiers to sustain it until the enemy moved off. Greaves was virtually blind with specs smashed. Both radios were destroyed. so he had to organise a foot party to march four miles to Garvagh RUC to summon support. Jack, Battalion Signaller and briskest of soldiers was today crushed against Land Rover by a police car in the dark at a VCP Leg severely fractured.

Dec 18: Sergeant's Mess party at Ballykelly. Felt very honoured to be invited and heard many good yarns. These are the best of all the army parties but you need a stainless steel tummy to survive.

Dec 22: The fearless and popular Sammy Armour RUCR killed by car bomb outside his house on Crewe Road Maghera. He leaves a wife and three little boys. Met Brigadier Bryan Webster at site at midday. A pitiful scene. His body still in the car. Christmas presents scattered on ground around it.

Other Christmastides there has been a truce declared in advance by the IRA. Haven't heard of one this year. On matters like this they tend to keep their word but we never take the risk of believing them or let down our guard. Regular units usually stagger Xmas and celebrate a few days early.

Dec 24: Private Jack hurt and hospitalized by a car which tried to crash through a road block set up to protect Security Forces at the Armour funeral. Will be much missed as one of or keenest soldiers who regularly attended five or six nights a week. Enormous funeral for Reserve Constable Samuel Armour.

Presbyterian Minister Sidlow McFarland spoke inspiringly at just right pace of Sammy as a father, brother, son and husband. He quoted a student poem;

Waste of life, Waste of love, Waste of body, Waste of mind

1030: In to Fort Garry . Talked to Int. men, to sentries and helped organize guard for Jack in hospital. Quite a competition to do this. Xmas Eve Drinks in Junior Ranks Club.[6]

Dec 25 1976: Xmas Day; Special boxed lunches of festive fare come from Ballykelly one for each soldier. All are laid out on Junior Ranks Bar table, plus lots of goodies the boys bring in like home-grown turkeys, ham and chicken. At 2 pm Simon Firth, CO of the Glosters, literally dropped in at our cottage. As his helicopter landed on the lawn, our children's donkey was so surprised it jumped over a three foot wooden fence! Simon had in the best tradition already served meals to soldiers, eaten and drunk at three different locations. Christmas can be toughest day of the year for battalion officers. He had bite of plum pud with us (Simon not the donkey) and then sky-high again with four more visits to go. We've often dined in Simon's quarter and partied at his Mess. Friendships like this do a lot to make the present horrors bearable.

Casualties in Periods Covered by Diary Above

Deaths in our area in 16 months Jan 76 to April 77 –
UDR 12: RUC 4: RUCR 2: Regular Soldiers 3: Prison Officers 1: Civilian businessmen 2.
Total for year 24.
Six of the UDR deaths came in seven months, probably mostly at hands of the Bellaghy gang. Without UDR guards and patrols, it would have been many times worse.

Provincial Totals for 1976

UDR < 15 plus 4 ex-.members; Regular soldiers; 14 and Police; 24.

From Official Account of 5th Battalion in UDR Journal 1977

'The gruelling, usually unspectacular, hard work has continued as ever and when there has been a call out the response has been invariably excellent. No one will forget the bitter days in November 1976 when Captain Ronnie Bond, Lance Corporals Jimmy Speers and Private Winston McCaughy died within four days. Deep anger characterised the mood in the battalion.'

Footnotes

*1: I'm sure the TISO meant every word of it but I never heard of him
    afterwards.*

2: Feb 17. Worcester and Sherwood Foresters reconnaissance group.

*3: April 7. Beating Retreat is an army musical occasion, recalling the days of
    walled towns when the garrison band used to play to call in foragers from
    outside before the gates were shut for the night .*

*4: Sept 12: Bruce Willink,. a most helpful man, was later a UDR CO. We saw
    him again for a third time as Deputy Commander 8 Bde .*

5: Dec 11: The 19 year old was later convicted of this shooting.

*6: Dec 24 : Jack was later most unwillingly invalided out for a minor arm
    malfunction.*

CHAPTER TEN

A COMPANY COMMANDER'S DIARY 1977

SHOOTINGS AND SKI RUNS

'Through joy and blindness he shall know,
Not caring much to know, that still
Nor lead nor steel shall reach him, so
That it be not the Destined Will.'

Into Battle. Julian Grenfell

Jan 1: New Year's Day. A busy one. Heard on 8 oclock news that IRA extends list of legitimate targets to include police families, civilian searchers at security checkpoints and businessmen. Nice of them to let us know. More work for their assassins. As far as we are concerned, since they are trying to kill all the UDR all the time it doesn't make much difference; they will continue to pluck our feathers one by one. That's all that they can militarily achieve.

Ski Patrol; Three inches of snow round the house, more on the hills which have been white for days. I've been longing to get up there. Yesterday I gathered up the old wooden skis we keep in the attic for occasions like this. They run much better on the slushy snow you find here than modern short ones.

11 a.m. Equipped a G Coy four man heli-ski patrol. Got dropped on a Sperrin peak in brilliant sunshine by an RAF Wessex. Helped fodder sheep and take food to a couple of isolated farms.

Finished with a downhill run of almost 1000 feet on a rough track A few protruding rocks to dodge or bounce off but the old skis don't mind, and no bones broken. Lifted from bottom to do it again. Gave Wessex crew a large bottle of whiskey. Hoped they wouldn't drink it before flying us back to base

A really good morale boosting outing; we all came back with faces glowing from that marvellous mountain air.

In evening I visited Bobby H., OC B Coy Royal Hamps, based in Kilrea RUC Stn, to express sympathy over death of their Intelligence Sergeant. He was in a Sioux Chopper doing a low pass to examine woods by River Bann, two miles north of Portglenone Bridge. The Sioux hit low wires with rotor. Both crewmen got clear. Pilot in flak jacket swam to bank. Sergeant was seen near bank then disappeared. Had a pistol on him. Hamps recovered his brief case full of mug shots and Intelligence records at Portna five miles downstream .

Jan 5 1977; Heard today of three RUCR houses and cars booby trapped since Xmas period. Each defused by the ATO team now based Magherafelt. Increasing use is being made by IRA of radio-controlled bombs.

Sat 8th: Colonel John Levey, South Staffs and currently Deputy Brigade Cdr and his wife Jackie with us for lunch. He is very worried about situation and knows that Brigade need more man power most urgently. Weather back its normal muggy mildness John helped paint my boat and we planned summer sailing.

Jan13 Thursday Intelligence briefing in Fort Garry; 8 to 12 pm. It was largely a farce; Army just milking us for info. for their own Ops. A badly managed negative meeting. They give nothing back for us to work on. So often I've witnessed a newly arrived battalion intelligence officer (sometimes a junior lieutenant) expecting an experienced police detective who has been at it for years to spill all his beans at first request. This in spite of the fact that at least one regular unit, prior to departure, dumped all its Intelligence records on a public tip. A few were noticed by a friendly dustman -others had been removed by a not-so-friendly Shinner. Thereby many sources must have been blown

Jan 14 Friday; Heard at 10 am that Reserve Constable James Greer RUCR was murdered by bomb in car outside his house on Ford Road, Innisrush. He was leaving to go to work at the bacon factory in Ahoghill. His bride of four months had left earlier to go to work in Ballymena. Found by his father who heard the explosion. I went along to scene feeling particularly upset because some of the wife's family, who live in a farm beside Black Loughs bog, work in Upperlands. Saw the car split open and, Greer's face blackened by blast; his lower body was luckily hidden from view.

Jan 16 Sunday 3 PM, Left friends we were entertaining at home for lunch to attend funeral of Greer at Innisrush. Experiencing a great rage at this incident. No indications of RUC success. They inhibit UDR and Army. Achieve nothing themselves. Now four murders in seven weeks here plus two attempts. No follow up. No arrests. Appalling.

Ken Newman, new head policeman, appeared at funeral. He is a wee man with slanty eyes and twisted mouth. When I complained of police inertia he said 'I suggest you inform yourself – they are working very hard'

To which I replied 'They are achieving nothing here; I quote the views of the local population'.

Bryan Webster at 8 Bde HQ told me he had been all set to snatch a local gangster known to be going to have Xmas lunch with his mother at his house in Bellaghy. Special Branch, or more likely NIO, would not allow them do this raid.

At the funeral Greer's distraught wife wearing a white beret looked like a school girl and I felt terribly sorry for her.

No NIO representative visible at funeral but the ex-unionist minister Bill Craig was among crowd .

Jan 17 th: Attend RUC Ops conference, Magherafelt. This ended in drinks and conviviality, a good antidote to present succession of fatalities. Inspectors Eric Lasgow and Doulter most helpful

Jan 19: Tom Arbuthnot and Tommy Read building garage on hard standing for my car in a hurry. Can't afford it, so overdrawn with current level of school bills, but it's life or death just now to have car protected. My son Miles during holidays has been putting a hair across various doors and mudguard arches to detect any interference by bombers. Feel I just want to stay alive, ie not be booby trapped, at least until tomorrow, then I'll have five days safety while on business in England. Anyway I've done most of things I want to do with my life ....
Grandfather's pocket size .38 revolver may be a lucky talisman, having been carried by the family thro' a lot of wars. It's old and worn but I keep it on me day and night. I test fire it often and have never had a jam

Jan 20: Adams of B Coy badly wounded in legs by booby trap in car in Derry today. Doc says may lose a leg but will probably survive.

Jan 22: Home to June from a UK sales trip. Is there a booby trap in our lane? I suppose chances are 400-1 agin' me being picked on tonight; but still an uncomfortable feeling. Nylon fishing line against your knee; Bang! It's all over.

Jan 23 Sunday: Private Alan Smith G Company shot at outside his council house in Maghera Taken to hospital with severe wound in hand and very badly shaken but at least alive. No police follow up.

Jan 25; Booby trap on policeman's car near Tamlaght failed to detonate

Jan 27: Sunday. Heard while on mobile that Patrick McNulty, RUC Special Branch, Derry, shot dead in his car as he approached his house.

So tired when we got back at 2am to Ops room that I could hear my own voice talking as if it belonged to another person. Promised June that I would resign before year end.

Feb 1: Ronnie Linton G Coy fired on coming out of his home lane but survived.

Feb 2 Jeff Agate, civilian, director of Du Pont, shot dead outside his house in Talbot Park, Derry

Feb 6: Much scurry and flurry for Commander UDR inspection Brigadier Mervyn McCord. With 56 companies to visit, I wonder how he gets around—once in a two year tour, I suppose. All seems to have gone well.

Feb 8th: Colonel Ian brings his relief Joe Hordern round to be introduced. He is to take over in May. Tall, erect and keen-eyed, Joe seems affable enough, with the manner of a brigadier, a contrast to Ian's quiet approach.

This is one of the recurring wrenches of UDR life—the severed contacts with regulars. By the time you get to know and like someone --he's off.

Feb 23 1977: Learned this evening that the affable Major Peter Hill shot dead outside his house in Daphne Gardens, Derry, at 6.30. It happened as he was returning from work. Peter, the easy going commander of A and B Company, might have been targeted as much as a prominent business man as from UDR membership. His family own a large department store in Derry. Peter had transferred from an elite TA unit, The North Irish Horse, to join the UDR in 1970 . His wife Ruby was a great supporter of the battalion and always a popular figure at Mess parties. Peter told me that, with feelings similar to my own, he had applied to resign from UDR some weeks back. After seven years of service he was cut down with true irony the day after his release.

Today nearer home two men on a motor bike (allegedly of the ASU that has tried so hard to shoot members of Linton Family) drove down Hall Street.Maghera A girl in café saw them, ran out and shouted a warning: Millard dodged behind a building and escaped. Bike-born heroes panicked , didn't follow up, and fled.

Feb 26 Saturday: Battalion Study Day, Ballykelly. Some regular officers took part in a political discussion. One, putting on a travesty of an Ulster accent, quoted the saying; 'Ulster will fight and Ulster will be right' and attributed it to Ian Paisley. I had to point out that it was Randolph Churchill's and that we Unionists have been resisting absorption into a hostile environment for more than a century.

Feb 27; Crocket, postman from Tamlaght shot at. He saved his life by feigning death. Sgt Willie Currie drove me to annual UDR conference and study weekend at Ballykinler Camp, County Down. General David House addressed us. Came across as an attractive and serious man, not the dogmatic senior officer. Said he was not inhibited by politics but by the laws and practices of democracy. I didn't entirely believe that but he is clearly doing a conscientious and competent job.

NIO conspic. by its absence. Newman the Chief Con. had been billed to speak but gave the need to attend the funeral of an

Colour Sergeant David Purvis receives his British Empire Medal

C.S.M. Hughie Patterson (left) is congratulated by
Brigadier Harry Baxter.

Inspector as an excuse. Generally assumed he couldn't face the criticism to be expected from UDR

March 8: Dinner at Lisburn HQ with Brigadier McCord, Commander UDR. (Aka 'Merv the Swerve'). General Young there saying that he is handing over more and more to RUC. I say 'Yes, but police are not making use of powers . Eg No follow up after local killings'.

The general replied 'Trouble is they lack personalities to carry out Newman's plans'. That sounded like a lame excuse.

March 10: A Signals W/O was servicing a security lookout camera on a pole top above a police station near Derry on a moonlit night. RUC patrol changing over at midnight saw him conspicuous in a white shirt against sky. The IRA's first burst missed . WO unclipped safety belt; started slide down, but shot thro' heart. Second man with him escaped unhurt.

Private Ian, G coy, awarded GOC Commendation for bravery and quick action during an attempted street hold up in Maghera.

March 15 1977: Heard at 11am the sad sad news that the fearless Private David McQuillan shot dead at 8.40 am. He was waiting for a lift on Main Street, Bellaghy. near the Diamond to work on a building site. A group of children including David's 14 year old son witnessed the attack. David tried to run into Castle Street but was cut down by shots from a cowardly gunman. His son picked up his pistol as he lay and tried to fire it.

I recall David being a victim of a near miss in a bungled attack five years ago when a vehicle he was in with two workmates was ambushed near Leitrim, Magherafelt in 1972. Many shots were fired on that occasion but no one hurt

His mother, who worked for a Bellaghy doctor, told him of the mental torture of expecting an attack day after day.

'We were so sure Dave would be attacked; it was almost relief when it happened'

5 PM; UDR call-out; whole area covered all night.

Mar 17: With G coy patrol which brought in a hi-jacked Jaguar left on road near Waterwalls, Ballymacpeake

Sgt Alan Benton MBE, RUC Portglenone, helpful as usual[1]

March 18: Visited Major Colin Willington UDR to see wooden bomb case which fell off his car as he backed out of garage. Yet another nylon cord to inner tube valve booby trap; in this case the knot had slipped.

The Scene of Crime policeman had said to Colin, 'Someone out there doesn't like you. Someone up top does'. No one will ever have a narrower escape

For David McQuillan's funeral I dug out my father's WW11 service dress and Sam Browne, hopefully for last time.

David's home was in a cul de sac on a council estate. I joined a small group of officers in uniform. As the coffin came out we saluted, watched by weeping women.

The Lord Lieutenant, Colonel Michael McCorkell, was there and the High Sheriff. A most striking sermon from Bishop Robin Eames lifted my mind. He made me forget I was in church at a funeral as he spoke of the goodness of our Lord finishing dramatically, 'God Be with you, David!'. That made us all feel that He was.

A big lift is planned for dawn tomorrow. Raids by several police parties to be covered by UDR checkpoints.

March 19th: One of our cordon cover sections under Corporal Hughie came under fire early this morning. They were sniped at on a Y junction in light of headlamps which were deliberately kept full

up by a motorist . Luckily no casualties. A G Coy patrol ran over
a road mine. There was a partial explosion only : no casualties.

MAR 23:   An F Coy Private was shot at outside a house on the
Curran to Magherafelt road 'He dove through a window to escape',
said my informant, 'and was not seriously hurt'.

Mar 25th: CTP (Cocktail Party) at Battalion Headquarters Some
UDR officers like these functions, some who despise the art of small
talk feel they are a fete worse than death. But all are expected to
attend. I got into a corner in good company and had my hand read
by a the wife of a King's officer. She had witchy green eyes and red
hair and was very comforting as regards my survival; but it was
a little disturbing how much about my past she knew and couldn't
possibly have guessed!

The odd occasions when we mess dine are always enjoyable, tho' bad
for the liver.   Going back to some old ones I recall a Scottish
Lieutenant Colonel with us as a guest Johnny, one of our
youngsters had learned a thing or two and was able to crawl under
the table. A friend created a diversion at other end and Johnny
removed the guest's stocking dagger It is the sort of thing that
could happen in his own Mess but with us the Jock was off his
guard. Cost him quite a few drams to retrieve it!   Earlier still the
great Leng when a Brigadier came into somebody's party at
Ballykelly via the window in drag and wearing a long blonde wig
He had supporter armed with a bag of buns, I think,. and fired them
with considerable accuracy at the great and good. But he'd left his
general's hat unguarded in a cloakroom and afterwards it couldn't
be found......

The best diver of those days was Alastair Roberts DWR who could go
head first over four armchairs and roll out unbruised. Army life

was never quite the same after he and has beautiful wife Carolyn went back to the mainland..

Mar 31: Big intelligence conference at Magherafelt arranged by Lt Colonel Bob Long. 1 ,8 and 5 UDR invited. Col Bob started by saying; 'No Int has ever been received yet from RUC Special Branch. A little only from Criminal Investigation Department (CID)'. We need more to act effectively.' He was clearly frustrated. An RUC Inspector outlined the three Active Service Units in our area –that means thirty local men on the run –but very short of weapons and explosives. He warned 'There will be more murders, specially on anniversaries'

IRA bounties for shooting a policeman, a regular and a UDR soldier are quoted as £5,000, £3,000 and £1,000. The price tickets vary from time to time.

This was a valuable meeting and our team contributed fully. Harry, an old friend and I.O. of 8 UDR, Tyrone provided good advice on ways of assimilating info .when it came in and much more ....

April 1: Attended enjoyable anniversary dinner in Belfast City Hall. Myles Humphrey ,the mayor, was the only guest and showed in his speech that he appreciates the work the 250 UDR officers present are doing. Security for the evening clearly a big risk but all passed safely. George Lapsley and I have developed a habit of dancing on the table on such occasions but in these grand surroundings it might have been taken as Lese Majeste, so we refrained.

April 6 1977: Heard early today that another man from the battalion has been shot in Derry. Details gradually followed. Lance Corporal Gerald Cornelius Cloete (pronounced Clote-ey), B

Coy, was on his way to work at the Dupont Factory, Maydown near Derry when gunmen rammed his car. He was a cool brave man who had disregarded warnings and took sensible precautions. He tried to get out and fight but the Terrorists put six shots into him. Originally from Gillingham he'd been in the Royal Navy from 1946 to 1961 and married a Derry girl.[2]

April 8 1977: Snow and sleet; last effort, one hopes, of a long cold winter John McCracken and Kenneth Sheehan, Special Group RUC shot dead at Gortgilly on main Magherafelt- Moneymore Road. They were pursuing a Volkswagen.which failed to stop at their signal. The VW crashed but occupants unhurt got out and opened fire with automatic weapons. Sounds like work of Bellaghy outfit. Constable Stuart, RUCR, brother of our Sergeant Willie. ambushed near Elk Bar, on Toome Road. He was driving a council lorry when shooting started . Not realising he'd been hit he drew his personal protection pistol and started to dismount. His wounded leg wouldn't support him and he found himself lying on the ground . Then seeing a gunman coming round rear of lorry to renew the attack. Stuart very gallantly drove him off with shots from his pistol. After the gunman fled he managed to climb back into cab and call assistance.

APRIL 9. Three Hamps soldier injured in ambush near Moneymore quarrie . after it an IRA volunteer was believed to be wounded and in hiding Big cordon set up by Jocks and ourselves along perimeter roads but no arrest

April 12: A good capture! I went into Fort Garry to leave a note for the incoming Black Watch. Just as I was departing a voice in Ops Room exclaimed, 'We've got two!'. Then came a concise order from Lieutenant Colonel Bob Long to Major Alan Sithers RGJ.

'Go and take charge of the search '.

Alan went out by Land Rover at once and I followed by mini van. On arrival we heard the sequence of events --- An army patrol had been staking out an arms dump for some time in a spinney beside a Gaelic Football Field at Doonan. This morning they spotted two gunmen coming to collect weapons. They fired but appear to have missed, then reported Contact by radio. Their own QRF Land Rover arrived swiftly. As the soldiers in it debussed they saw two gunmen hiding in the ditch. One gunman runs left but find himself heading straight towards another approaching Land Rover. He fires three shots from the hip, then is hit. He falls, gets up, tries to run, is hit again, screams in agony and is arrested.

The patrol commander advances from a stand of fir trees across the football field towards the road. He sees the second gunman spring from cover and run right. The man is hit and screams, 'Mother!', but picks himself up and escapes into the wood. The patrol finds his rifle on ground, then spot a third gunman crouching in ditch and arrest him. They find two Armalites and a Remington Woodmaster with telescopic sights in the dump beside where stones had been rolled together at edge of the wood to form a Sangar.

As we arrived the first gunman. lay on the ground, his head rolling from side to side as he licked his lips, gabbled and moaned. The left leg of his rough trousers had been pulled up and showed the yellow of a field dressing applied to the knee. A tear in his blue shirt showed another wound in his side.

The name he had mumbled was Kennedy but the ginger hair and pale blue expressionless eyes soon identified him as prominent on the Wanted List. In confirmation of evil intent a paper in his pocket had names and addresses of three G Company men.which it appeared his unit had been tasked to kill.

Army marksmanship had not been up to its usual standard but the intercept was a considerable success. Many lives were saved by the patience of the soldiers who had lain concealed beside that dump for untold days. 'That makes it all worth it,' said a six foot six Hamps drum major, a coloured man of great athletic skill.

April 14: On Patrol with a Black Watch platoon now based in G Coy Huts -- a grand bunch. Johnny Maxwell, a brilliant mathematician with a cheerful grin and an untidy mass of black hair[3] of Killyleagh, is their officer.

Malachi Conway, our brave, efficient and kindly CSM, complained day or two ago of pain in head. He had rarely been ill in his life but died in hospital this evening of a brain tumour.

April 17: All day on Magilligan range. Enjoyed it but grudge the time away from home. Got back in time for supper with (sons) Bruce and Miles, their last evening at home before end of holidays. Roy Mason NI Sec announces Conrate ie full time UDR to recruit up to 2,500

April 18: A collection for Malachi's widow was generously supported. He was carried by a UDR uniformed bearer party to be buried at Glen Catholic Chapel, a mile out of Maghera. The priest asked us to remove the Union Flag from the coffin, reasonably enough when he explained that he allowed no political flags inside his church. The Regular platoon left Fort Garry today as army re-disposes for UDA strike

April 19: Farewell lunch for Colonel Ian and his wife June at our house. We will miss them a lot. Ian failed to qualify for the Queen's Jubilee Medal by one day; it was awarded on a mean scale --only to those in command on her birthday. That was the day Joe Hordern took over. The medal should have gone to all those serving at time of her Coronation and still doing so – E.G. the likes of me! Joe tried hard to turn the medal over to Ian but wasn't allowed.

April 20th: Wednesday Conference with Maghera police sergeant Dick Arlow, an old and tried friend. He has been in charge there throughout our tenure. 'Station Sergeant', which the position he holds, was an old Dublin Metropolitan Police rank which, sadly I think, was never adopted by the RUC.

April 30th: Road Patrol with Billy Patterson. We examined very large mine crater. It extends full width of Tobermore- Glenshane Road, ten feet deep in reddish mud. Found possible parts of case in nearby hedge. It had been a culvert bomb set for one of our Land Rovers but exploded by the IRA when no target had appeared and the detonation system become unreliable

May 1: Sunday Bob Long MC, Royal Hamps to lunch. He is an outstanding CO who has pulled the Battalion amazingly together and is ready to co-operate with us in all activities. Then to UDR in evening for meeting with Greenfinches re having better facilities at Fort Garry. The Paisley Strike supposed to commence at midnight.

May 2: Support seems patchy. Power cut off only for short periods.

May 3: Warnings. 'Bomb in your Office'. to William Clark and Sons, (my family linen business) at 0755 ,1230 and 1630. They didn't sound convincing but after last one we closed.

May 5: Visit by General Dick Trant, CLF. He was jocular and informal with lots of four letter expletives. Tendered very sincere thanks for help of the UDR. 'Call me or my ADC direct if you have a problem' Underneath he was probably anxious as whether there was any to support for the strike within UDR. In our case minimal We didn't telephone him for help of course but his attitude was admirable.

Andrew Myrtle. new 8 Bde Brig. called later, also positive and relieved at apparent failure of strike. The Brass were worried that the UDR would be ineffective against UDA road blocks.

May 6: RRF back into Fort Garry

May 10: Battle of Toome; loyalists tried today to block main road near bridge. Put to flight following arrival of milk lorry full of bottles; ideal ammo for Nationalist opposition.[*]

May 15: Things seem to be quietening down a bit. Strike now seen to have failed. Mainly because power workers refused to back it. A relief. A new bit of graffitti by one of our Jock comrades

> 'I'm only a sentry in a sanger
> As much use as a wire coathanger
> If only I could use my gun
> By God. I'd make those buggers run'

May 16: Robert Nairac, Grenadier Gds, captured and murdered on Border. I compose my letter of resignation. 'To facilitate promotion of younger officers' used to be a good reason quoted in the Navy. Really I'm worn out and my private affairs neglected to point of chaos. It's time for a break.

May 31: Meet Airey Neave at lunch with Sir Norman Stronge at Tynan Abbey - Tipped as next NI Secretary if Conservatives get back in. A very experienced soldier and full of determination to beat the bombers.

July 31: Mailed my letter of resignation as promised June I would four months back

Aug 10: Her Majesty The Queen's visit to University of Ulster. It is said to contain several active service units on the campus, so situation is taut. Miles of barbed wire laid down at last minute and check points all over county. Wild Goose, my boat. volunteered as part of patrol in Northern Approaches. We were on our way to St Kilda at the time!

Aug 25 Did eagle patrol with (son) Milo* on detachment from Sandhurst.[5]

August 27 1977 My resignation came through with unexpected speed – Mixed feelings. But know I am handing over the company to a first class man. Can stay on the reserve for a spell.

A remark overheard as I passed the guardroom on my way out made me realise that I'd probably timed my exit right. 'He wasn't a bad fella, when he was at himself'. But perhaps they were talking about a neighbour who'd been buried the day before .

Three Final Diary Extracts

Six months later

Nov 2 1977: My God, they're at it again! Lieutenant Walter Kerr of F Company, a young bank official, was this morning desperately wounded by a booby trap as he backed his car out of his garage. Both legs were amputated in Mid Ulster Hospital but this failed to save his life

Great sadness.

Feb 8TH 1978: Our windows rattled at breakfast time . Yet another bomb...... It seemed to be in the direction of Maghera. We heard within half an hour from the guard commander the awful news that my friend Corporal Willie Gordon had been killed by a car bomb outside his house. He lived in Grove Terrace a hundred yards from Fort Garry. This murder was an ENORMITY. The bomber could not fail to have known that children would be at as much risk as their father when he attached his mercury tilt-switch to the front wheel. Willie was a School Attendance Officer and took his two older children with him each day to drop off as he started on his round. Willie's beautiful twelve year old daughter Leslie sitting in the front seat was killed instantly. His son Richard in the back was blown out through a window, appearing at first dead. His younger daughter three year old Lindsay had come out to wave the family off. Her legs were covered in blood from several gashes.

Richard soon came round but appeared to have lost one eye and suffered severe scorching. His hearing is affected.

Willie was good section leader, a brave soldier and a convivial and much liked member of G Company. He had been guard commander the night before and walked home just after midnight. In the face of threats and intimidation Willie Gordon had refused to give up his part in the defeat of terrorism. The whole battalion is once more in mourning.[5]

Shoot out At Fallagloon

March 17 1978: St Patrick's Day . We heard on 8 o'clock news. ' Two members of Parachute Regiment wounded after stopping a car west of Maghera'.

Learned mid- morning from a colleague in UDR that it took place on Ranaghan Road, a wiggly country lane which leads north off the A5 where it climbs straight up the mountain face towards Glenshane Pass.

This is in 'Grid Square Mike[+]. The UDR been banned from it for a month.'Sounds like a relief party on the way to an observation patrol got ambushed', said my informant

'One of the soldiers is pretty bad. Terrorists not yet caught. Three UDR patrols were in the area last night but none were used in the follow up. That sickens the company off. We're getting far too many static guards at present; it makes morale low'. The army wanted that arrest for themselves. The best of soldiers can be much prone to jealousy.

March 18 Saturday: Hear that a wounded man been picked up close to site of the gun battle. Great relief. He'd been lying out all night in sub-zero temperature. Now in Mid Ulster Hospital. Won't speak to anyone, not even nurses when they say, 'We're Catholics'.

Later at Ebrington I got fuller account. An ambush had been put in on a tip-off to watch a safe house where terrorists were expected. They saw two men approaching in what looked like army uniform. Decided to challenge as thought it might be UDR. Fifteen Armalite shots was instant reply. L/C David Jones was hit in the stomach and liver and knocked over, but managed to wing both terrorists as he fell. Smyth his comrade was hit also in the stomach. A car was heard driving away and it was assumed that it had taken at least one of the wounded.

Glosters set up a cordon at dawn. During the search blood from different groups was found so it was certain that two men had been hit.

By midday the Glosters were about to give up, convinced that both wounded had gone Private Walnut was sent back to Tac HQ to bring up some tea. Walnut had been in cells the day before on a charge of appearing dirty on parade. He was released only to go on the search. Now he wandered off with a dog handler and it was he who spotted a figure propped against a tree trunk in a deep wooded gully. It was fifteen freezing hours since that volunteer had been wounded but his attitude in the face of his enemies was of bold defiance.

He'd made nearly six hundred yards and lost much blood before he managed to put a tourniquet on his leg. His weapon was found hidden under a bush. Perhaps he'd put pepper down because the dog that had followed his trail some way appeared to lose the scent .

If he'd made another hundred yards he'd have been outside the cordon.

Private Walnut's charge was dismissed!

This interception broke up the Bellaghy gang for a spell . Killings in our area declined *.

Here endeth my diary extracts for 1976 ,1977 and early 1978 also my brief career in the UDR.

Spiritually I remain in the UDR for the rest of my life.

For those who soldiered on many adventures and hardships lay ahead

Footnotes to Chapter Ten

1: *See details of this in Chapter four*

2: *Cloete was the last battalion death for six months but we were not to know this at the time.*

3: *Next time I saw the McBains was guarding a pile of luggage at Gatwick airport en route to Kano, en route for an appointment as directing staff at the Nigerian Command and Staff College.*
After this Colonel Ian was Commander Recruiting and Liaison in Scotland until he retired from the army in 1983. He then assumed a Retired Officer appointment in Edinburgh Castle. During this Colonel Ian joined his brother Colonel Stuart McBain (a Royal Scot) as assistant commentator for the Edinburgh Military Tattoo. He finally retired inl 1998. Major Sammy Hudson has been assiduous in keeping in touch by phoning the Mc Bains every New Years Day. In December 2001 I enjoyed a splendid dinner cooked by June at their Edinburgh home.

4: *Johnny, from Killyleagh Castle, County Down, was sadly later murdered while, assisting a free lance photographer friend and his wife in the Arabian desert. All three disappeared.*

5: *A republican song included following verse*
    Wee Black Bobby's jeep
    Lies fifty fathom deep
    If you want your JCB back
    Send for Red Adair.
    (Red was a famous repairer of burst oil wells)

6: *My son Miles aged 17, later commissioned as a Greenjacket, was home*
    from a preliminary course at Sandhurst. No door on the chopper so we were
    able to dangle our legs over the side and get a much improved view ; spotted
    several potential terrorist hide-out sites. Also two new snipe bogs up in hills
    to try out next season. In the long run the bogs will, I hope, prove the more
    rewarding find.

7: *The surviving children echoed the bravery of their father, also their*
    grandfather John Watt, a soldier in both world wars. They made good
    recoveries. After many skin grafts, eye and ear surgery, Richard is a
    quantity surveyor and Lindsay has worked far from home in Australia.

8: *There is a lengthy account of this incident in Ten Men Dead by David*
    Beresford. The volunteer was convicted of the murder of Corporal Jones
    and sentenced to life imprisonment. He was reputed to have earlier killed
    Corporal Willie Gordon and his ten year old daughter Leslie among a total
    of eleven, mainly security forces, in the Maghera area. Never released, he
    died aged 27 on 15 May 1981, as the second hunger striker.
    Two weeks later on May 25 '81 Private Alan Ritchie, F Coy was killed in
    an ambush probably in retaliation for the death of this multiple killer.

CHAPTER ELEVEN
LEST WE FORGET

Thirteen Years from 1977 to 2000

'They stood up for right against wrong because they believed in the system, believed in democratic Government; believed they might have to pay the price but ultimately there would be justice. Now they've been betrayed.'

Willie Frazer on the UDR after losing several close relatives to PIRA murderers. Quoted by Martin Fletcher 'An Outsider in Ulster'. The Times May 3 2000

'Under Entirely New Management' was the sign outside Fort Garry in October 1977. Major Billy Patterson, the youngest of three UDR brothers from Culnady, took command. G Company went from strength to strength. It continued to recruit well and was noted for efficiency on training as well as operations. The Inter-Company Championship came to Fort Garry in five separate years.

Pipers from G formed the bulk of the battalion band which won many regimental prizes. In 1978 G Company in the UDR Regimental Competition took 'everything except the table cloth'. That meant the prizes for best piping, drumming, marching and to WO II Davy of Tamlaght the accolade as smartest Pipe Major. That company band went on to win 4th place in its class at the world championship in Scotland. A dozen bottles of finest old Upperlands poteen was taken to Scotland as trade goods by the support party. They were much appreciated by certain Highland police bands. Our boys were of course too smart to do more than sip it. One told me afterwards that he couldn't remember much about the celebrations but the bits he did remember he'd never forget!'

Our company pipers did recover sufficiently to assist shortly afterwards 5 UDR to win the Royal Scottish Pipe Band Association World Championship against 126 entrants.

The regiment with eleven battalions was now of divisional strength. Posts of Lieutenant-Colonel North and Lieutenant-Colonel South were created to help the Commander keep in touch. Part-time UDR officers occupied both positions. Later Sir Dennis Faulkner KBE was promoted

full Colonel and appointed Representative Colonel Commandant of the
Regiment.

The part timers who wanted to climb were showing that they could
reach the top. Cross postings from one battalion to another, rare in early
days, became common. Captain Paul Murray, whom we knew as a good
soldier in G. transferred to the elite 8 UDR in Dungannon. There he did
us proud when he became commander of one of their companies. He'd
survived an ambush near Gulladuff with us when bullets fired from less
than ten yards cut through the Land Rover close in front and behind him
as well as the driver.

The End of Fort Garry

On June 30th 1980 the G Company Maghera base was closed down.
This was during a major Treasury demand for defence economies. The
flag on Fort Garry was saluted and lowered for the last time before
Company marched out. Then its corrugated iron bastions were pulled
down and interior messes, offices, bunkrooms, stores and Junior Ranks
club, where so much intensive life and sadly death had occurred were
scrapped.

'Was the million pounds spent on Fort's construction and
enlargement worthwhile?' I asked that question of a senior planner as we
watched it being dismantled.

'Well, a single bomb in Maghera could have cost a lot more than a
million. So if you stopped one or two of those the arithmetic was all
right' he replied. I am sure we did.

G Company returned to Fort William from which it had sprung. This
was now a large establishment ringed in fifteen feet corrugated iron
walls. They were painted an unattractive shade of khaki and enclosed a
world class Ops Room, large drill hall, tunnel range, roomy
accommodation for the Messes, stores and weapons. Outside was a
helipad as well as huts that would hold a regular company when needed.
The merger was known as FG Company. That name was to be a short-
lived placebo, the usual device when units or commercial companies are
sold or merged.

CITATIONS

Citations were regularly put forward by company commanders and
awards sometimes filtered through. Ronnie Linton of Maghera was one

of the first to join the Regiment in April 1970 On January 21 1977 he was fired on as he was driving down the lane from home on the way to duty at Fort Garry. He luckily escaped injury. The gunmen appeared to have been scared off by a neighbour armed with a shot gun.

Now a marked man Ronnie continued his service as lance corporal. Two and a half years later on September 21 1979 on business he was driving his mini-van from Maghera to Swatragh to visit a customer. As he entered the village he was alerted by the sight of an unfamiliar car at the roadside but decided to continue. After completing the call he drove on up the village street towards Garvagh. Three shots were fired at him from ahead. One of these punctured a front tyre. A second burst of fire followed. One shot struck the windscreen, narrowly missed Ronnie and passed out through the window beside him. He was injured by flying glass, and by fragments of another bullet which struck a seat support and lodged in his left leg. In spite of these injuries he drove two miles to the nearest house where he would be sure of a safe reception. From there he telephoned the police before attending to his wounds. Six shots had struck his vehicle. A follow up showed that ambushers had

Brigadier David Miller presents Champion Company Trophy

been posted to cover his exit whichever way he turned after the business call. In April 1980 he was awarded the G.O.C's Commendation for Courage and Devotion to duty.

On May 24th 1983, Lance Corporal Ronnie was attacked for the third time. At am he unlocked the shop where he worked in Hall Street Maghera and entered an inner office to switch on lights. As he turned to come out he found a gunman pointing a pistol directly at him. Two shots followed but both missed Ronnie dropped to the floor at the same time as drawing his own pistol and returned fire. Not the sort of thing assassins expect to put up with. This one, with poor spirit, ran out the door and disappeared down the street. Ronnie however had on advice to change his place of employment but continued to serve in the UDR.

In October 1992 for his twenty two years of loyal service in the most difficult circumstances, Ronnie was awarded a well deserved Mention in Despatches.

In an associated incident Raymond Linton, and his brother Kenneth, were visiting a relative in Tamneymullan. As they were leaving they were fired on by gunmen at about 20 metres range. The car received eight hits, three near the radiator, one through the windscreen and four on the driver's side doors. Raymond was hit in the leg. They carried on to Maghera and reported the shooting to the RUC.

Crime Special branch then went to the house. As they started to look for the fire position there was an explosion. The remains of a 2lb device of commercial explosive, a timer and empties were found in secondary cover nearby. Raymond had recently bought his car from Ivan Linton, G Coy, and this may have been an attempted assassination on what was thought to be a member of the UDR. The Lintons were examples of the best sort of UDR soldiers, skilled, quick-witted and undeterred by enemy threats.

A tangible success came some three months after the merging of F and G Companies.

A Brilliant Interception

At 11. 30pm on 2 Sept 1980 an E Company patrol was ambushed by terrorists armed with four automatic rifles near Swatragh. Platoon Sergeant David Purvis of FG Coy was ordered to take his patrol towards Slaghtneill, five miles from the ambush and look out for movements of suspects through the area.

Using his local knowledge Davy selected a particular cross roads and set up a hidden check point. There he maintained a silent watch - no smoking, no movement - and remained undetected close to several houses whose occupants could have been expected to pass word to terrorists on the move if they had realised that the Army were in the area.

Eventually at 2.30 a.m the lights of a solitary car were sighted coming up the brae face. Sergeant Purvis decided that this was the one to stop and stepped out onto the road at considerable risk of being fired on. In the car were three young men, one of whom he recognised as top of the Wanted List. The patrol kept the three apart and in due course the police arrested them on suspicion of having taken part in the ambush. They had no arms. It could be assumed that they had disposed of these two hours earlier before heading for home. This capture cooled the ardour of would-be killers for months.

For his personal courage, loyalty and devotion to duty on this and many other occasions Sergeant Purvis later received a specially well deserved British Empire Medal. Brigadier Prosser, 8 Brigade wrote in congratulation saying,

'Men of your calibre form the backbone of the Ulster Defence Regiment and those under your command can take pride in your award for their efforts under your leadership'.

More Gallantry

F Company won two Queen's Gallantry Medals — Captain David Evans for dashing forward at great risk to save children from a burning car which could have exploded at any minute. David, a tall handsome natural leader was later badly wounded in the leg in an ambush in 1994. He will walk with a limp for the rest of his life.

On the evening of 3 Feb 1991 a Tobermore household was held at gunpoint by a terrorist who had tricked his way in. The husband was taken out and tied into the seat of a stolen van. He was told that his wife and child would be shot if he didn't deliver the bomb in the back into Fort William, Magherafelt. His wife was likewise threatened with death if she made any move to report for half an hour.

Once through the outer gate of the Fort and hemmed between by 14 foot high wriggly tin walls and the inner gate the driver yelled 'There's a bomb in the car'.

Corporal Speers was Guard Commander. He ran forward and released the driver. Two minutes later the bomb went off. Much blast damage to buildings but no one injured. Speers had risked his life for his friend and never was a decoration more richly deserved.

It was not long before the gap now left in Maghera security was made obvious by a fresh spate of killings. They came in August and September 1981.

On 24 July John Hazlett, a civilian resident of Maghera, was mistaken for an ex-UDR soldier working beside him and gunned down while painting a wall in his home town. The IRA went so far as to admit the mistake. The Presbyterian minister remarked at the funeral 'Apologies cannot bring sparkle to a tear-dimmed eye or bring joy to a desolate family'.

A Narrow Shave

A few days later in August 1981 an Upperlands UDR man, Nigel McGonigle, had an escape as narrow as any. This was in the village main street. He had driven half a mile from work, stopped to drop off a friend, then as usual entered a gate in a low wall leading to the gravel outside his parent's house. A car, which had been in waiting, drew up at the kerb behind him. The gunman poked an automatic rifle through the passenger window and fired a burst at point blank range. Incredibly he missed. The intended victim with extraordinary agility leapt some seven feet at one bound and gained the roof of a corrugated iron garden shed. Temporary cover at best. Slipping down at the rear to find better he expected another burst of fire, or to see the gunman coming round to close the range. Nothing happened. Later a magazine was found on the footpath. The would-be killer had knocked it off as he fired and failed to stay to pick it up.

More Murders

Three weeks on — Saturday 12 September 1981 at about 5 oclock Private Alan Clarke a full time UDR soldier from Upperlands, aged 20, was walking down Hall St, Maghera. He was off duty and wearing just jeans and a T shirt, so clearly unarmed. A bullet from behind fired by an on-the-run terrorists left him mortally wounded.

Two days later Reserve Constable Johnnie Proctor of Upperlands, a former member of the UDR, carried his friend Alan's coffin to burial. A few hours after that it was Johnnie himself who 'bought it'. He was gunned down coming out of the Mid Ulster Hospital after visiting his wife June and new born son.

These acts of mayhem and murder came from a gang recently released from jail, one of whom had sworn vengeance for his brother who had been killed while attempting to ambush an army patrol.

A CLF Inspection that was Different

Swatragh village, always a potential hotspot , had been transferred at some time prior to 1980 from F/G Company area to that of E Coy, Coleraine. The two companies maintained a friendly rivalry and this loss of a traditional source of contacts ruffled the Magherafelt boy's feathers a bit. But after all 75 percent of E Company's TAOR was in peaceful holiday country along the north coast, so fair's fair - let them have it!

So it came to pass that Commander Land Forces General Chiswell accompanied by Brigadier Peter Graham, brand new UDR Commander and a firebrand, arrived on November 8th 1982 on a planned inspection.

Captain Pat in South Derry Ops Room, Magherafelt deployed patrols with all her skill and moved them round in squares, circles and parallels, from one intersection to another with speed and verve.

A pair of E Company Land Rovers from Coleraine was vectored to pass south along the main street of Swatragh at 50 yard spacing and 30 mph. A sniper fired at the rear of the back one. He failed to kill but the shot knocked the muzzle off a soldier's rifle. Some fire was returned and flares fired but no hits claimed.

One Shot Willie, deciding that was all for the night, slung his rifle over his shoulder and walked up the street towards the pub.

Two mobiles would never have followed each other on a normal night, but anything to impress a general. So along comes another mobile patrol from Garvagh detachment. Quick eyes discerned the gunman. Two soldiers disembarked to give chase. In the pub yard they saw an outhouse door moving and dashed into what might have been a booby trap or a rifle on the aim at point-blank range. Boldness paid. Instead, they made an arrest after little more than token resistance.

The general and the commander approaching Swatragh from Magherafelt saw two cars speeding in the opposite direction and assumed they contained escaping gunmen. Generals love to get in on some action – makes them feel young again! They turned and gave chase, pistols drawn, overtook and forced the cars to pull in.

Luckily, or unluckily, it was the police escort with the prisoner; felicitations instead of shots were exchanged. CLF was impressed with the night's work.

So were G Company and didn't grudge Garvagh their laurels, specially since the man arrested lived almost in Upperlands.

'It'll be a while before the crows shit on him', was one soldier's comment.

Close Calls

A month later on March 5th 1982 at about 8.30 pm Corporal Stanley, a big handsome fellow with a ready smile, noticed that he was being followed as he drove away from Magherafelt Hospital towards Knockloughrim. As he drove along the main Belfast Derry A5 Road, his wife was beside him and his brother Private Harold in a rear seat, he kept a close eye on a car that stuck close behind. At 70 mph he saw with some horror the pursuing car pull out to overtake. As the car drew alongside a gunman in the back could be seen preparing to fire.

Stanley's quick wits now saved three lives. He braked. This to put the attacker off aim but he recovered enough to get off a three round burst. If anybody ever escaped death by a millimetre it was Stanley. One bullet went through both fleshy parts of his chest, scoring his breast bone in between; another hit the steering wheel and caused splinters to enter his eye and arm. His wife's clothing was cut by so many splinters that she thought at first that a shot gun had been used. It turned out to be shards of glass. Harold was badly wounded in his left shoulder.

The gunmen did not return and the brothers, after some delay, were taken off to the military wing of the Musgrave Hospital in Belfast. There they could recover under the protection of armed guards and there two days later I found them looking cheerful and well cared for.

Stanley was a marksman. At this time he had won the battalion individual medal three years running and narrowly failed to get into the Queen's Hundred at Bisley. This high honour he would almost certainly have attained a month or two later. A wrist weakness and the loss of his right eye took the top edge off his shooting but after recovery he continued to make some good practice.

He is still serving as a sergeant in the Royal Irish Regiment as I write in 2001 and has given much assistance from his remarkable memory for dates and places.

Charles Moore

We didn't see much of the media. At one time the UDR was getting such a bad press that all such contact was banned. But when the Deputy Editor of The Daily Telegraph came to stay in September 1982 as a guest of my son, it seemed too good an opportunity to miss. Our families had been friends since Charles' father Richard stood for the North Antrim Westminister seat in 1970 general election. He and the sitting member my brother Henry, a moderate Unionist, were beaten by Ian Paisley. Henry and Richard met at my house the day afterwards for a convivial post-mortem. Now this was a social visit but pleasure might be combined with a little business. There wasn't time to consult HQ. And if we had they'd have either forbidden or wanted to run the whole thing and killed the spontaneity. Policy at this time was to play down army work and beef up the police.

G company dressed Charles in combat kit and took him out on patrol. It was good for his and the soldier's morale. A penetrating and laudatory article followed. Probably the best ever written about the Regiment. (See Appendix Two)

'From where', HQ asked,' did that guy get his info?' Plenty of guesses. The adjutant came over the mountain and quizzed the boys. But nobody split.

Later in1982 Major Sam Hudson MBE retired having completed twelve years of arduous service, most of it as a liked and respected company commander.

Moneysharvan Mine

Next year a police car was mined at Moneysharvan. It was being driven from Maghera towards Swatragh when about two hundred yards north of the Grillagh junction a charge blew it into a adjoining field. You can see to this day the repair marks where it struck a post and rail fence en route. Incredibly neither constable was seriously hurt. The command wire was soon found leading towards a house on a nearby hill. A search revealed a man hiding in the roof-space. He denied any knowledge of the bomb.

'Why the hell were you hiding up there?', he was asked
With quick wit he replied
'Well, I was going with the wife and when I heard footsteps I thought
they were her oul' man coming home'.

BUTCHERY

On Saturday Dec 17 1983 Lance Corporal Brownie McKeown was
finishing work as a butcher at Smith's Supermarket on Garvagh Road ,
Maghera. He'd done three and a half years service -- in G Coy first, later
in F. His son aged 13 was working with him that day to earn some
pocket money for Christmas.

Father and son were in their Mini ready to drive away when two
gunmen appeared in front of the car. They had clearly been tipped off
and in waiting. One fired several shots through the windscreen. The
gallant Brownie was killed instantly.

The gunmen retired briefly and then came back with the clear
intention of killing his son. A small hole in the windscreen showed
where the bullets entered Some passed through the brave boy's s hair as
he crouched down but he miraculously escaped injury. This ruthless
cruelty was said to be work of a terrorist who was afterwards shot by
Special Forces near Dunloy.

G and F lose their Names

The combined companies had been in 1982 renamed A Company.
This looked neater in the Battalion order of battle. But the pride and
Esprit de Corps which G and F had built up over twenty years suffered.
In 1984 Major Billy Patterson retired after 14 years of exemplary
service. An officer on transfer from One UDR, Ballymena, a
schoolmaster by profession, took over as OC.

By 1986 some brilliant detection by RUC O Division had put most of
the principal local terrorists into jail. Others who had moved south were
picked up and held by co-operation with the Civic Guards. A welcome
gap in attacks followed. It lasted for more than two years. Then the
Cabinet conceded early releases and in 1989 blood started once more to
flow.

This happened as Major Alan Reid, a man full of charm and smiles,
as burly as a Churchill Tank, took over as OC. He led with skill and
enthusiasm and never let the enemy find things easy.

The Threat to Service Firms who Work for the Army

On 8 March 1990 Sergeant Tom Jamieson, an experienced section leader, on his way home at the wheel of cement mixer lorry owned Henry Brothers. The firm did Army Maintenance work and had come under threat when the IRA said that any employees of contractors to security forces were legitimate targets. Several members of Jim Henry's family and staff had been wounded or shot. But Jim resolutely refused to go back on his contracts and Tom as bravely backed him up.

On this occasion IRA gunmen took over a house on the Stewartstown - Coalisland Road and lay in wait. Tommy had narrowly survived an earlier ambush when on patrol near Gulladuff in company with Corporal Paul Murray when several bullets penetrated his Landrover. But this time his luck had run out. As he passed the ambush point the gunmen fired rapid volleys. Several bullets hit poor Tommy in the head and heart. No less than 84 empties were later picked up. Aged 30 Tommy was married to an Upperlands girl Margaret nee Kirkpatrick who had earlier been my most efficient secretary and helper. So this was a doubly sad death.

On the evening of December 1st 1990 Bertie Gilmore, a civilian excavator driver who had some time back completed twelve years as sergeant in the Garvagh platoon of E Company, was sitting with his wife in a car viewing the site of their new bungalow. Gunmen drew alongside and fired two bursts of machine gun bullets. He was killed and his wife severely wounded.

Just two days later on December 3th 1990 another civilian David Shiels was attacked outside the family farm on Crewe Road, Maghera. He was living in a mobile home at the time while building a house. As David fell dead his baby and wife had the narrowest of escapes from the hail of bullets which went clean through the thin walls. It was claimed later by the IRA that they had mistakenly believed that he was a Reserve Constable. This was not accepted by the stricken family. A moving appeal for information from either community as to the killer was issued by his brother George who also wrote the following lines.

'Who has the right to take life
And mould a widow from a wife?
Who has the right to leave a father
Three score ten and old and grey
Grief-stricken to his dying day ?

Who has the right to leave a mother
Full of sadness for our brother   ?
Who has the right to leave a child
Without the warmth of a father's smile ?
We have the right to ask men why
They came with guns to make us cry.

(Coleraine Constitution 15 12 1990).

The blame for these latter deaths lies with the politicians who continually showed the enemy that violence pays. England, in the words of Conor Cruise O'Brien, continued her effort to tiptoe away from Northern Ireland without quite seeming to do so. The Peace Process became a cover name for appeasement.[1]

The Reaper struck again eleven months later on November 6 1991. Private Michael Boxall was a Permanent Cadre soldier sent from Ballykelly to do guard duty in Magherafelt. He swapped jobs with a part timer who was due to go out on a mobile but wanted to stay in to see a football game. The sortie was planned as a joint RUC/UDR patrol but the police at the last minute opted out. Between Bellaghy chapel and village the patrol came under fire from a mortar- type device. Michael was killed instantly by the missile and fell on top of another soldier. This man was wounded in the leg and head but poor Michael's fall probably saved his life.

A pitiless crowd in Bellaghy stopped the ambulance coming through and it had to do a long detour to help the wounded. That turned out to be the last security forces death in the area until the time of writing in the year 2002.

There were of course many   narrow escapes but a lot of these tend to go unrecorded. Under this heading few could outnumber the record of Jimmy Burry. When he was a Corporal in G Coy a road mine in Ballymaguigan exploded under his Land Rover. Luckily the detonator only went off. Later with the RUCR in the Special Patrol Group on Oct 10 1984 he survived a mortar attack on a Carrickmore base when the man beside him was killed.

As point man hundreds of yards ahead of an RUC foot patrol Jimmy triggered off the an explosion of a charge in a turf bank. He saw it disintegrate upwards as a claymore exploded beneath it . Somehow the blast passed over him and he survived a lethal situation. But he needed 90 stitches and a spell in intensive care before returning to duty with no outward signs of injury.

A narrow squeak of another sort came when in 1985 Corporal Jimmy was driving through Derry in the course of his employment at a modest 50 mph.

Blue lights flashed behind him. An RUC Patrol Car was signalling stop. Jimmy realised he was in a 30 mph limit. A stocky policeman with a big jaw looked in through the window.

'Are ye still in?' he asked fiercely. 'Sure I am', said Jimmy relieved. It was Rowlands, an HQ Instructor, who had recently transferred to the RUC!.

'Well you better get to hell out of here at the right speed. There's a policewoman just behind me and she'll have your guts if she nabs you'.

UDR men stuck together!.

But the end of the Ulster Defence Regiment by that name was nigh.

MARCH PAST

New Colours were presented to the UDR on its 20th Anniversary in 1991 by Her Majesty The Queen. Royal courage was admired and the parade was dignified and moving, as it should have been. It had been two years in the planning. But by 1991 talk of amalgamation and disbandment were in the air and inevitably the day was seen by many as a curtain call.

Far worse things can happen to a regiments than to be annihilated in battle. There is commonly some honour in that situation followed by rapid recruiting. A sadder fate is to be wiped at the stroke of a pen by bargaining minister or a penny-pinching civil servant.

By 1991 there were various reasons for a major reduction in the strength of The Ulster Defence Regiment. Most European armies were being pruned following an apparent end to the Cold War. Some ten infantry battalions in all were to be cut from British Army strength. Let us say that the move in NI was led by the Treasury as part of a major overall services cutback. What the other factors were you may guess.

'Men who ne'r smelled powder
Affairs of State decide.
Soldiers are expensive things
Defence an empty pride.'

Northern Ireland Command was faced with the unpleasant prospect of the disbandment of one or possibly both battalions of the Royal Irish

Rangers as well as all the UDR. Also the closure of Ballykinler Camp in County Down, St Patricks Barracks in Ballymena and many smaller bases.

After stiff negotiations, conducted in strict privacy by a three man committee, whose names remain secret, over many months, it was calculated that UDR and Rangers could both be afforded -- if administered jointly. This merger was seen as less destructive than annihilation. The Rangers themselves had been born as an amalgamation of three splendid regiments. The Inniskilling Fusiliers, The Royal Ulster Rifles and The Royal Irish Fusiliers. These, the pride of Ulster, had been known and loved for generations as The Skins, The Stickies and The Faughs.

Twenty four days after the Queen's Colour Parade Northern Ireland Minister Tom King announced that the UDR would be amalgamated with the Rangers. The forced marriage, to take place on 1 July 1992, was blessed with an honourable name -- that of The Royal Irish Regiment which had been disbanded at the end of World War One after long and distinguished service under the Crown. Most military men were delighted to see it resurrected, but without necessarily wanting their own parent regiment to disappear as part of the price.

Younger UDR soldiers, particularly those in full time service, welcomed the move. For them it gave enhanced chances of promotion and overseas postings with the full time Royal Irish Battalions. Regular officers of the Royal Irish were to see the amalgamation is an enhancement of all aspects of career, training and conditions for the part timers.

Most of those with long part- time UDR service welcomed the change as much as turkeys welcome Christmas. The regiment we had joined was recruited to do one job in one country for time indefinite. Its training had progressively been changed to that of regular infantry, ready to do anything in any part of the world at a moment's notice. Brigadier Baxter has vividly drawn attention in his Foreword to the hazards of such demanding training for part timers, particularly for older members. Politically it is argued that the move increases the chances of survival of the three part-time Royal Irish Battalions which are currently all that is left of Ulster Defence Regiment. Ex-UDR soldiers I have talked to set little store by this alleged increase in tenure. Perhaps the attitude comes from the serviceman's inbuilt distrust of politicians.

Now however we must play the ball where it lies.

How effective was the UDR?

In general its perseverance over two toilsome and perilous decades as an essential component of the security forces was enough to persuade the IRA that bombing alone would not work. The resultant Republican change to more political methods has lead to the present so called peace. Killings and maimings continue but at a much lower rate, so many lives have been saved. Whether this form of peace is of long term benefit to Northern Ireland as a community is an open question. In making it possible as an experiment The UDR has been highly effective.

As killers of terrorists I can only quote figures of two battalions I know personally. Harry Stevenson in his excellent book '8 UDR' recorded that in the 22 years of very active service his elite Battalion suffered 27 fatal casualties and shot dead only one terrorist.

To my knowledge 5 UDR did not get even one confirmed kill. Those figures show the cripplingly restrictive effect of the Rules of Engagement, and the high discipline of the two Battalions who obeyed them to the letter. I am sure other battalions did the same or better.

Each battalion spoiled hundreds of enemy operations and put a lot of men behind bars. Good work it was, and not our fault that those men are nearly all out now and many can be seen swaggering around their old killing grounds.

The Colours of the 5th Battalion Royal Irish of which some Maghera and Magherafelt had become members were presented in October 2000 and were laid up the next month. This must have created an additional UDR, sorry Royal Irish record - to have owned the shortest serving Colours in military history.

The 5th Battalion was disbanded some seven years after the amalgamation in December 2000. Its few remaining soldiers were transferred to what had been the 4th Battalion in Omagh. That made an inconveniently long drive - 40 miles in some cases - from home to barracks - and hence there were more resignations. The donors of table silver, paintings and saltires to the battalion messes received a letter asking them if they would like their gift to be returned or sold off for the benefit of Benevolent Fund. Some were returned. Some are now in a private museum near Garvagh.

I had the job of returning the silver horse presented by Lieutenant Colonel Robin Faulkner, 16/5th Queens Royal Lancers, a sailing friend and one of our later Commanding Officers.

The Ulster Defence Regiment Association flourishes and continues the camaraderie which sustained us in bad times. Its most important function is, in cooperation with the Benevolent Fund, to offer help to ex-soldiers in need.

The UDR in one sense is in good company - the men who manned Derry's walls in 1690 got neither pay nor rations after the siege was raised. Wise soldiers have low expectations. Any thanks from a government they have supported are rare.

Of Northern Ireland Simon Jenkins remarked in The Times in June 2001 *'There was never a British colony so abused by its distant rulers'*

Having seen the 'Bs' destroyed by a studied campaign of lies and vilification lapped up by gullible politicians, the UDR never seemed to me, as a historian to be destined for a long life. That Regiment of which we all became so proud and fond lasted only 22 years --- . It had a short life but the one a soldier would ask for — continuous active service.

The good news is that 4 Royal Irish Regiment based at the picturesque St Lucia Barracks, Omagh, is now strongly recruited and in excellent spirit. I saw this at first hand when their Commanding Officer did me the honour of an invitation to represent County Londonderry in taking the Salute after Beating Retreat on September 2002.

What of the future? All countries or factions at war find it necessary to misrepresent or demonise those they oppose. In a civil strife this is probably more easily and thoroughly achieved than in an international one. The process of attempted dis-honourment of the UDR by our foes will be on-going. It remains important for the children and grandchildren of UDR soldiers in days ahead when we hope that hatred in Ireland will have died its own death that the deeds and attitudes of their forbears who risked life and gave up leisure to protect them and their fellow citizens should be truthfully recorded.

The regiment had about two hundred and sixty fatal casualties. Of these fifty seven were murdered AFTER having resigned. The risk continues to ex members, perhaps for all their remaining lives. The fatalities in F and G Companies are recorded in the Roll of Honour which follows. Twenty seven in all died in the battalion to which they belonged. And many other wounded men and women bear scars, physical and mental, which will be painful to their dying day.

What can an individual do to help raise an adequate memorial to these deaths? How can we make sure that the dead are well thought of by future generations? Without a positive effort they could within fifty years fly forgotten as a dream. My answer as a writer has been to compile, with much help from surviving comrades, an account of some of the doughty deeds of the local ones. That way those of us still around can live at peace with our well-beloved fallen comrades. So I hope this book will act as a memorial, 'by their ain folk', not some remote academic, to all who served throughout the Fifth Battalion. And specially, since I knew them almost all personally, those who served in F and G Companies. When UDR men and women get together, as they will continue to do for many a year, there is a feeling of being in elite company. These are the men and women who held Ulster for a generation — held it for Ulster people who minded deeply about patriotism, religious freedom and honour.

These were the men and women with the guts and skill to beat the IRA. If there'd been twenty thousand of them and Government backing they'd have done it..

What is the commonest remark of those ex-UDR soldiers I meet today ?

'I wouldn't have missed it'.

Let us make as sure as possible that the Brave Men and True who gave so much in return for so little are held in unfading memory for their youth and laughter and unquenchable courage.

Footnote

1.   MEMOIRS. CONOR CRUISE O'Brien. P 436

ROLL OF HONOUR

UDR soldiers killed in or from the Maghera and Magherafelt area

Private	PORTER	Samuel	SHOT	22 November 1972
Private	ARRELL	John	SHOT	22 January 1976
Private	McCUTCHEON	John	SHOT	1 Apri 1976
Staff Sergeant	LENNOX	Robert	SHOT	2 April 1976
Private	SCOTT	Robert	BOMB	30 July 1976
Lance-Corporal	SPEER	Jimmy	SHOT	9November 1976
Private	McQUILLAN	David	SHOT	15 March 1977
Lance-Corporal	CLOETE	Gerald	SHOT	6 April 1977
Lieutenant	KERR	Walter	BOMB	2 November 1977
Corporal	GORDON	William	BOMB	8 February 1978
Private	RITCHIE	Alan	SHOT	25 May 1981
Private	CLARKE	Alan	SHOT	12September 1981
Corporal	McKEOWN	Brownie	SHOT	17 December 1983
Sergeant	JAMIESON	Thomas	SHOT	8 March 1990
Private	GILMORE	Bertie	SHOT	1 December 1990
Private	BOXALL	Michael	MORTAR	6 November 1991

Some ten members of UDR in the area were severely wounded.

Royal Ulster Constabulary

Constable	PURVIS	David	SHOT	5 May 1973
Constable	DAVIES	Noe	BOMB	24 May 1975
Detective-Constable	LOVE	David.	BOMB	6 October 1975
Constable	CASKEY	Alan	SHOT	4 May 1982
Superintendent	HARRIS	Alwyn	BOMB	8th October 1989

Royal Ulster Constabulary Reserve

Constable	EVANS	Cliff	SHOT	5 January 1976
Constable	HAMER	William	SHOT	12 February 1976
Constable	ARMOUR	Samuel	BOMB	22 December 1976
Constable	GREER	James	BOMB	14 January 1977
Constable	PROCTOR	John	SHOT	14 September 1981
Constable	FINLAY	Winston	SHOT	30 August 1987

Associated Civilian Deaths

GORDON	Leslie (aged 12)	BOMB	8 February 1978
SHIELS	David	SHOT	3 December 1990
WATTERS	Alexander	SHOT	16 March 1997

Total 5 UDR Deaths 1970 until the Truce - 27

'It is intrinsic to the nature of bravery that the hero should be the last man to describe himself as brave. Selflessness is of the essence of bravery as the brave man acts for the benefit of others. The true nature of the hero is selflessness to act that other may live.'

BREHM AND NELSON. EBURY PRESS

'There is a bright inheritance in the sky
For those who bravely live or bravely die'.

CHRONOLOGY

THE PHASES

PHASE ONE: 1966 to 1969	NICRA and Civil Violence
PHASE TWO: 1970 to 1976	ARMY PRIMACY
	UDR Formed.
	Build up of terrorist activity
PHASE THREE : 1976 – 83	RUC PRIMACY
	Continual concessions to terrorists
PHASE FOUR 1983 to 1992	APPEASEMENT
	Numerous UDR assassinations
	Ends with AMALGAMATION of UDR and Rangers
	as Royal Irish Regiment
2000 :	DISBANDMENT OF FIFTH BATTALION
	Royal Irish Regiment

THE DATES

1969:	October:	Hunt Report advises disbandment of USC and disarming of RUC.
		UDR created by White Paper.
1970:	April I	UDR becomes operational .
		Phoney War period
		F Coy strength 45 .

1971:   **Year of Internment**
March: James Chichester- Clark resigns as PM
May 8:   First Regiment and Battalion casualty.
      A Coy Land Rover mined near Border at Killea.
August: Army called in. 800 men interned.
      Followed by enormous increase in terrorist activity
      and setting up of No Go areas.
21:       First IRA man shot by army in Derry

1972:   **Year of the Car Bomb**
Jan 30:   Provocative crowd activity in Derry leads to major
      incident. with Parachute Regiment and wave of Catholic anger.
      British Embassy in Dublin burned down.
March 4:   Captain Marcus McCausland, D Coy, murdered
March 24:   Stormont Government disbanded
      Direct Rule from Westminster by Northern Ireland Office
      F Coy strength reaches 220
June: Two week truce while Government talks to IRA .
July: Bloody Friday: IRA kill 22 in Belfast
August: Operation Motorman clears No Go areas
      Three weeks full UDR Mobilisation

October:	G Coy formed in Maghera.
November 22:	Pte Samuel Porter G Coy shot outside his house in Ballinahone

1973 **Year of the Greenfinch**
Women's UDR recruited up to 500
Constable David Purvis son of a member of G Company shot in
while on duty in Enniskillen.

1974 **Year of the Booby Trap**
Sunningdale Agreement wrecked by Workers Strike
Oct: General Frank King opens G Coy's new custom-built HQ.
CGS visits G Coy.
Dec: G Coy captures most wanted man west of Bann.
Constable Davies killed by pressure plate booby trap at Moyola
Bridge

1975 **Year of Frustration ------ Truce on-- Truce off -**
All Internees out
Nov 25: Pte Robert Stott shot in Derry
G Coy has minimum of contacts, finds or arrests
Lt Col Ian McBain becomes CO of 5 UDR.

1976: **Year of Assassins**
Worst year for local killings
Police Primacy under way
Jan 22: Pte. John Arrell shot. Clady
Battalion HQ moves to new building beside tarmac at Ballykelly.
April 1: Pte. John McCutcheon shot Toomebridge
2: Sgt. Bobby Lennox shot near Gulladuff
July 30: Pte. Robert Scott killed by booby trap near Ballyeglish.
Nov 7th: Capt. Ronnie Bond short near Derry.
Nov 9th: Lance Corporal Jimmy Speer shot in Desertmartin
Dec 22: S/ Con Samuel Armour killed in car by nylon line booby trap
in Maghera

1977: **A Change of Company Commanders.**
Feb 23: Major Peter Hill shot dead at door of his house in Derry
March 15: Pte David McQuillan shot dead,. Bellaghy, on way to work
April 6: L/C Gerald Cloete shot dead in Derry
12th Special Forces wound and capture gunman in Gortinure.
May: Paisley strike fizzles out after a few days
Sept : G Company taken over by Captain Billy Patterson
Nov 2: Lt. Walter Walter Kerr killed by a booby trap on his car at his
home in Magherafelt

1978 :

Feb 8:   Corporal Willie Gordon and his daughter killed by car booby trap
               outside their house in Maghera

March 17   Special Forces ambush IRA killers on Glenshane Pass.
               Leading Bellaghy gunman arrested by Garda and held in prison
               until 1982

1981:

May 25:   Pte Alan Ritchie shot.

Sept 12:   Pte Alan Clark shot

1982:   Major Sammy Hudson resigns after twelve years.

1983

Dec 17:   Pte Brownie McKeown shot outside a supermarket,Maghera

1989:   F and G Coys amalgamated

1990

March 8:   Sergeant Thomas Jamieson shot near Stewartstown .

1991

Feb 3:   Proxy Bomb blows up gate of Fort William Magherafelt

July 23:   End of UDR announced.. Regiment to be amalgamated with
               Royal Irish Rangers to form Royal Irish Regiment.

2001:   The Derry Battalion, 5 R.Irish, disbanded. A few men go to
               Four Royal Irish in Omagh
               Large mortar bomb narrowly misses Officer's Mess building at
               Ebrington Barracks.

2002:   Sept. Huge Bomb bound for the North intercepted near Newry

'This is the truce, the whole truce, and nothing but the truce!'

Appendix One

THE FORMATION OF THE 5th BATTALION, THE ULSTER DEFENCE REGIMENT

By Colonel George Lapsley MBE
(* in following lines means now deceased)

The activation of the Regiment and the Fifth Battalion was due in April 1970. Before that many men with TA or 'B' Special backgrounds were travelling round County Derry looking for recruits. In some areas like Fermanagh and Tyrone the 'B' Specials joined 'en bloc' but in other areas where unfeeling senior Army personnel were at work (as in parts of Derry) whole companies of good recruits were lost because of the fact that their older Sub District Commandants and sergeants were turned down for age or other reasons. The men were loyal as always to their own officers.

There were supposed to be six companies in Co Londonderry:

Three in Derry City -- A Company on the west side under Major Hamilton,* B Company in the Waterside under Major Anderson* and C Company in Claudy under Major Gilbert Craig*.

After a couple of years A and B were amalgamated and based in Ebrington Barracks. under Major Peter Hill*. Major Dougy Caldwell took over C. Later the bases at Duncreggan and Claudy closed and the two remaining companies were based in Ebrington Barracks as recruiting dropped away, especially on the west side of Derry City.

The original Company Commanders of A, B and C were ex 'B'Special District Commandannts. There were no others with the experience to take the load.

D Company under Major Cartwright, ex RAF and Royal Artillery TA was formed in Ballykelly and stayed firm until the end.

'E' Company was supposed to be in Coleraine but was not started until April 1970 because there was no armoury available. Then the strange decision was made that a company from 1 UDR in Ballymoney, County Antrim would recruit from Coleraine. George Lapsley ex Royal Navy and RA (TA) was sent away from Coleraine to Derry to be Second in Command of the Battalion. At this time men kept their weapons at home and eventually after a year someone had the bright idea that an armoury was not all that important but a company in Coleraine was. Immediately Major Lapsley headed for Coleraine to command E Company based in a dilapidated 'B' Hut in Macosquin.

F Company was in Magherafelt under Wallace Clark then Major Sammy Hudson. This like D Company lasted until the bitter end with an extensive new building and helipad. By 1971 there were six companies. In 1972 another, G by name, was added in Maghera RUC Station. It survived for eight years until the rationalisation started and then moved to be merged with F Company in Magherafelt.

Big changes were happening in Coleraine as the old hut in Macosquin was soon too small for the growing company and Laurel Hill House appeared on the market. This has been home to the Henry family and appeared in good condition but later damp and dry rot was found and enormous sums had to be spent on repairs and extensions. E Company eventually became the largest company with 9 Officers and 269 men. Its detachment in Garvagh was a very strong 24 Platoon. Lt (Later Major) Ivan Cromie was in charge.

The other platoons were 21 Plt, the 'Seasiders'. 22 Plt from the town side of Coleraine under Lt Jim Simpson*, ex 'B' Special and one of the bravest and most respected of men: 23 Plt. The 'Killowens' under Lt. Victor Hamill (later Lieutenant Colonel) led 22 Plt who eventually took over from Major G S Lapsley when he left in 1976 to again become Second in Command of the Battalion and later go to Lisburn as Lt Col (North).

The sad end of the story is that after thirty years E Company and the beautiful Laurel Hill are gone along with the unique 5th Battalion. Only a mixed gathering remains at Ballykelly attached to 4 Royal Irish.

These in the hour when heaven was falling
The hour when Ulster's Union cracked
Took up a military calling
Risked their all...
And then were sacked'

With apologies to AE Housman

The Company Commander and Malachi

Appendix Two

GOING TO WAR AFTER A DAY AT THE OFFICE
By Charles Moore (Editor, Daily Telegraph) 1982

Mention the UDR to an Englishman and, if he has heard of it at all, he will as likely as not be under the impression that it is 'one of those Protestant terrorist organisations'. In fact, the Ulster Defence Regiment is an essential part of the security forces. It is also the largest infantry regiment in the British Army and the regiment with the longest record of continuous active service since the Napoleonic wars.

The UDR was born out of the chaos resulting from British indecision over the disorders in the province at the end of the 1960's. Believing the largely phoney accusations made by Republicans and repeated in the Press, the Government of Harold Wilson disbanded the 'B' Specials (the Ulster Special Constabulary), the men most vital in the defeat of previous IRA campaigns. Thanks to the insistence of the military that some equivalent of the "B men" were essential to internal security, the Government reluctantly formed the UDR, the first seven battalions of which became operational in April 1970.

Although it bears many similarities to the "B" Specials, the UDR is part of the Army, and therefore subject to military discipline, training and rates of pay. Its members today (who include women members, known as "Greenfinches") are young, fit some Specials were definitely antique – and properly equipped. According to the Regular Army officers posted to command the 11 battalions, they are now the equal, if not sometimes the superior, of Regular battalions.

The character and organisa5tion of the UDR is unique. Its full time commanding officers are all from the Regular Army, a precaution which is a little offensive of Ulstermen, but which has not caused much friction. But most of the officers, both in the permanent cadre (full-time 2700) and part-timers (4500) and all of the men, are Ulstermen.

For all the training, most of the work of the UDR is routine and undramatic. The regiment does not go in for the undercover operations of parts of the Regular Army, nor for any of the detection and arrest work of the RUC. Like the 'B' Specials, it is not trained to deal with riots. Since 1977, when the RUC took the lead again in security operations, the UDR has acted upon its instigation, and has become trusted enough to be the part of the army called upon by the RUC in the first instance of trouble in two-thirds of the province.

I went out in a country area with a UDR night patrol. We travelled in two vehicles, one with an armoured gun-turret. In my Land-Rover was an officer, one "Greenfinch" (always used to search women at security checks) and two men. We all wore bullet-proof jackets.

Typically, we patrolled small towns and country roads. At one corner I was shown the spot where one of our number had been shot at from a passing car while off duty. After the first shot missed, the would-be assassin's magazine jammed, and the young UDR man, only feet away, was able to scramble to safety. On one road out of a strongly Republican village our party set up a vehicle checkpoint (VCP). Each car was stopped, and when not known to the men the driver was asked to produce means of identification and to say where he was going. Number plates were checked on the spot over the radio with the RUC computer. The men asking questions were covered at all times by their companions. Since it was shortly after pub closing time, some unco-operativeness was to be expected, and sure enough, one car load of four teenagers giggled, complained and refused to answer questions. With scrupulous politeness, the UDR man asked them to get out of the car for it and them to be searched. When they eventually gave their names, a check with the computer revealed that one of them was the brother of a terrorist on the run; but there was no call for further questioning and the driver was allowed to continue. She did so, hooting angrily into the night.

Such trivial incidents are often the pretext for trumped-up, complaints against the UDR. But, as one officer told me, the need for politeness is something very successfully drummed into his men; finding terrorists is that much harder when rudeness provokes hostility. Nevertheless, provocation is sometimes severe. Often when a UDR man has recently been murdered, Republicans stopped at a checkpoint will say something like, "glad we got one of your boys the other day".

Patrols similar to the one I joined, together with guarding and escorting duties, make up most of the work of the UDR. What is remarkable is that, for the part-timers, the work is usually undertaken after a day in a civilian job. Men return from their night patrols at two or three in the morning, and then rise for ordinary work at seven or eight.

It is the danger which is the most striking aspect of a UDR man's work. It is an unglamorous sort of risk. The chance of going "into battle" and being killed is low, that of being shot from behind a hedge as you bicycle home, very high. Of the 123 UDR killed up to August this year, more than 100 have been murdered off duty. UDR men live at home, unprotected except perhaps by their own gun. The keenest recruits are often farmers and people living in country districts where ambushes can be set up with the greatest of ease. Nor is leaving the regiment any guarantee of safety. Whether through ignorance or policy, the IRA frequently murders ex-UDR men. As for Roman Catholics who dare to join, the risks are terrible. When the UDR was set up it was supposed to be "non-sectarian" and it initially achieved a Catholic membership of 18 per cent. Persistent intimidation has now brought that down to an official figure of 3 per cent, though the real one is probably larger, due to the number of Catholics who join "incognito".

Families suffer worse than the members of the regiment themselves. Wives sometimes have nervous breakdowns, fiancées sometimes insist that their men get out. The UDR has a 24 hour capability, and a corresponding 24 hour exposure to danger which has lasted the whole of its history.

But for the most part, the very risks and tribulations seem to strengthen the UDR's morale. Although much of the work is monotonous, officers say discipline is good, and men say they do not get bored. Those ready to take the risks of joining are convinced of the importance of whey they do. Once in, most stay. A close social life binds the regiment together (there are even a good many husbands in the UDR whose wives are also members). They are not easily daunted.

Due to the slight lessening of terrorist activity, and the IRA's targets, the UDR is changing. In areas such as Antrim and North Down, where recruitment is high and terrorist activity low, UDR men are often sent off to help police and colleagues in more dangerous areas, where, in the works of one officer "it feels like being the 7th cavalry in Indian country". Such movement can only be taken so far; if the UDR were to lose the advantage of its immense local knowledge, it would be infinitely less effective. With the RUC usually posting policemen to areas where they are not local, it becomes all the more important that the UDR retain its intimate link with the neighbourhoods in which it operates.

It is not only for the defeat of terrorism that the UDR is essential. It is as important in satisfying the aspirations of the loyal population. The military instinct is very strong in Ulster people. In recent years, desperate frustration has sometimes forced that instinct into illegal channels. The UDR turns the instinct to best effect by protecting the State and the people from those who would destroy them.

It commands the same sort of loyalty and affection as did the Home Guard in Britain during the Second World War, and does a job that is more dangerous and testing. The UDR is an institution that any politician should be proud to foster; a force of law deeply rooted in the people. Yet it is no thanks to any politician that it is a success.

APPENDIX THREE

SOURCES

Published

Ambush James Adams and Morgan and Bambridge
A Testimony to Bravery . John Potter
British Army in Northern Ireland . Barzilay.
Dirty War by Martin Dillon
British Army in Ireland. Dewar
Days that are Gone. Sir Patrick Mc Crory
Dead Ground. Raymond Gilmour
Memoirs of a Statesman. Faulkner
Fetch Felix By Col Derrick Patrick Hamish Hamilton
Faith and Duty: Curtis M M
Hansard 12 12 78. Biggs Davidson
Hope Against History Jack Holland
Holding the Line John Hermon
IRA Targets and Tactics by Bowyer Bell
Linenhall Library Political Files
Lost Lives. Mc Kittrick and others Mainstream Presss
Northern Ireland A chronology 1968 1999 - Bew And Gillespie
Security Forces in NI. Tim Ripley: Osprey Military
The IRA. Tim Pat Coogan
The Filibusters. John Lodwick Methuen 1947
The Irish War and Who Dares Wins by Tony Geraghty
The RUC. Dillon
25 Years of Terror: Martin
The B Specials Admiral Sir Arthur Hezlet
UDR: Ryder
8 UDR: Harry Stevenson

Regimental Magazines

Defence UDR Magazine, 1972 to 1976
Visor, Checkpoint, NI Regular Army, with some mentions of UDR
Guards Magazine
Public Eye; RGJ
Rampages; Worcesters and Foresters
Tiger Rag; Royal Hamps

APPENDIX FOUR

8 INFANTRY BRIGADE COMMANDERS SINCE 1972

1969 – 1971	Brig JAC Cowan MBE
1971 – 1972	Brig APW McClelland OBE
1972 – 1974	Brig JDF Mostyn MBE
1974 – 1975	Brig D Houston OBE
1975 – 1977	Brig BC Webster
1977 – 1978	Brig AD Myrtle MBE
1978 – 1980	Brig CT Shortis OBE
1980 – 1982	Brig WKL Prosser MBE MC
1982 – 1984	Brig CB Mattingley OBE
1984 – 1986	Brig MIE Scott DSO
1986 – 1988	Brig MRI Constantine OBE
1988 – 1990	Brig JW Parker OBE
1990 – 1992	Brig JCB Sutherell OBE
1992 – 1994	Brig AMD Palmer
1994 – 1996	Brig NJ Cottam OBE
1996 – 1998	Brig SD Young CBE
1998 – 2000	Brig PE O'R-B Davidson-Houston OBE
2000 -	Brig PR Newton

GLOSSARY

My apologies for the length of the following . It could have been twice as long and still not covered all the abbreviations we encountered. The number with which one had to become familiar in training indicates the effort needed.

ANFO:	Ammonium Nitrate and Fuel Oil. One of several varieties of HME --home made explosive
ASU:	IRA active service unit;usually an isolated cell, small in number.
ATO:	Ammunition Technical Officer: man responsible for dealing with UXB (unexploded bombs) in car, culvert, parcels and many other forms and often fitted withcunning booby traps AKA:also known as Felix
BDE:	Brigade
BK:	Ballykelly (or Ballykinler)
BN:	Battalion
BORU:	local name for unemployment allowance
BRICK:	4 man patrol
BRUDR:	Brigade UDR Reserve
B SPECIALS:	See USC below
CLAYMORE:	Mine used by terrorists to discharge shrapnel as part of an ambush
CIVVY:	Civilian
CO:	Commanding Officer
COY:	Company
CPC:	Civilian Patrol Car
CLF:	Commander Land Forces
CTP:	Cocktail Party. Used sometimes as a 'Hullo, we're here' when a regiment accompanied by wives and families first arrives.
COME-ON:	Faked bomb report,car accident or any incident to draw Security Forces into an ambush.
CONRATE:	UDR soldiers serving full time (as opposed to part time) Comprised almost half the Regiment in the final year.
CSM:	Company Sergeant Major
DMSU:	RUC Mobile Support Unit
DOC:	Decent ordinary Criminals (as opposed to terrorists)
DWR:	Duke of Wellington's Regiment
ENCLAVE:	Salient area west of between river Foyle and Donegal
FELIX:	Ammunition Technical Officers responsible for de-fusing or otherwise disposing of terrorists bombs See ATO.
FFR:	Fitness for Role Annual Inspection
FORT GARRY:	G Company HQ adjoining RUC Station, Maghera
FORT WILLIAM:	F Company HQ in Magherafelt.
FORT GEORGE:	Regular Army Base in Derry at junction of Strand and Buncrana roads

FPTE:	Female Private
GARDA SIOCHANA:	Civic Guards. The Police of the Irish Republic
GPMG:	General Purposes Machine Gun aka 'Gimpy'.
GREENFINCH:	Female UDR soldier .Established in 1973
GOLDFINCH:	Nickname for Senior Greenfinch.
HQ:	Headquarters
HV:	High Velocity
IED:	Improvised explosive Device
INFIDELITY ALLOWANCE:	Local name for Invalidity allowance!
INLA:	Irish National Liberation Army
INT:	Intelligence
INTREP:	Intelligence Report---- occasionally humorous.
	Eg 'Two gunmen seen to run away - one six foot six, other four foot nine. RUC are searching high and low'
	Another time -- 'Intelligence no trace' (meaning No Criminal Record) came through tagged onto the name of a harmless and particularly clever neighbour. I sent him a copy.
IRA:	(Don't you know anything?) Irish Republican Army
KOB:	Kings Own Borderers
KP:	Key Point, one that needs to be guarded
LR:	Land Rover
LRB:	Londonderry Roulement Battalion
	Roulement applied to a regular battalion doing a short tour, usually four months, unaccompanied by families.
	This would be in support of the garrison battalions who did two year accompanied tours.
MOD:	Ministry of Defence
MOLAR:	Quartermaster, Rations etc.
NCO:	Non commissioned Officer
NIO:	The Northern Ireland Office which ruled the Province after the abolition of Stormont in March 1972
O-GROUP:	Orders Group; Summoned by a Commander at any level to issue instructions
ONE PIP WONDER:	Newly commissioned Second Lieutenant.
OPS ROOM:	Operations Room, a Communications and Control centre.
OWN GOAL:	Self inflicted casualty --also known as 'Blue on Blue'.
OPS ROOM:	Operations Room, a Communications and Control centre.
OWN GOAL:	Self inflicted casualty -- also known as 'Blue on Blue'.
OIRA:	Official Irish Republican Army. The 'Stickies '
OC:	Officer Commanding: Eg Company Commander
ODS:	Off duty soldier; Favourite IRA target
ORBAT:	Order of Battle
PGF:	Prison Guard Force-in our case Magilligan on Lough Foyle
PIG:	One Ton Humber Armoured troop carrier.

PIRA :	Provisional Irish Republican Army -The 'Provos'
PPW :	Personal Protection Weapon. Pistols issued to UDR personnel after 1972.
PRUDR:	Provincial Reserve UDR.
PVCP:	Permanent Vehicle Check point
PMO :	Principal Medical Officer
Proxy:	Bomb delivered by driver under durance or threat to his family.
PRUDR :	Provincial UDR Reserve
PSI:	Permanent Staff Instructor
QM:	Quartermaster ; Officer in charge of supplies
QRF:	Quick Reaction Force
RSM:	Regimental Sergeant-Major
RE :	Royal Engineers
Recce	Reconnaissance
REME:	Royal Electrical and Mechanical Engineers
RGJ:	Royal Green Jackets
R Hamps:	The Royal Hampshire Regiment
R Irish R:	Royal Irish Regiment
RMP:	Royal Military Police
RRF:	Royal Regiment of Fusiliers
SAPPER:	Royal Engineers
SB:	Special Branch. RUC Anti-Terrorist Department.
SF:	Security Forces — Regular Army, UDR, RUC and RAF.
SIB	Military Police Special Investigation Branch.
Sitrep:	Signaleese for Situation Report at various levels. Brigade HQ issued one daily.
SKINS:	Nickname for Inniskilling Fusiliers, 27th of Foot. Our esteemed local regiment
SLR:	Self Loading Rifle
SMLE:	Short Magazine Lee-Enfield; Standard British Infantry rifle in WWI and WW11; in use by UDR during early years.
SMG:	Sub-machine gun eg Sterling or Sten
STAG:	Period on guard or other duty
TAC HQ:	Tactical (hence temporary) HQ.
TISO:	Training, Intelligence and Security officer
RUPERT BEAR:	Reconnaisance platoon or section
SANGAR:	Originally a North West Frontier term for a breastwork of rocks, now used for any small strong point or guard post of sandbags or bricks.
SUNRAY:	Commander at any level
TAOR:	Tactical area of responsibility
TSMG:	Thomson Sub Machine Gun or Tommy Gun
UDR:	The Ulster Defence Regiment
UVF	Ulster Volunteer Force
UDA	Ulster Defence Association Formed 1971Banned in 1992

UFF:	Ulster Freedom Fighters sometimes used as Cover name by UDA.
USC:	Ulster Special Constabulary, Also known as The 'B 'Specials, more often referred to by those neighbours who relied on them for protection as 'The ' B's' or The 'B Men'Name arose from the original 1920 categories of Police Reserves--- A Specials Full Time, B Part Time, and C Elderly men employed on static guard duties only.Of these only the B Specials survived until 1970.
VCP:	Vehicle Check Point
WO2:	Warrant Officer Second Class
WOOFERS:	Nickname for our good friends the Worcester and Sherwood Foresters Regiment

INDEX
(bold indicates killed by terrorists)

BOOKS BY WALLACE CLARK

GUNS IN ULSTER
A personal history of the B Specials
Second Edition 2002 with added photographs and fresh
information to expose the lies promulgated by the enemies
of this dedicated force.
ISBN 0950 090 421X

LOCAL HISTORY

Rathlin — Its Island Story
Northern Ireland's only inhabited offshore island
More history and more massacres than any other island of its size.
Third edition 1998
ISBN 0-948 25476-4

Linen on the Green
The story of Upperlands, a mill village which has been producing Irish linen since
before 1736. Hardback.
ISBN 950 9042 0 1

Upperlands Visitors Guide
36 page guide illustrated in colour to Ireland's oldest linen village

VENTURESOME VOYAGES

Sailing Round Ireland
Reprinted 2002
A classic circumnavigation in 1976, starting and finishing at Portrush
aboard Wild Goose, the family's 40 year old wooden yawl.
Third edition with an update
ISBN 0-950 90422-8

Sailing Round Russia
A voyage in the same boat as above by the author's son Miles
to North Cape, then via the Rivers Volga and Don, to the Black Sea.
This was the first ever voyage of its sort by a non-Russian craft.
Illustrated with colour photographs of the standard of the National Geographic
Magazine which sponsored the voyage
ISBN 0-9509 042-1
Hardback 0-9509042-2-8

The Lord of the Isles Voyage
Six weeks rowing and sailing a replica sixteenth Century Galley from Galway to
Stornoway in 1992
ISBN 0-950-1758-6-2

Signed copies available from
Wallace Clark Booksales, 115 Kilrea Road, Upperlands, BT46 5SB
Telephone: 028 796 43737 Fax: 028 796 45944 or 796 43693